The rainforest edge.

$79.95

DATE			

The rainforest edge

Plant and soil ecology of Maracá Island, Brazil

This book presents some of the most important research and findings of the Royal Geographical Society's Maracá Rainforest Project, one of the largest research efforts ever mounted in Amazonia, involving scientists from Brazil and from Britain.

It focuses in particular on ecological dynamics at the forest–savanna boundary, which are crucial to explaining how rain forests work and how human interventions modify the rainforest ecosystem. After an introduction to the Maracá area, which lies on two great biogeographical boundaries, leading ecologists and geographers cover in depth key elements in Maracá's ecological dynamics: savanna ecology; physical environment, forest structure and floristics; litter and nutrient cycling; the nitrogen cycle; soil nutrients and organic matter; and regeneration in forest gaps. They also examine soil degradation and consider how to establish a geographic information system for resource management of the area. *The rainforest edge* is a major contribution to our understanding of the ecology of the world's most diverse and fascinating ecosystem, and to how humanity's activities are changing them.

This book will be essential reading for ecologists, geographers and their students.

John Hemming is Director and Secretary of the Royal Geographical Society and was leader of the Maracá Rainforest Project.

The rainforest edge

Plant and soil ecology
of Maracá Island, Brazil

edited by John Hemming

Manchester University Press
Manchester and New York

Distributed exclusively in the USA and Canada by St. Martin's Press

Copyright © Manchester University Press 1994

While copyright in the volume as a whole is vested in
Manchester University Press, copyright in individual chapters
belongs to their respective authors, and no chapter may be
reproduced wholly or in part without the express permission in
writing of both author and publisher.

Published by Manchester University Press
Oxford Road, Manchester M13 9PL, UK
and Room 400, 175 Fifth Avenue,
New York, NY 10010, USA

Distributed exclusively in the USA and Canada
by St. Martin's Press, Inc.,
175 Fifth Avenue, New York, NY 10010, USA

British Library Cataloguing-in-Publication Data
A catalogue record for this book is available from the British Library

Library of Congress Cataloging-in-Publication Data
The rainforest edge : plant and soil ecology of Maracá Island, Brazil
/ edited by John Hemming.
   p. cm.
  ISBN 0-7190-3477-9
   1. Rain forest ecology – Brazil – Maracá Island (Roraima) 2. Soil
ecology – Brazil – Maracá Island (Roraima) 3. Maracá Island (Roraima,
Brazil) I. Hemming, John, 1935– . II. Title: Rain forest edge.
QK263.R35 1993
581.5′2642′098114–dc20   93–10964
                                                       CIP

ISBN 0 7190 3477 9 *hardback*

Typeset in Hong Kong
by Graphicraft Typesetters Ltd., Hong Kong
Printed in Great Britain
by Biddles Ltd, Guildford and King's Lynn

Contents

Figures

Tables

Contributors

Thomas C. D. Dargie is an ecological and environmental consultant, based in Scotland and previously a lecturer in the Department of Geography, University of Sheffield. He was a member of the Land Development team on Maracá.

Michael J. Eden is a lecturer in the Department of Geography at Royal Holloway College, University of London, and was a member of the Land Development team on Maracá.

Peter A. Furley is Reader in Tropical Soils and Biogeography at the Department of Geography, University of Edinburgh, was the leader of the Land Development team and a soil scientist with the Ecological Survey on Maracá.

John Hemming is the Director of the Royal Geographical Society, and was the leader of the Maracá Rainforest Project and a member of the Land Development team on Maracá.

Duncan F. M. McGregor is Senior Lecturer in the Department of Geography at Royal Holloway College, University of London, and was a member of the Land Development team on Maracá.

Robert H. Marrs is the Director of the Botanic Gardens, University of Liverpool, and was a member of the Forest Regeneration team on Maracá. At the time of writing, he was based at the Institute of Terrestrial Ecology, Huntingdon.

Stephen Nortcliff is a Senior Lecturer in the Department of Soil Science at the University of Reading, and was a member of the Soils and Hydrology team on Maracá.

Christopher J. Place is a computer officer in the Department of Geography at the University of Edinburgh, with special responsibility for remote sensing.

John Proctor is a Reader in the Department of Biological and Molecular Sciences at the University of Stirling, and was the leader of the Forest Regeneration team on Maracá.

James A. Ratter is a Senior Principal Scientific Officer at the Royal Botanic Garden, Edinburgh, and was the joint leader of the Ecological Survey team on Maracá.

Daniel M. Robison is a researcher in the Department of Soil Science, University of Reading, and was a member of the Soils and Hydrology team on Maracá. At the time of writing, he was a researcher in the Agroecological Studies Unit at the Centro Internacional de Agricultura Tropical (CIAT), Colombia.

Sheila M. Ross is a lecturer in the Department of Geography at the University of Bristol, and was a member of the Soils and Hydrology team on Maracá.

Duncan A. Scott is now at D. W. S. Atkins (Consultants) Ltd., Glasgow, and was a member of the Forest Regeneration team on Maracá. At the time of writing, he was a research student in the Department of Biological and Molecular Sciences at the University of Stirling.

Jill Thompson is working for the Overseas Development Administration from the Department of Plant Sciences, University of Aberdeen, and was a member of the Forest Regeneration team on Maracá. At the time of writing, she was a lecturer in Biological and Molecular Sciences at the University of Stirling.

Nelson A. Q. Vieira is a lecturer in the Department of Sociology and Anthropology at the Federal University of Minas Gerais, Belo Horizonte, Brazil, and was a member of the Land Development team on Maracá.

Glossary

caatinga	dry wooded vegetation on white sandy soil.
campo	savanna grassland.
campo cerrado ('dense' or 'closed' campo)	arboreal or shrubby savanna.
campo limpo ('clean' campo)	open savanna grassland, cleared of trees.
campo sujo ('dirty' campo)	savanna before clearance.
catena	a grouping of soils linked by topography and drainage. Catenary changes occur step by step.
cation	positively-charged ion.
CEC	cation exchange capacity.
CL	confidence limits.
cmol	centimoles (= milli-equivalents).
colonião	*Panicum maximum* Jacq., used as cattle pasture.
cover value index	relative dominance plus relative density, used as an estimate of vegetation cover.
dbh	diameter at breast height.
deliquescent tree	a tree which shows continuous low branching of the trunk, producing a wide bushy form.
ECEC	effective cation exchange capacity.
ecotone	transition zone between different vegetation communities.
edaphic	relating to soils.
GIS	geographic information system.
ground-truthing	fixing and describing conditions and locations on the ground for interpretation of satellite imagery.
hylaean	high Amazonian canopy forest.

IBDF	Instituto Brasileiro de Desenvolvimento Florestal (Brazilian government's forestry department).
INPA	Instituto Nacional de Pesquisas da Amazônia (National Amazon Research Institute).
LSD	least significant difference.
M	molarity.
micro-kjeldahl	apparatus used in total soil nitrogen analysis.
meq	milli-equivalents.
MSS	Multi-Spectral Scanner.
n	number
NOAA-AVHRR	National Oceanographic and Atmospheric Administration – Advanced Very High Resolution Radiometer.
planation	erosion and degradation processes that plane or level the topography.
point-centred-quarter technique	standard plotless technique for surveying vegetation.
ppm	parts per million.
SE	standard error.
SEMA	Secretaria Especial do Meio Ambiente (Special Secretariat of the Environment).
seral	a plant community representing a stage in succession.
sheetwash	overland flow of precipitation in unchannelled form.
TEA	total exchangeable acidity.
terra firme **forest**	slightly elevated forest, not subject to seasonal flooding.
TM	Thematic Mapper.
turbation	disturbance of soil by physical and biological processes.
vazante	seasonally flooded areas covered in weedy vegetation.

1 *John Hemming*

Introduction: the Maracá Rainforest Project

Maracá is one of the world's larger riverine islands. It is formed by the dividing and rejoining 60 km downstream of the Uraricoera River, a northern headwater of the Rio Branco, which in turn flows into the Rio Negro, which enters the main Amazon River near Manaus (Figure 1.1). Maracá Island is roughly triangular, measuring 25 km at its widest, and its area is somewhat over 100,000 ha.

Such is the flatness of the vast Amazon basin, that the channels embracing Maracá are at an altitude of only about 100 metres above sea level, whereas the rivers have to flow for 2500 km before they enter the Atlantic Ocean. The unexplored centre of the island has forested hills that rise to some 350 m.

This uninhabited island is in a scientifically interesting location, on two great biogeographical boundaries. Maracá is close to the transition between the Amazon basin and the Guiana Shield. The latter is one of the world's oldest geological formations, home of Mount Roraima (2875 m) and other sandstone table mountains, and related to similar formations in Africa that antedate the breakup of Gondwanaland and westward drift of South America. Situated at the northern edge of the Amazon River system, Maracá Island lies on Pre-Cambrian rocks on the southern slopes of the Guiana formation.

This location explains the island's geomorphology, as outlined in Chapter 8 by Furley, Dargie and Place on remote sensing, and in Chapter 10 by Robison and Nortcliff interpreting the geomorphology from an analysis of its soils (also Robison & Nortcliff 1989). Geomorphologically, Maracá divides roughly into four zones (Figure 10.1.a). To the north-east, where most of the research described in this book was carried out, the land is generally flat and about 5 m above the upper level of the surrounding rivers. The central third of Maracá is the catchment of a fan of small streams called Nassasseira that flow north-eastwards into the Santa Rosa Channel of the Uraricoera. Most of these streams dry up during the dry

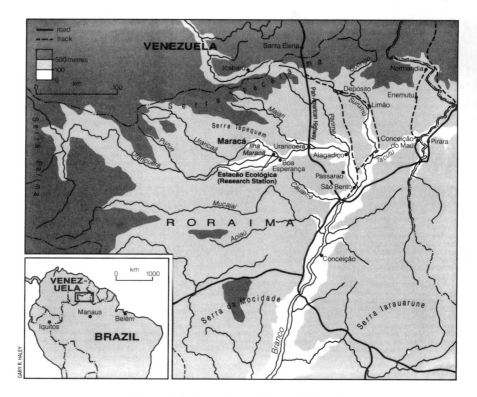

Figure 1.1   Location of Maracá Island.

season, October to late April; but this part of the island is extensively flooded during the rains.

The highest hills occur in the south-centre of Maracá. This area is still largely unexplored, but from the air it has a varied vegetation. The pedologists Robison and Nortcliff, who managed to penetrate these hills, describe in Chapter 10 their finding of a variety of soils and parent materials. The south-central hills give rise to another stream, the Igarapé de Pedra Sentada (Balanced Rock Creek), that flows northwards to the north-western side of the island. The lower part of this stream is seasonally flooded, but its valley is generally well drained. This drainage is related to sub-surface ridges of granite. At the south-western tip of Maracá Island, there are two ridges of granite hills enclosing another seasonally flooded valley. This granite formation gives steep relief to the land under the forest. It continues onto the mainland north-west of the island and causes the Uraricoera to cascade over the magnificent Purumame Falls. José Mauro Martini of the Brazilian government department of mineral production made a study of the geology of rocks in the rivers surrounding Maracá (Martini 1988).

Pedologists and geologists found a complicated pattern of rocks and soils on Maracá. The low forests of the eastern end rest on a layer of conglomerate-type material with rounded pebbles cemented together by quartz and iron. In places, this is capped by a layer of very sandy drift. Around the edges of the island and on the seasonally flooded Pedra Sentada valley, there are large areas covered in alluvial and colluvial deposits of clay. These in turn are interspersed with deposits of coarse sand. In the central highlands, a different clay drift deposit contains fewer weatherable minerals and appears to overlie a deposit of ironstone. To the east are soils directly related to residua of fresh rock. On the low ridges, the parent material is granite. But elsewhere, on steeper hills, it is metamorphic rocks such as schist, gneiss and quartzite.

Maracá Island lies on another major biogeographical boundary, between tropical forest and savanna. To the west are thousands of kilometres of unbroken and largely undisturbed forests – of the Parima Hills, beyond them in Venezuela the upper Orinoco, and west of it the headwaters of the Rio Negro and in Colombia other north-western tributaries of the Amazon. To the east and north are great natural savannas, grasslands covering 54,000 sq km of the upper Rio Branco in northernmost Brazil, the Rupununi plateau of southern Guyana, and the Gran Sabana of south-eastern Venezuela. The eastern tip of the island projects into the edge of these grasslands.

There are some 480 ha of unflooded savanna on Maracá, so that it proved a useful place to study the enigmas of the forest–savanna boundary. In Chapter 2, John Proctor discusses the formation and underlying soils of both the unflooded campo savannas and the seasonal savannas, which include rank herbaceous *vazantes* (seasonally flooded areas). In Chapter 7, Peter Furley and James Ratter examine the factors that appear to have caused the sharp transition between forest and savanna, both at two sites close to the ecological station near the eastern end of the island, and also at some *vazante* clearings that occur in many parts of Maracá. They conclude that seasonal flooding and differences in soil properties are the prime factors. This study summarises and complements other papers on forest–savanna boundaries in many parts of the tropics, including Maracá Island, which are published in a book edited by Drs Furley, Proctor & Ratter on the nature and dynamics of such boundaries (Furley, Proctor & Ratter 1992).

Ninety per cent of Maracá's 100,000 or more hectares are covered in forest, which varies considerably partly as a result of the underlying soils and flood conditions. The intensively studied eastern end of the island has a low forest cover. The continuous canopy here is at 20–30 m, with occasional emergents such as the kapok tree (*Ceiba pentandra*) which rise to 40 m. Most tree species in this forest have slender trunks and only 12 per cent of the species are supported by triangular buttress roots. On Maracá as a whole, the density of trees and the number of tree species are comparable to other Amazon forests. However, large areas to the north of the island are unusual in being dominated by only one tree species: the 40-m *Peltogyne gracilipes*. For a detailed analysis of Maracá's vegetation, see Milliken & Ratter 1989.

Despite a long dry season (September to April) and relatively low annual rainfall averaging some 2300 mm, Maracá's eastern forests are evergreen, tropical moist forests with only 6 per cent of their trees deciduous. A peculiarity of this forest is that it grows on extremely weak, sandy soil, and yet its trees do not have a dense root mat to ensure efficient nutrient cycling. Also, these trees do not spread all their roots horizontally to collect all possible nutrients from decomposing surface litter. Some of Maracá's trees put roots down into the weak soil. In Chapter 6, Sheila Ross describes chemical characteristics of soils under forest and savanna at the eastern end of the island. She then examines changes to decomposition and soil chemistry, and rates of erosion, under different conditions of forest clearance.

Another peculiarity of the island's eastern forest is its lack of epiphytes but abundance of lianas. Only 15 per cent of its trees were found to have epiphytes – a scarcity due to the long dry season, which deprives these perching plants of a water supply. On the other hand, creepers are abundant, particularly Bignoniaceae (*Jacaranda* family). The water-carrying liana *Pinzona coriacea* (Dilleniaceae) is common, as is the 'Swiss cheese' plant *Monstera dubia* with its leaves perforated by round holes. There are many *Passiflora longiracemosa* and various *Bauhinia* species, with their undulating corkscrew stems that can reach 100 m in length. Strangler figs are also abundant. In Chapters 3 and 4, the Forest Regeneration team from the University of Stirling, which was led by Dr John Proctor, describes the structure of some semi-evergreen parts of this forest, in which 45 per cent of trees are deciduous, and such forest's relation to litter and nutrient cycling. Dr Rob Marrs joins this team in Chapter 5, in a detailed description of rates of soil mineralisation and nitrification under undisturbed forest, artificial gaps and across the forest–savanna boundary.

Maracá Island may have had some Indian inhabitants in the last century, and a handful of settlers lived at its eastern tip in the mid-twentieth century (Hemming 1990a, b). Most of the island, however, was and is uninhabited and therefore contains fauna that is becoming scarce in forests exposed to human interference.

The entire island and islets in the surrounding rivers were designated as a protected area in the 1970s, and the custodian SEMA (Special Secretariat of the Environment) decided to build a permanent research station close to Maracá's eastern, accessible end. SEMA has now been incorporated into the Brazilian government's new environmental protection agency IBAMA. The Maracá ecological station is one of the finest purpose-built research facilities in tropical America, and it continues to be admirably maintained by its administrator, Mr Guttemberg Moreno de Oliveira.

Few scientists had taken advantage of the excellent facilities on Maracá, until the Brazilian Secretary of the Environment, Dr Paulo Nogueira-Neto, invited the Royal Geographical Society to organise an ecological survey of this rich reserve. In his letter of invitation, Dr Nogueira-Neto wrote: 'Our basic objective is that research should be undertaken to provide a full understanding of the ecosystems that exist there. We want to obtain a general ecological survey of the research station in the following disciplines: geology, geomorphology, soil studies, climate, hydrology, vegetation and fauna.' Once such data were obtained, the reserve could be zoned and recommendations made for future research. Indeed, Dr Nogueira-Neto later explained to the author that it was a condition of the island's reserve status that it *must* be studied – otherwise, it risked losing its protection and being invaded by frontier colonisation. (Hemming 1989; Hemming, Ratter & Santos 1988; Hemming & Ratter 1993).

In accepting this challenging invitation, the RGS asked for permission to carry out four research programmes alongside the ecological survey requested by SEMA. One such programme was called Soils and Hydrology. Under the leadership of Professor John Thornes, then head of the Geography Department of the University of Bristol, this group conducted a series of experiments to see how much water and nutrient entered soils of the forest floor under different conditions. Some study plots had the canopy removed, others the lower vegetation, others the root-and-litter mat. These three plots were all situated some 2 km from the ecological station's buildings. Within them, the Soils and Hydrology team studied four processes: soil hydrology – movement of water on the surface and below ground; soil erosion; decomposition of leaf litter; and soil chemistry. Some of the results of this work are presented in this book. The Soils and Hydrology team involved nine Brazilian and six British scientists. Together with their scientific technicians, they spent 617 days on their field work. Dr Ross's Chapter 6 describes part of this team's research.

Another team whose research is reported here is the Forest Regeneration programme, led by Dr John Proctor of the University of Stirling. Two members of this team, Dr Jill Thompson and Duncan Scott, spent a full thirteen months on Maracá, collecting samples and recording regeneration processes in a series of artificial clearings. During the main thirteen-month phase of the Maracá Rainforest Project, the four British and four Brazilian scientists of this group together with their eight scientific technicians worked a total of 1262 days. With funding from the British Overseas Development Administration, this programme worked for a further three years in laboratory analysis of their samples, and in further annual monitoring of their field plots.

A third research programme took advantage of Maracá's location close to Roraima's natural savannas, to study the settlers who are active on this colonisation frontier. This programme, which we called Land Development, involved seven British and three Brazilian scientists working a total of 393 days. It was funded by The Ford Foundation and led by Dr Peter Furley of the University of Edinburgh. Most of its results are published in a volume edited by Dr Furley, called *The Rainforest Frontier: Settlement and Change in Brazilian Roraima*. Included here, however, is a paper by Michael Eden, Duncan McGregor and Nelson Vieira about their studies of the damaging effects on soils of forest clearance and introduction of cattle pasture on ranches across the southern channel from Maracá Island.

Another research programme was Medical Entomology, led by Dr Victor Py-Daniel of INPA in Manaus (Instituto Nacional de Pesquisas da Amazônia, Brazil's great rainforest institute). His team did valuable work on insects that transmit three common Amazonian diseases, malaria, onchocerciasis and leishmaniasis. However, none of its papers is included in this volume.

The programme that involved by far the largest contingent of scientists was the Ecological Survey. This was the team studying various aspects of the island's flora and fauna, to comply with the invitation from Dr Nogueira-Neto of SEMA. This programme was led by Dr James Ratter of the Royal Botanic Garden, Edinburgh, but the majority of its 101 scientists and 41 scientific technicians were Brazilian. Most came from INPA, the Royal Geographical Society's partner in organising the Maracá Project. The many researchers on this Ecological Survey worked a total of 3438 days. Some of their findings are published in a companion volume to this one, edited by William Milliken and Dr Ratter.

As Director of the RGS, I personally led the Maracá Rainforest Project. It developed into the largest multi-disciplinary research effort ever organised in Amazonia by any European country, with 148 scientists and 55 technicians working a total of 6075 days in the field during the main phase, plus additional later work by the Forest Regeneration team and by individual researchers. The Project was maintained by a 17-person administrative team, which worked for 1337 days, and it was visited by 107 teachers, students, media and other visitors. It thus involved a total of 327 people spending 8245 days at Maracá during the Project's main phase from February 1987 to March 1988.

The Maracá Rainforest Project may be compared in size to the longer Minimum Critical Size of Ecosystems Project (now called the Biological Dynamics of Forest Fragments Project) of INPA, WWF/US and the Smithsonian Institution. This research effort works on fazendas north of Manaus and some 900 km south of Maracá, and there were exchange visits between individuals from that and our projects. Tom Lovejoy and Rob Bierregard devised these studies of the ability of different-sized areas of forest to continue to function after surrounding forests have been felled.

Thus, in a sense, it mirrored the research of our Forest Regeneration programme. Another large research effort was the ten-year Projeto Flora Amazónica, led by Professor Ghillean Prance when he was at the New York Botanical Garden. This project sent teams of botanists to collect in many parts of Brazilian Amazonia, including Maracá; but it was of course concerned only with botanical inventory.

References

Furley, Peter A. (ed.), (1993), *The Rainforest Frontier: Settlement and Change – Brazilian Roraima*, London, Routledge.

Furley, Peter A., John Proctor and James A. Ratter (eds.), (1992), *The Nature and Dynamics of Forest–Savanna Boundaries*, London, Chapman & Hall.

Hemming, John H. (1989), The Society's Maracá Rainforest Project, Roraima, Brazil, *The Geographical Journal*, 155:1, 1–12.

— (1990a), How Brazil acquired Roraima, *The Hispanic American Historical Review* (Durham, NC, USA), 70:2, 295–326.

— (1990b), *Roraima: Brazil's Northernmost Frontier*, Research Paper 20, London Institute of Latin American Studies, University of London.

Hemming, John H., James A. Ratter and Ângelo A. dos Santos (1988), *Maracá*, São Paulo, Empresa das Artes.

Hemming, John H. and James A. Ratter (1993), *Maracá, Rainforest Island*, London, Macmillan.

Martini, José Mauro (1988), *Projeto geologia – Ilha de Maracá*, Manaus, Departamento Nacional de Produção Mineral.

Milliken, William and James A. Ratter (1989), *The Vegetation of the Ilha de Maracá*, Edinburgh, Royal Botanic Garden.

Robison, Dan and Stephen Nortcliff (1989), The soils and geomorphology of the Ilha de Maracá, Roraima: the Second Approximation, in J. A. Ratter and W. Milliken (eds.), *Maracá Rainforest Project, Preliminary Report, Soils/Solos*, Edinburgh, Royal Botanic Garden.

The savannas of Maracá

Introduction

Maracá Island is situated at the zone of transition between the Amazonian forest and the Rio Branco–Rupununi savanna. The island has an area of about 101,000 ha and is mostly forested. It has several patches of savanna, and the forest boundaries of some of those at its eastern end have been studied by a number of authors (Furley & Ratter 1990; Marrs *et al.* 1991; Milliken & Ratter 1989; Thompson *et al.* 1992; Ross *et al.* 1992; Ross, this volume). My present aim is to give a synthesis of this work, to reassess some earlier conclusions about the causes of the Maracá savannas, and to relate them to the most recent general savanna model of Sarmiento (1992).

Sarmiento regards all neotropical savannas as variants of a 'moist' type. (The true 'dry' types of savanna which occur under an annual rainfall of less than 700 mm are widespread in Africa and Australia, but absent from the neotropics where low woody formations lacking perennial grasses tend to be found in regions experiencing such a low rainfall.) Within moist savannas, Sarmiento recognises at least three major ecological types: seasonal savannas with an extended water shortage in a dry season and where water excess is absent or unimportant; hyperseasonal savannas where water excess and water shortage occur annually; and semi-seasonal savannas which suffer from an extended period of water excess without any long period of water deficiency. Sarmiento believes that the three types form a catena or chain, with seasonal savannas on the higher positions on coarsely-textured soils, hyperseasonal savannas on silty soils of intermediate positions, and semi-seasonal savannas in the lowest areas on clay soils. On Maracá the first two types have been identified (Thompson *et al.* 1992). Semi-seasonal savannas probably exist there (for example in the lower parts of the formerly grazed areas on each side of the field station causeway in the south-east of the island) and may be a component of some of the *vazantes* and other hyperseasonal savannas discussed in this paper. However in the absence of more measurements of water table depths I have regarded the wetter savannas described in this paper as of the hyperseasonal type.

Climate

Maracá has an alternating wet and dry climate which falls in the 'Aw' category defined by Köppen in 1936. This, according to Sarmiento & Monasterio (1975), is more favourable for savanna than forest. The nearest long-term weather station to Maracá is in Boa Vista, 130 km to the south-east. Records from 1923 (Instituto Nacional de Meteorologia/ Delegacia Federal de Agricultura em Roraima, unpublished) show a mean annual rainfall (1923–88) of 1696 mm. The wet season is mainly from April to September. Rainfall data are available for Maracá for two years. From 1 April 1981 to 31 March 1982 (Moskovits 1985) the rainfall was 2385 mm (cf. Boa Vista 1711 mm); from 1 April 1987 to 31 March 1988 (Thompson *et al.* 1992) the rainfall was 1822 mm (cf. Boa Vista 1299). If these differences from Boa Vista are near the average then we may tentatively assume that Maracá has had a mean annual rainfall of around 2300 mm. Monthly mean minimum temperatures on Maracá ranged from 22.2 °C to 24.7 °C and mean maxima from 36.6 °C to 39.8 °C in 1987–88 (Thompson *et al.* 1992).

The difference in rainfall between Maracá and Boa Vista is likely to reflect the overall regional constraint on the advance of the forest into the savanna. Maracá is mainly forested, while Boa Vista has little forest. This paper is concerned with local forest–savanna boundaries as they occur on the island.

The types of Maracá savannas; their boundaries with forests and associated soil changes

Furley & Ratter (1990) recognised three types of savanna from their preliminary surveys of the eastern part of Maracá. They termed these: hyperseasonal savannas; island savannas of mostly dry campo or *campo cerrado* (open arboreal savanna); and *vazante*. I shall discuss the main features and soils of each and add the case in which a described savanna (Ross *et al.* 1992) is a catena involving the first two types.

Hyperseasonal savannas

Hyperseasonal savannas have periods of soil waterlogging and soil water deficit which reinforce the seasonality of the climate in causing very wet and very dry conditions in alternation. According to the model of Sarmiento (1992), savanna, but not forest, can tolerate these fluctuations in soil water.

Furley & Ratter (1990), Marrs *et al.* (1991) and Thompson *et al.* (1992) worked on a transect across such a savanna near Santa Rosa. Details of the vegetation along the transect are given by Milliken & Ratter (1989) and summarized by Thompson *et al.* (1992) who refer to it as transect 'A'. The transect runs roughly south-west to north-east from a low-stature secondary evergreen forest (trees up to about 20 m high) across a savanna in a shallow depression (up to about 2.8 m below the forest) and on to a higher-stature secondary semi-evergreen forest (trees up to 34 m high). There is a transitional zone (about 40 m wide) of marginal woodland and low scrub as one passes from the evergreen forest into savanna grassland (*campo limpo*) (Sarmiento 1983). The opposite boundary is wider, with a zone of low scrub and dense thicket roughly 100 m wide between the savanna grassland and the semi-evergreen forest. Only the term savanna grassland (*campo limpo*) has a formal definition (Sarmiento 1983). The rest of the vegetation zones are named according to J. A. Ratter (personal communication, 1992) and supersede those terms used by Furley & Ratter (1990) and Marrs *et al.* (1991). The profile diagram in Thompson *et al.* (1992) shows many detailed differences from the sketch in Furley & Ratter (1990) and supersedes it also. It must be mentioned that transect 'A' is unusual in the diffuseness of its boundaries because of the low scrub and dense thicket. These vegetation types are local in the Santa Rosa area and absent from the transect of Ross *et al.* (1992) described later.

P. A. Furley dug a series of soil pits along the transect and measured the water depths in them from 17 March 1987 to 1 April 1988 (Thompson *et al.* 1992). The pits were all dry by 18 December, when the water in them had sunk below their bases (about 120 cm from the soil surface). There was a good correlation between wet-season water levels and the vegetation zones, which agreed well with the hyperseasonal model.

Four replicate soil samples (0–10 cm deep) were collected from each of the vegetation zones in the wet and dry seasons (Thompson *et al.* 1992). Judging from these samples the transition from forest to savanna on transect 'A' was associated with textural changes, with the savanna grassland having more clay and less sand than the forests. The correlation with the vegetation zone was not exact, however, since one of the sets of samples from low scrub had less clay and more sand than those from the semi-evergreen forest.

There were few consistent chemical differences along the transect. Available phosphorus (but not total phosphorus) was least in the low scrub and savanna grassland samples, and this coincided with their higher exchangeable acidity and lower base saturation. There was a tendency for nutrients (e.g. available phosphorus) to be more available and pH to be higher in the wet season. Marrs *et al.* (1991) obtained good correlations with the vegetation zone for nitrogen mineralization and nitrification along the transect. The forests seem likely to be much better supplied with inorganic nitrogen. The processes of nitrogen mineralization and nitrification are clearly sensitive to waterlogging, but it is important to note that the differences in these processes between forest and savanna were maintained in the dry season.

The results of Thompson *et al.* (1992) show some differences from those of Furley & Ratter (1990), who studied the soil pits which were used for the water depth measurements, and which were also analysed for chemical and physical variation. The differences in results probably reflect local soil heterogeneity, and to some extent differences in analytical methods, but Furley & Ratter (1990) also found high exchangeable acidity levels in the non-forest areas.

A second boundary between forest and hyperseasonal savanna – the 'Angico' transect – was studied by Furley & Ratter (1990). This transect was 40 m long. It ran down a forested slope of about 25°, then flattened out as it crossed an abrupt transition with a '*Curatella americana* dominated arboreal cerrado' to savanna grassland on channelled flat ground. In this case the savanna soil had a lower pH, percentage organic carbon, available phosphorus, exchangeable bases and cation (positive ion) exchange capacity, and higher exchangeable acidity, than the forest soils. Furley & Ratter (1990) consider however that these surface soil parameters are unlikely 'to have determined the boundary'. They emphasize the importance of seasonal flooding. In 1987–88 the limit of the seasonal flooding of the savanna coincided with the limit of the forest trees and moreover 'detailed examination of the soil profiles showed that mottling (indicating at least periodic gleying) exactly coincided with the rooting depth at about the forest margin'.

Seasonal ('island') savannas
The term 'island' savannas was used for isolated, discrete savannas within the forest and for savannas 'which surround the wet hyperseasonal savannas at Santa Rosa and elsewhere' (Furley & Ratter 1990). In the latter situation they can hardly be called 'islands', however. They seem to correspond to the seasonal savannas of Sarmiento (1992) with dominant perennial grasses which 'overcome an extended period of water shortage induced by rainfall seasonality' but where 'water excess is absent or unimportant'. I propose that the term 'island' be replaced by 'seasonal'.

A transect ('B') which traversed forest and seasonal savanna at Santa Rosa in a roughly north–south direction was studied by Thompson *et al.* (1992). Here the savanna occurred on raised ground which was higher than that under the forest. The soils along the transect were predominantly sandy or of a loamy sand texture, but became more silty at the wetter southern end. There was no low scrub nor dense thicket, and the forest–savanna boundaries were abrupt. The forest at the southern end was a type of swamp forest which includes some 'buriti' (*Mauritia flexuosa* L.f.)

palms which indicate a high water table close to their bases for much of
the year. Water was observed to flow through the forest for the whole of
the wet season. At the northern end of the transect there was evergreen
forest continuous with that at the south-west of transect 'A'. The seasonal
savanna on transect 'B' was of the tree/shrub type with *Curatella americana*
by far the commonest woody species.

The savanna is up to 2.2 m higher than the lowest part of the evergreen
forest surveyed at the end of transect 'B' and up to 0.7 m higher than the
swamp forest. Surface observations in very wet periods in July 1989 and
July 1991 suggest that most of it is rarely, if ever, flooded. On 15 September 1987, when the water levels were high, the tree/shrub savanna pits on
transect 'B' had water depths ranging from 29 to 106 cm below the surface.
On the same date the four low shrub pits and the savanna grassland pit in
the central part of transect 'A' had water depths from 14 to 51 cm below
the surface. In July 1991 transect 'A' was flooded to depths of over 1 m
while transect 'B' was not flooded.

Soil analyses were less detailed for transect 'B' than for transect 'A' and
did not include studies of inorganic nitrogen dynamics. There was a large
increase in percentage sand, moving from the swamp forest into savanna.
The transition from evergreen forest to savanna at the north end of the
transect was not accompanied by any soil textural changes. The swamp
forest had a much higher loss-on-ignition and much higher concentrations
of total nitrogen, phosphorus and exchangeable cations. Nutrient concentrations in the seasonal tree/shrub savanna were generally low (except for
samples from the southernmost pit in this vegetation, close to the swamp
forest). Exchangeable potassium, calcium, and magnesium were at relatively
high concentrations in the evergreen forest sample, while available
phosphorus and pH showed no clear trends along the transect.

Furley & Ratter (1990) described the seasonal savanna grasslands along
the 'Preguiça Trail' (about 10 km south–west of the Santa Rosa savannas):
'Despite their isolation, these island campos contain characteristic arboreal
cerrado species.' Their soils are 'extremely sandy-textured with high porosity and drainage potentials'. The data show that although they had a
similar pH (*c.* 5.0 in water) they had much lower exchangeable base concentrations than the *vazante* and nearby forests, much lower carbon and
nitrogen, and a relatively high exchangeable acidity.

Vazantes

These seem to be a special type of hyperseasonal savanna which Furley
& Ratter (1990) described thus: 'valley-like features containing a dense
layer of herbs, herbaceous climbers and grasses and occupying seasonal
streamlines through tall forest. The forest–marginal shrub boundary is
extremely sharp and is coincident not only with the morphologically distinct seasonal streamlines but also with a very characteristic soil change

from well-drained sandy soils in the forest to poorly-drained clay-rich soils in the *vazantes'*. In the example studied in detail by these authors, the *vazante* soils had much higher soil organic matter, exchangeable cations, and a slightly lower pH than the soils under the surrounding forests.

Catenary savannas

A catena from seasonal to hyperseasonal savanna occurred on the transect studied for a short period during the early part of the wet season of 1989 by Ross *et al.* (1992). This transect is in the Santa Rosa savanna area and is about 900 m south of transect 'A' studied by Thompson *et al.* (1992). The lower parts of Ross *et al.*'s transect, including their 'dry campo' and 'wet campo', are hyperseasonal tree/shrub savannas structurally different from any vegetation on transect 'A'. The upper part of the transect, including their 'transition zone' and 'dry savanna', is savanna grassland of the seasonal savanna type but less woody than the savanna on transect 'B'. The *terra firme* forest of Ross *et al.* was taller and probably older secondary forest than the evergreen forests of transects 'A' and 'B'.

Water depth measurements made by Ross *et al.* (1992) showed the expected trend, with the lowest levels under the evergreen forest and the highest under the hyperseasonal savanna. Soil pH showed little difference between vegetation types along the transect while there was a trend in soil organic carbon from low values in the tree/shrub savanna to high values in the forest. There were low total nitrogen concentrations along the whole transect and lower carbon–nitrogen ratios in the savanna than in the forest.

As reported by Marrs *et al.* (1991) for transect 'A', the evergreen forest was likely to be better supplied than the savanna with nitrate nitrogen. For ammonium nitrogen (unlike Marrs *et al.* 1991), Ross *et al.* (1992) found the savanna on their transect better supplied than the forest. It must be re-membered that the conclusions of Ross *et al.* are based on samples taken on one date only (in the early wet season) whilst the data collected by Marrs *et al.* spanned a year, and that the latter authors did report one occasion (in the transition between the dry and wet seasons) when there was a greater rate of nitrogen mineralization in the savanna grassland than the forest.

The causes of the Maracá savannas

Human influence

Furley & Ratter (1990) made no mention of the possible influence of man on Maracá. However, the Santa Rosa savanna is known to have been near the site of a large Indian village destroyed in the 1880s (Koch-Grünberg 1917). The area has had human occupation since then. Thompson *et al.* (1992) reported the remains of a manioc-grating station near transect 'A' and other signs of human occupation on transect 'B'. The Santa Rosa savanna was burned regularly until about 1980 when the last farmer left the area. The hyperseasonal savanna grassland at the end of the 'Angico' transect of Furley & Ratter (1990) was burned regularly and grazed by several hundred cattle until 1980 (Proctor & Miller 1993). The latter authors also give evidence of past human occupation well inland on Maracá which might have influenced the seasonal ('island') savannas and *vazantes*.

Furley & Ratter (1990) reported the 'discovery of well-established trees, characteristic of the savanna, currently lying well within the forest boundary'. There are individuals of the savanna tree *Curatella americana* 'over 10 metres into the forest'. They 'appear to be no more than 10 years old which would therefore represent a rapid rate of advance'. This observation is consistent with the view that the forest is now advancing into savannas which may themselves have been to some extent man-made.

One is forced to conclude that man has had some influence on the present distribution of the Maracá savannas. This is now taken into account in the following discussion of the hyperseasonal (including *vazante*) savannas and seasonal savannas.

Hyperseasonal savannas (including vazantes)

Although their soil chemical analytical results differed to some extent, both Furley & Ratter (1990) and Thompson *et al.* (1992) used the same water-table data set, and agreed that wet-season water levels have an overriding influence on the position of the forest–savanna boundary. This model is likely to apply to the 'Angico' transect and the *vazantes* of Furley & Ratter (1990). The best correlations between soil chemistry and vegetation were those involving the supply of inorganic nitrogen (Marrs *et al.* 1991) and nitrate (Ross *et al.* 1992). Of all mineral nutrients, nitrogen supply seems the likeliest to have a role in determining the boundary between forest and savanna but it needs further work to prove this. In any case, it is likely to be subordinate to water levels since these are a major determinant of the mineralization and nitrification processes. Ross *et al.* (1992) investigated a series of soil chemical and biological attributes including soil microbial biomass, soil faunal numbers, and soil respiration. All of these were related to moisture in the upper soil horizons, and the authors provided further insights into interactions involving soil water and both nutrient supply and soil organisms. The limits of waterlogging will vary from year to year and it is important to realize that the detailed data of Furley & Ratter (1990) and Thompson *et al.* (1992) were for 1987–88 which seems to have been a relatively dry year. The good correspondence between gleying and the transition from forest to savanna observed on the 'Angico' transect by Furley & Ratter (1990) is likely to be less clear elsewhere (as Furley (1989) showed for example at the north-east end of transect 'A') because gleying features are not well-developed in many coarse-textured soils.

Some evidence of the lethal effects of flooding on non-tolerant trees was obtained in July 1991. Eighty-one tree seedlings, tagged in permanent plots at the boundary between savanna and the semi-evergreen forest near Santa Rosa, were inundated for a few days in the first part of the month. By 20 July 1991 after the water had subsided, nineteen of the seedlings were dead or moribund. The adult trees were apparently unharmed and there was no evidence that they had suffered mortality as a result of similar floods in 1989. No similar mortality occurred in seedlings in unflooded areas. A few years of low water levels and the absence of fire may allow tree seedlings to establish to the point where they survive waterlogging, and as a result the hyperseasonal savanna will tend to become forested. The high evapo-transpiration of trees will tend to lower the water level and hence facilitate their expansion into hyperseasonal savannas. Any natural or man-induced burning or grazing activities which damage the trees might have a reverse effect and thus favour hyperseasonal savannas. (A similar argument has been used to explain the expansion of European bogs following forest clearance (Moore 1987).)

Seasonal ('island') savannas
Furley & Ratter (1990) have argued that the coarsely sandy soils of the seasonal (island) savannas may be so low in nutrients that they limit the advance of forests. Sarmiento (1992) also suggested that an important cause of these savannas was low nutrients along with droughts. However the data of Furley & Ratter (1990) show concentrations of exchangeable cations under 'tall forest' which are not greatly dissimilar from those under 'campo' (savanna). The idea of the importance of low soil nutrient availability receives some support from the data of Thompson et al. (1992) along their transect 'B'. Total exchangeable bases were higher in the forests than in the tree/shrub savanna there, although available phosphorus showed no clear trends and total phosphorus was strikingly low in the evergreen forest. The comparisons of the seasonal savanna soil with those under types of depauperate Amazonian heath forests made by Furley & Ratter (1990) seem not to be valid. The base saturation of the drier savanna soils on Maracá is around 50 per cent and their pH about 5.0. Both these values are higher than those of heath forest soils – which are podzolized and not developed under such seasonal conditions as on Maracá (Thompson et al. 1992).

The role of excessive drought in accounting at least partly for the seasonal savannas is supported by some evidence. The upper parts of transect 'B' are certainly drier than the swamp forest, although only one pit in the tree/shrub savanna had water depths as low as those in the evergreen forest at the northern end of the transect. Furley & Ratter stress the

coarse sandy nature of their seasonal ('island') savannas and it is possible
that all these seasonal savannas have prolonged soil moisture deficits which
inhibit forest colonization. Anthropogenic factors may have played some
part in the formation of the seasonal savannas as discussed earlier, and
transect 'B' (Thompson *et al.* 1992) is known to have been in a highly
disturbed area, for example. It should be emphasized that the causes of the
seasonal savannas are not mutually exclusive, and nutrient shortage,
drought, and man might have been involved singly or in all combinations
as envisaged by Sarmiento (1992). The occurrence of seasonal savannas
which 'surround the wet hyperseasonal savannas at Santa Rosa and
elsewhere' (Furley & Ratter 1990) might even simply result from the
occasional outward and limited spread of fire from a hyperseasonal core
savanna. Finally, the possibility has been put forward by Furley & Ratter
(1990) that the seasonal savanna communities on Maracá may be relics
which are gradually being overtaken by forest. They may possibly represent
'the last relict outposts of the supposed Pleistocene savannas'.

Distinguishing seasonal and hyperseasonal savannas
The catenary transition between seasonal and hyperseasonal savannas is
bound to be a continuum, and intermediates will always be found. Furley
& Ratter (1990), through tracing savanna distribution from satellite imagery, suggested that at least some seasonal ('island') savannas might represent old streamlines where past or present water excesses may occur.
W. Milliken (personal communication, 1992) observed flooding in some of
these savannas during the wet season of the relatively dry year 1987. A
sample pit dug in July 1991 near the forest in the seasonal savanna ('dry
campo') part of Ross *et al.*'s (1992) transect had water about 10 cm below
the soil surface. These and other observations pose the important question
of how frequently, at what level, and for how long the water must remain
before it has an ecological effect. No data are presently available to determine this. It should be mentioned that S. M. Ross (personal communication, 1992) has observed organic mottlings in the surface horizons along
transect 'B' which may have been made by earthworms in unflooded conditions. At greater depths in the same profiles she observed ochreous
discolourations indicating iron depositions. The relationship between these
features and present-day water tables remains to be elucidated. W. Milliken
(personal communication, 1992) regards all Maracá savannas as significantly
influenced by soil waterlogging, but in the absence of detailed studies I
prefer to keep the distinction of Sarmiento (1992) between the extremes
of seasonal savanna, where waterlogging may briefly occur but have no
important effect, and hyperseasonal savanna, where waterlogging is prolonged and has a pronounced effect. Much further work is necessary before
the role of waterlogging can be more fully understood.

Conclusions

There are several important questions about the Maracá savannas, particularly the seasonal savannas, which need more intensive and longer-term studies on more sites than hitherto. Since the island has a wide range of savanna types, which have apparently mobile boundaries with forest, and has fully protected status, it has the potential to become a key site for savanna research. Studies of the long-term dynamics of savanna and other Maracá vegetation sites are important, and other research should include: palynology of the sediments of the island's few small lakes; studies of $^{13}C/$ ^{12}C quotients in the soil organic matter; and studies of soil micromorphology.

Acknowledgements

Dr P. A. Furley, Mr W. Milliken, Dr J. A. Ratter, Dr J. Thompson and Dr S. M. Ross are thanked for comments on the manuscript.

References

Furley, P. A. (1989), The soils and soil–plant relationships of the eastern sector of Maracá Island (appendix 5), in Milliken, W. & Ratter, J. A. *The Vegetation of the Ilha de Maracá*, Edinburgh, Royal Botanic Garden, 229–76.

Furley, P. A. & Ratter, J. A. (1990), Pedological and botanical variations across the forest–savanna transition on Maracá Island, *The Geographical Journal*, 156, 251–66.

Koch-Grünberg, T. (1917), *Von Roroima zum Orinoco. Ergebnisse einer Reise in Nordbrasilien und Venezuela in den Jahren 1911–1913*, 2, Berlin, Ernst Vohsen Verlag.

Köppen, W. (1936), Das geographische System der Klimate, in Köppen, W. & Geiger, W. (eds.), *Handbuch der Klimatologie*, 1, Teil C. Berlin, Gebrüder Bornträger.

Marrs, R. H., Thompson, J., Scott, D. A. & Proctor, J. (1991), Soil nitrogen mineralization and nitrification in *terra firme* forest and savanna soils on Ilha de Maracá, Roraima, Brazil, *Journal of Tropical Ecology*, 7, 123–37.

Milliken, W. & Ratter, J. A. (1989), *The Vegetation of the Ilha de Maracá*, Edinburgh, Royal Botanic Garden.

Moore, P. D. (1987), Man and mire: a long and wet relationship, *Transactions of the Botanical Society of Edinburgh*, 45, 77–95.

Moskovits, D. K. (1985), *The Behaviour and Ecology of Two Amazonian Tortoises* Geochelone carbonaria *and G.* denticulata *in Northwestern Brazil*, Ph.D. thesis, University of Chicago, USA.

Proctor, J. & Miller, R. P. (1993), Human occupation on Maracá Island: preliminary notes, in Milliken, W. & Ratter, J. A. (eds.), *Maracá: Ecology of an Amazonian Rain Forest* (in press), Manchester, Manchester University Press.

Ross, S. M., Luizão, F. J. & Luizão, R. C. C. (1992), Soil conditions and soil biology in different habitats across a forest–savanna boundary on Maracá Island,

Roraima, Brazil, in Furley, P. A., Proctor, J. & Ratter, J. A. (eds.), *Nature and Dynamics of Forest–Savanna Boundaries*, London, Chapman & Hall, 145–70.

Sarmiento, G. (1983), The savannas of tropical America, in Bourlière, F. (ed.), *Ecosystems of the World 13: Tropical Savannas*, New York, Elsevier, 245–88.

Sarmiento, G. (1992), A conceptual model relating environmental factors and vegetation formations in the lowlands of tropical South America, in Furley, P. A., Proctor, J. & Ratter, J. A. (eds.), *Nature and Dynamics of Forest–Savanna Boundaries*, London, Chapman & Hall, 583–601.

Sarmiento, G. & Monasterio, M. (1975), A critical consideration of the environmental conditions associated with the occurrence of savanna ecosystems in tropical America, in Golley, F. B. & Medina, E. (eds.), *Tropical Ecological Systems: Trends in Terrestrial and Aquatic Research*, New York, Springer-Verlag, 223–50.

Thompson, J., Proctor, J., Ratter, J. A. & Scott, D. A. (1992), The forest–savanna boundary on Maracá Island, Roraima, Brazil: an investigation of two contrasting transects, in Furley, P. A., Proctor, J. & Ratter, J. A. (eds.), *Nature and Dynamics of Forest–Savanna Boundaries*, London, Chapman & Hall, 367–92.

3 *Jill Thompson, John Proctor and Duncan A. Scott*

A semi-evergreen forest on Maracá Island I: Physical environment, forest structure and floristics

Introduction

Maracá Island (3° 20′ N, 61° 20′ W) is situated in the Uraricoera River, a principal headwater of the Rio Branco, in Roraima. The island is 60 km long and 15–25 km wide and has an area of about 101,000 ha. It is mostly covered with evergreen lowland rain forest but its east end is at the zone of transition between the Amazonian rain forest and the Rio Branco–Rupununi savanna. There are several small savanna areas on Maracá itself (Furley & Ratter 1990) and very locally, semi-evergreen forest. The island is now uninhabited but, as is discussed later, the forests at its east end are likely to have had human disturbance in the past (Proctor & Miller 1993).

The evergreen forest on a plateau in the east of Maracá has been intensively described and studied for nutrient cycling and regeneration (Scott *et al.* 1992; Thompson *et al.* 1992a, b). During the course of this work, a smaller-scale study was made of the semi-evergreen forest. The area of the semi-evergreen forest on Maracá is very small and no plot replication was attempted. The lack of replication means that any conclusions must be accepted with caution, but the study was deemed worthwhile because of the shortage of ecological information about this forest type. A 50 × 50 m plot set up in this forest type is described here and compared with the evergreen forest. Litterfall and nutrient cycling in the semi-evergreen forest plot are discussed by Scott, Thompson & Proctor (this volume).

Physical environment

Climate

The nearest long-term weather station to Maracá is in Boa Vista, 130 km to the south-east. Records from 1923 (Instituto Nacional de Meteorologia/ Delegacia Federal de Agricultura em Roraima, unpublished) show a mean annual rainfall (1923–88) of 1696 mm. The wet season is mainly between April and September. Rainfall was recorded daily in a clearing next to the Maracá field station at 0700 hours from 20 March 1987 to 31 May 1988 in a standard (7.7 cm diameter) rain gauge of which the upper rim was 110 cm above the ground. The total rainfall between 1 April 1987 and 31 March 1988 was 1822 mm (the Boa Vista rainfall was 1299 mm). Moskovits (1985) measured rainfall (2385 mm) on Maracá for the same period in 1981–82 (cf. Boa Vista 1711 mm). If these differences from Boa Vista are near the average then Maracá has probably had a mean annual rainfall of around 2300 mm since 1923. During the present study the wettest month was May 1987 with 371 mm and the driest was April 1988 with 0.1 mm. Occasional but fairly regular heavy rains were a feature of the dry season. Eleven days with more than 5 mm of rain occurred between 15 October 1987 and 24 March 1988 when a rainfall of 25 mm was followed by a very dry spell of 44 days until 37 mm fell on 8 May 1988.

Temperature records were made at 0700 daily in a Stevenson screen in the field station clearing from 5 September 1987 to 31 May 1988. These records unfortunately did not span the wettest part of the year but they included some very wet days. The monthly mean maxima ranged from 36.6 °C in September 1987 to 39.8 °C in April 1988 with the highest temperature of 42.0 °C recorded on 1 February 1988. There was a sharp decrease in May 1988, when the lowest daily maximum of 26.5 °C (9 May 1988) was recorded – coinciding with the onset of the wet season. Mean minimum temperatures were less variable than the maxima, and ranged from 22.2 °C in March 1988 to 24.7 °C in April 1988. The lowest minimum recorded was 20.0 °C on 20, 22–24 and 28 March 1988, and the highest was 28.0 °C on 23 April 1988.

Soils
The soils under the semi-evergreen forest plot are sandy loams in the surface horizons and sandy clays in the deeper layers. They had no surface organic horizon nor root mat. Details of the chemistry and texture of soil surface (0–10 cm depth) samples are given in Table 3.1.

Materials and methods

Forest description
The plot of 50 × 50 m was set up in a typical area of a small patch of semi-evergreen forest about 1 km from the river at Santa Rosa. The plot was marked out and sub-divided into twenty-five (10 × 10 m) sub-plots which were used as a sample grid. The diameters of all trees (at least 10 cm dbh) were measured on one occasion in March 1987. The measurements were made at breast height (1.3 m) except for those trees with large buttresses or prop roots which had their diameters measured 30 cm above the protrusions. Where trees had multiple stems (each at least 10 cm dbh) each

Table 3.1 Mean soil chemical and physical properties in surface (0–10 cm) samples from a 50 × 50 m plot in semi-evergreen forest and from three plots (means with ranges in parentheses) of the same size in evergreen forest on Maracá Island, Roraima, Brazil. There were ten soil samples from each plot.

		Semi-evergreen forest	Evergreen forest
pH	(log units)	4.7	4.9 (4.8–5.0)
Loss-on-ignition	(%)	3.0	1.02 (0.95–1.08)
N_{total}	(mg/g)	1.1	0.46 (0.44–0.50)
P_{total}	(mg/g)	0.18	0.061 (0.052–0.073)
$P_{extractable}$	(μg/g)	6.7	5.1 (4.7–5.4)
$K_{exchangeable}$	(m-equivs/100g)	0.19	0.066 (0.051–0.078)
$Na_{exchangeable}$	(m-equivs/100g)	0.001	0.048 (0.0096–0.104)
$Ca_{exchangeable}$	(m-equivs/100g)	0.73	0.23 (0.15–0.37)
$Mg_{exchangeable}$	(m-equivs/100g)	0.56	0.18 (0.13–0.25)
$Al_{exchangeable}$	(m-equivs/100g)	0.041	0.007 (0.004–0.012)
$H_{exchangeable}$	(m-equivs/100g)	0.122	0.36 (0.29–0.41)
CEC	(m-equivs/100g)	1.60	0.85 (0.75–0.99)
Base saturation	(%)	89.9	55.5 (47.4–70.6)
Bulk density	(g/cm^3)	1.42	1.38 (1.27–1.56)
Clay	(%)	12.7	11.9 (9.8–15.5)
Sand	(%)	56.3	87.9 (82.8–90.9)
Silt	(%)	31.2	3.7 (2.3–5.6)

was measured separately. The trees were identified initially in the field by J. A. Ratter and co-workers, and further identifications were made on collected specimens.

Each tree in the plot was scored for the following attributes:

- deciduous or evergreen (J. A. Ratter, personal communication, 1992);
- simple, pinnate, bi-pinnate or palmate leaves;
- buttresses (greater than 50 cm);
- presence or absence of epiphytes above and below 5 m bole height;
- percentage cover of bryophytes in a 10 cm-wide band between 1.5 and 1.6 m high on the bole.

Lianas (more than 1 cm dbh) were counted in all 10 × 10 m sub-plots. A transect (60 × 7.5 m) of mature forest (of which 50 m were within the plot) was selected for a profile diagram of trees over 6 m high.

Surface soil sampling and analysis
One surface (0–10 cm) soil sample was collected at random from each of ten randomly selected 10 × 10 m sub-plots on 25 April 1987. Each soil

sample was air-dried and sieved through a 2 mm mesh, and 100 g sub-samples were returned to Stirling for chemical analysis. pH was measured in a mix of one part soil to two parts deionized water, shaken for two hours and allowed to stand for one hour. Loss-on-ignition was measured on oven-dried sub-samples after heating at 375 °C for 16 hours. Total nitrogen and phosphorus were extracted from 1.5 g sub-samples of soil digested in a mixture of 6 ml concentrated sulphuric acid (containing 0.1 per cent selenium as a catalyst) and 3 ml of '100 volume' hydrogen per-oxide. The nitrogen and phosphorus were measured colorimetrically by Technicon auto-analyser: nitrogen was determined using sodium dichloroisocyanurate as the chlorine source, and phosphorus was deter-mined using molybdenum blue. Available phosphorus was extracted from 10 g sub-samples of soil by 50 ml Melich solution (a mixture of 0.05 M hydrochloric acid and 0.0125 M sulphuric acid) and analysed using a similar auto-analyser technique to that used for total phosphorus. Exchangeable cations were leached from 10 g sub-samples of soils by ten successive additions of 10 ml of 1 M ammonium acetate solution adjusted (by the addition of acetic acid) to pH 4.8 (mean soil pH), and were analysed by atomic absorption spectrophotometry, using an air/acetylene flame for sodium and potassium and a nitrous oxide/acetylene flame for calcium and magnesium. For analyses of total acidity and exchangeable aluminium, 10 g sub-samples of soil were leached by ten successive additions of 10 ml of 1 M potassium chloride solution. This was then treated with 0.0025 M sodium hydroxide solution and phenolphthalein indicator to measure total acidity. After 10 ml 1 M potassium fluoride had been added to the titrated solution, another titration with 0.005 M hydrochloric acid gave the values for exchangeable aluminium. Cation exchange capacity was calculated from the sum of total exchangeable cations plus total acidity.

Soil particle-size analyses were made on 50 g of soil samples using the pipette method of Black *et al.* (1965). Bulk density was measured in January 1988 (during the dry season) at two points. A metal box with dimensions of 30 × 30 cm was inserted into the soil to a depth of 10 cm, and the soil excavated, weighed in the field and then corrected to dry weight in the laboratory.

Results

Forest description

The profile diagram (Figure 3.1) gives an impression of the overall appearance of the forest plot, and descriptive data for it are given in Table 3.2. The tallest tree recorded in the plot was about 40 m and none exceeded 70 cm diameter. Deciduous trees accounted for 45 per cent of the individuals. There was a relatively high density of trees and small lianas, and a small proportion of trees with pinnate or bi-pinnate leaves.

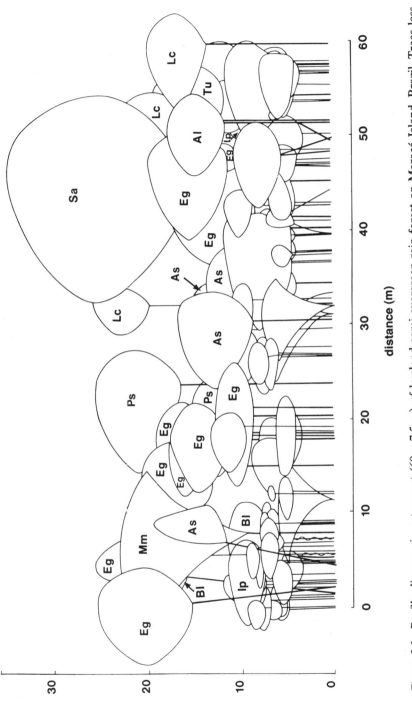

Figure 3.1 Profile diagram in a transect (60 × 7.5 m) of lowland semi-evergreen rain forest on Maracá Island, Brazil. Trees less than 6 m excluded. Symbols for trees over 10 cm dbh: Al, *Alseis longifolia*; As, *Apeiba schomburgkii*; Bl, *Brosimum lactescens*; Eg, *Ecclinusa guianensis*; Ip, *Isertia parviflora*; Lc, *Lecythis corrugata*; Mm, *Maximiliana maripa*; Ps, *Pouteria surumensis*; Sa, *Simarouba amara*; Tu, *Tabebuia uleana*.

Table 3.2 A comparison of features of trees (≥ 10 cm dbh) and lianas (> 1 cm dbh) in the semi-evergreen forest plot with those from six plots (means with ranges in parentheses) of the same size in evergreen forest on Maracá Island.

Feature	Semi-evergreen forest	Evergreen forest
Tree density (per ha)	600	419 (340–476)
Tree basal area (m² per ha)	21.6	23.8 (21.7–26.7)
Tree species no. (per 0.25 ha)	31	40 (33–47)
Trees with palmate leaves (%)	3.3	1.1 (0.9–1.7)
Trees with pinnate leaves (%)	7.9	19.7 (13.4–26.5)
Trees with bi-pinnate leaves (%)	0.7	0.6 (0.0–2.7)
Trees with buttresses (≥ 0.5 m) (%)	2.6	11.9 (8.2–15.7)
Trees with multiple stems (≥ 10 cm dbh) (%)	6.0	0.9 (0–3.4)
Trees with epiphytes (>5 m) (%)	9.3	14.7 (9.7–21.0)
Lianas (< 1 cm dbh) (per m²)	6.8	1.6 (1.6–1.6)
Lianas (≥ 1–< 5 cm dbh) (per m²)	0.8	0.5 (0.2–0.8)
Lianas (≥ 5 cm dbh) (per m²)	0.0	0.07 (0.0–0.2)

Thirty-one tree species were recorded from the plot (Table 3.3) which is relatively species-poor although the species–area curve is still rising (Figure 3.2). The Sapotaceae were the leading family with 25.5 per cent of the basal area, with the Lecythidaceae second with 16.1 per cent of the basal area (Table 3.4).

Soil analyses
The soil analytical results are given in Table 3.1.

Discussion

Comparisons with evergreen forest
Comparative data for the Maracá evergreen forests studied by Thompson *et al.* (1992a) are included in Tables 3.1, 3.2 and 3.4. Their data were obtained from an intensive study of six quarter-hectare plots in an area about 3 km south of the semi-evergreen forest. The soils (Table 3.1) under the semi-evergreen forest were much less sandy, higher in organic matter and total and available nutrients, and had a higher base saturation. Marrs *et al.* (1991) found that soil nitrogen mineralization rates and nitrification rates were higher in three out of four sampling periods in the semi-evergreen forest. Evergreen trees with their longer-lasting leaves are probably able to use nutrients more efficiently (Chapin 1980) and hence likely to be better adapted to poorer soils. The occurrence on relatively

Table 3.3 The tree (≥ 10 cm dbh) species (with the family in parenthesis) recorded from a 50 × 50 m plot in semi-evergreen forest on Maracá Island, Brazil.

Aegiphila sp. (Verbenaceae)
Alseis longifolia Ducke (Rubiaceae)
Amaioua corymbosa Kunth (Rubiaceae)
Apeiba schomburgkii Szysz. (Tiliaceae)
Bombacopsis quinata (Jacq.) Dug. (Bombacaceae)
Brosimum lactescens (Moore) C. C. Berg (Moraceae)
Casearia sylvestris Sw. (Flacourtiaceae)
Cecropia palmata Willd. (Moraceae)
Ceiba pentandra (L.) Gaertn. (Bombacaceae)
Cochlospermum orinocense (Kunth) Steud. (Cochlospermaceae)
Cordia sellowiana Cham. (Boraginaceae)
Ecclinusa guianensis Eyma (Sapotaceae)
Eschweilera pedicellata (Richard) Mori (Lecythidaceae)
Genioa americana L. (Rubiaceae)
Guazuma ulmifolia Lam. (Sterculiaceae)
Guettarda spruceana M. Arg. (Rubiaceae)
Himatanthus articulatus (Vahl) Woods. (Apocynaceae)
Isertia parviflora Vahl (Rubiaceae)
Jacaranda copaia subsp. *spectabilis* (Mart. ex DC.) A. Gentry (Bignoniaceae)
Lecythis corrugata Poit. (Lecythidaceae)
Maximiliana maripa (Correa) Drude (Palmae)
Maytenus sp. (Celastraceae)
Pouteria surumensis Baehni (Sapotaceae)
Pradosia surinamensis (Eyma) Penn. (Sapotaceae)
Rinorea brevipes (Benth.) Blake (Violaceae)
Sapium sp. (Euphorbiaceae)
Simarouba amara Aubl. (Simaroubaceae)
Spondias mombin L. (Anacardiaceae)
Swartzia grandifolia Bong. ex Benth. (Leguminosae)
Tabebuia uleana (Kranzl.) A. Gentry (Bignoniaceae)
Vismia cayennensis (Jacq.) Pers. (Guttiferae)

---

more fertile sites of forests with a relatively high proportion of deciduous trees has been reported from central Brazil by Furley *et al.* (1988) and Ratter *et al.* (1973, 1978).

The semi-evergreen forest had a higher tree density (Table 3.2) and was of smaller stature than the evergreen forests studied by Thompson *et al.* (1992a), which had trees up to about 40 m tall and up to 107 cm diameter, and a higher proportion of buttressed trees. The proportion of deciduous trees was much higher (45 per cent of the individuals) in the semi-evergreen forest than the evergreen forest (5.7 per cent, range 3.4–8.3 per cent).

The plots in both forest types are likely to be in old secondary growth

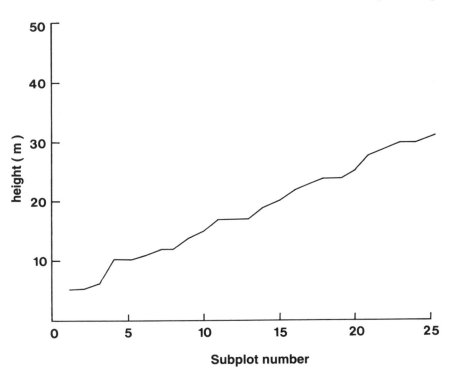

Figure 3.2   Species–area curve for trees (≥ 10 cm dbh) on a 50 × 50 m plot in semi-evergreen forest on Maracá Island, Brazil. The curve follows the order of enumeration of the twenty-five 10 × 10 m sub-plots within the plot.

(Proctor & Miller 1993). The semi-evergreen forest plot is almost certainly part of the light woods ('lichten Wald') described by Koch-Grünberg (1917) on his way to the Santa Rosa savanna. He described human occupation in the area, and there was small-scale occupancy there until 1980 (Proctor & Miller 1993). These occupants are likely to have had a considerable impact on the semi-evergreen forest, and its smaller stature and higher proportion of multiple-stemmed trees (Table 3.2) suggest that it may be more recently disturbed than the evergreen forest. The evergreen forest plots have remains of axeheads and pottery nearby and abundant charcoal in the soil, but have probably been undisturbed since before 1880 (Proctor & Miller 1993). There is no evidence that semi-evergreen forest is a seral stage in the recovery of evergreen forest from disturbance.

In the evergreen forest plots the Moraceae ranked first (thirteenth in the semi-evergreen forest) and the Sapotaceae ranked second (first in the semi-evergreen forest) (Table 3.4). The Burseraceae and Chrysobalanaceae, ranked third and fourth in the evergreen forest, were absent from the

Table 3.4 The percentage contribution of each family to tree (≥ 10 cm dbh) basal area in the semi-evergreen forest plot, and the mean contribution (with ranges in parentheses) of the same families to tree basal area on six plots of the same size in the evergreen forest on Maracá Island.

	Semi-evergreen forest %	Evergreen forest %
Anacardiaceae	1.50	0.87 (0.0–2.4)
Apocynaceae	0.06	2.67 (0.0–4.2)
Bignoniaceae	4.44	1.20 (0.0–3.1)
Bombacaceae	0.05	0.0
Boraginaceae	1.87	0.62 (0.0–2.8)
Celastraceae	0.20	0.05 (0.0–0.3)
Cochlospermaceae	2.85	0.0
Euphorbiaceae	2.92	0.57 (0.0–3.0)
Flacourtiaceae	0.02	0.82 (0.3–1.7)
Guttiferae	0.02	0.0
Lecythidaceae	16.1	2.55 (0.0–3.7)
Leguminosae	0.07	3.43 (0.0–7.9)
Moraceae	1.47	20.13 (13.2–31.8)
Palmae	11.39	5.12 (2.4–6.2)
Rubiaceae	6.04	3.10 (1.1–8.1)
Sapotaceae	25.47	18.47 (8.2–31.0)
Simaroubaceae	6.76	1.40 (0.0–4.9)
Sterculiaceae	5.00	0.0
Tiliaceae	12.45	2.8 (0.0–9.8)
Verbenaceae	0.18	0.25 (0.0–1.1)
Violaceae	0.21	0.0

semi-evergreen plot. There was a mean of forty tree species (range thirty-three to forty-seven) per quarter-hectare in the evergreen plots, which were all more species-rich than the semi-evergreen forest (Table 3.2).

Relationships with savanna
A transect across the boundary between the savanna and the semi-evergreen forest has been described by Thompson *et al.* (1992b). They concluded that the sharp boundary was related to the degree of waterlogging in the wet season. The savanna adjacent to the plot was of the 'hyperseasonal' type of Sarmiento (1983) which is waterlogged annually for several months. It is assumed that the semi-evergreen forest is intolerant of prolonged waterlogging, although adult trees there survived soil flooding for a few days in 1989 and 1991 during exceptionally high levels of the Uraricoera River. The savannas of Maracá have already been discussed by Proctor (this volume).

Acknowledgements

We thank Secretaria Especial do Meio Ambiente (SEMA) for their invitation to the Royal Geographical Society (RGS) to work on Maracá, and Guttemberg Moreno de Oliveira and other SEMA staff for much help. The RGS, particularly Dr J. Hemming, Mr S. Bowles, and Miss F. Watson, gave support in many ways. We thank the Overseas Development Administration for funding. Souza Cruz Ltd provided Jill Thompson with financial support. Dr J. Ferraz, Dr P. A. Furley, Miss S. Latham, Dr R. H. Marrs, Mr R. Miller, W. Milliken, J. A. Ratter, V. Viana and Dr S. Ross and technicians from Instituto Nacional de Pesquisas da Amazônia (INPA) are thanked also for their help.

References

Black, C. A., Evans, D. D., White, J. L., Ensminger, L. E. & Clark, F. E. (1965), *Methods of Soil Analysis*, Madison, American Society of Agronomy.

Chapin, F. S. (1980), The mineral nutrition of wild plants, *Annual Review of Ecology and Systematics*, 11, 233–60.

Furley, P. A. & Ratter, J. A. (1990), Pedological and botanical variations across the forest–savanna transition on Maracá Island, *The Geographical Journal*, 156, 251–66.

Furley, P. A., Ratter, J. A. & Gifford, D. R. (1988), Observations on the vegetation of eastern Mato Grosso, Brazil III. The woody vegetation and soils of the Morro de Fumaca, Torixoreu, *Proceedings of the Royal Society of London*, B: 235, 259–80.

Koch-Grünberg, T. (1917), *Von Roroima zum Orinoco. Ergebnisse einer Reise in Nordbrasilien und Venezuela in den Jahren 1911–1913*, 2, Berlin, Ernst Vohsen Verlag.

Marrs, R. H., Proctor, J., Scott, D. A. & Thompson, J. (1991), Nitrogen mineralization and nitrification in *terra firme* forest and savanna soils on Ilha de Maracá, Roraima, Brazil, *Journal of Tropical Ecology*, 7, 123–37.

Moskovits, D. K. (1985), *The Behaviour and Ecology of Two Amazonian Tortoises*, Geochelone carbonaria *and* G. denticulata *in Northwestern Brazil*, Ph.D. thesis, University of Chicago, USA.

Proctor, J. & Miller, R. P. (1993), Human occupation on Maracá Island: preliminary notes, in Ratter, J. A. & Milliken, W. (eds.), *Maracá: Ecology of an Amazonian Rain Forest* (in press), Manchester, Manchester University Press.

Ratter, J. A., Askew, G. P., Montgomery, R. F. & Gifford, D. R. (1978), Observation of forests of some mesotrophic soils in central Brazil, *Revista Brasileira de Botânica*, 1, 47–58.

Ratter, J. A., Richards, P. W., Argent, G. & Gifford, D. R. (1973), Observations on the vegetation of northeastern Mato Grosso I. The woody vegetation types of the *Xavantina-Cachimbo* Expedition area, *Philosophical Transactions of the Royal Society of London*, B: 266, 449–92.

Sarmiento, G. (1983), The savannas of tropical America, in Bourlière, F. (ed.), *Ecosystems of the World 13: Tropical Savannas*, New York, Elsevier, 245–88.

Scott, D. A., Proctor, J. & Thompson, J. (1992), Ecological studies on lowland evergreen rain forest on Maracá Island, Roraima, Brazil. II. Litter and nutrient cycling, *Journal of Ecology*, 80, 705–17.

Thompson, J., Proctor, J., Viana, V., Milliken, W., Ratter, J. A. & Scott, D. A. (1992a), Ecological studies on a lowland evergreen rain forest on Maracá Island, Roraima, Brazil. I. Physical environment, forest structure and leaf chemistry, *Journal of Ecology*, 80, 689–703.

Thompson, J., Proctor, J., Viana, V., Miller, R. P., Ratter, J. A. & Scott, D. A. (1992b), The forest–savanna boundary on Maracá Island, Roraima, Brazil: an investigation of two contrasting transects, in Furley, P. A., Proctor, J. & Ratter, J. A. (eds.), *Nature and Dynamics of Forest–Savanna Boundaries*, London, Chapman & Hall, 367–92.

A semi-evergreen forest on Maracá Island II: Litter and nutrient cycling

Introduction

Thompson *et al.* (this volume) have described a semi-evergreen forest plot on the east of Maracá, and contrasted its soils, structure and floristics with those of evergreen forest on the same island. The semi-evergreen forest occurred very locally and was on more nutrient-rich, less sandy soils, and was of smaller stature and less species-rich than the evergreen forest. Forty-five per cent of its trees (those at least 10 cm dbh) were deciduous compared with 5.7 per cent of the trees in the evergreen forest.

In this paper we report on a study of litterfall and nutrient cycling from the plot in the semi-evergreen forest and compare the results with those from a parallel study on the evergreen forest (Scott *et al.* 1992).

Materials and methods

Small litterfall
Small litterfall was collected in 1 × 1 m traps made of four pieces of wood, each 15 cm deep, with a fine (*c*. 1 mm) nylon mesh nailed to the base. The traps were supported on four legs so that the top was 1 m above the ground. Nine traps were placed in a stratified random design in the plot and litterfall was collected in them from 14 April 1987 until 12 April 1988. The traps were emptied at intervals of 13–15 days except for a period (in the dry season) of 26 days between 8 December 1987 and 5 January 1988.

At each collection the contents of each trap were placed in cloth bags and dried in a field oven at about 70 °C. After drying, alternate collections were sorted into four fractions as recommended by Proctor (1983):

- leaves;
- small wood (less than 2 cm diameter; pieces larger than this were broken off and discarded, separate bark fragments were included if they were less than 2 cm along their longest dimension);
- flowers and fruits;
- trash (unrecognizable plant debris under 2 mm and insect refuse)

Shortage of time prevented the sorting of the other collections beyond two fractions: leaves and the rest. There were twenty-five fortnightly samples for leaves, thirteen such samples for small wood, flowers and fruits, and trash. There were twelve unsorted non-leaf samples. All the sorted and partially-sorted collections were dried in the laboratory at Stirling at 85 °C and weighed separately for each trap.

Small-litter layer and decomposition quotient (k_L)

All small litter was removed from within a 1×1 m quadrat at nine positions selected in a restricted random design in the plot. There was no trash fraction since it was impracticable to sort out from the soil organic matter any fragments less than 5 mm along their longest dimension. Four small-litter layer collections were made (two in each of the dry and wet seasons). The collection dates are given in Table 4.2. The litter was dried in a field oven at about 70 °C and all the collections were sorted into leaves, wood and reproductive parts as described for the small litterfall. Each sorted fraction was redried in the laboratory in Stirling at 85 °C and then weighed separately for each quadrat.

The decomposition quotient (k_L) is an approximation of the proportion of small-litter layer decomposed in one year and is calculated by the equation:

$$k_L = I/X$$

where I is the annual small-litter input to the forest floor and X is the mean small-litter layer mass. k_L values for leaves, small wood, flowers and fruits, and total small litter were calculated.

Large-wood litter and standing dead trees

An estimate of large wood lying on the forest floor was made during the dry season on 11–13 January 1988. The mass of large wood (more than 2 cm diameter) was measured in nine 5×5 m sub-plots located in a restricted random design within the plot. All dead wood was collected where practicable from each sub-plot and sorted into three categories: $> 2-< 5$ cm diameter; $> 5-< 10$ cm; and > 10 cm diameter. Occasionally large pieces of dead wood were too heavy to move so these were measured and sub-sampled using a chain saw and weighed in the field using a spring balance. The weights were corrected to oven-dry (85 °C) weights from sub-samples dried and weighed in the laboratory.

All standing dead trees (over 5 cm dbh) were measured to estimate their volume. For those dead trees which had retained their branches, the following formula (Dawkins 1961, 1963) was used:

volume of wood and bark = tree height $\times$ basal area $\times$ 0.5

A conversion factor of 0.47 g dry weight per sq cm of fresh wood obtained by oven-drying nine sub-samples of measured dead wood (more than 10 cm diameter) was used to calculate the mass of the dead trees. It is accepted that at least some of the dead trees may have been hollow and hence their mass over-estimated.

Chemical analysis of small litter
Each sorted fraction and non-sorted non-leaf fraction of the oven-dried small litterfall samples from each trap was ground and then bulked for each fraction for each collection date. The fractions (all sorted) from the small-litter layer were ground and bulked for each of the four collection dates.

Sub-samples of 0.5 g for each ground litter sample were digested in a mixture of 6 ml concentrated sulphuric acid (containing 0.1 per cent selenium as a catalyst) and 3 ml of '100 volume' hydrogen peroxide (Allen *et al.* 1974). Analyses for potassium were made by atomic absorption spectrophotometry using an air/acetylene flame and for calcium and magnesium using a nitrous oxide-acetylene flame. Nitrogen and phosphorus were measured colorimetrically by Technicon auto-analyser where nitrogen was determined using sodium salicylate and sodium nitroprusside with sodium dichloroisocyanurate as the chlorine source, and phosphorus was determined using molybdenum blue. Every fourth sample was analysed in triplicate and differences between replicates never exceeded 10 per cent and were usually within 5 per cent. Analytical techniques were tested using a foliar standard supplied by E. V. J. Tanner. For nitrogen, phosphorus and potassium, our results were within 4 per cent, 1 per cent and 1 per cent respectively of those of Tanner (personal communication, 1992). Analyses of the same material have been made by a laboratory in California (Tanner, personal communication, 1992) for calcium and magnesium. Our results were exactly the same as theirs for calcium and differed by 2 per cent for magnesium.

Results

Small litterfall
The mean small litterfall was 6.87 tonnes/ha per year (Table 4.1). Small litterfall showed a marked peak in the dry season (Figure 4.1). Leaf litter was a mean of 74.8 per cent of the mass of small litterfall. The distribution of leaf litter throughout the year was similar to the total small litterfall (Figure 4.1). The seasonal pattern of the fall of flowers and fruits, trash, and small-wood litter was less clear, partly because only alternate collections were sorted. There were peaks for flowers and fruits in March 1987, October and November 1987, and February 1988. For small wood there was a marked peak in March 1988.

Table 4.1 The small litterfall (tonnes/ha per year) (± 95 per cent CL) estimated from nine 1 × 1 m traps in a semi-evergreen forest plot on Maracá Island, Brazil (a). The means (with ranges in parentheses) of a parallel study (Scott *et al.* 1992) in three evergreen forest plots (b) are also shown.

		litterfall fraction			
(a)	leaves	small wood (< 2 cm)	flowers & fruits	trash	total
	5.14±1.10	0.78±0.40	0.63±0.30	0.32±0.10	6.87±1.66
(b)	6.30	1.34	1.21	0.42	9.28
	(5.97–6.83)	(1.07–1.58)	(0.96–1.50)	(0.39–0.47)	(8.85–9.52)

Small-litter layer and decomposition quotient (k_L)
The estimated values of the small-litter layer are shown in Table 4.2. The mean total small-litter layer mass was 3.09 tonnes/ha. The litter decomposition quotient (k_L) values for the various components of small litter are shown in Table 4.3. They range from 0.79 for the small wood to 3.94 for the flowers and fruit.

Large-wood litter and standing dead trees
The large-wood litter was 8.68 tonnes/ha (Table 4.4) which includes values for eleven standing dead trees which had a calculated total mass of 2.96 tonnes/ha.

Mineral element concentrations and accession in the small litter
The mean concentration of mineral elements in the small litterfall are given in Table 4.5 and those in the litter layer in Table 4.6. The total small-litter layer concentrations of nitrogen, magnesium and potassium were lower than in the litterfall while phosphorus and calcium concentrations were similar. Leaf-litter nitrogen, phosphorus and calcium concentrations in the small litterfall and small-litter layer were almost identical. Table 4.7 shows that leaves are a principal accession pathway.

The k_L quotient for the mass of the small litter is less than the corresponding quotients for mineral elements (Tables 4.3 and 4.7).

Discussion

Small litterfall
The small litterfall mass lies at the lower end of the published range of values recorded for Amazonian forests (Table 4.8) and is less for all fractions than the litterfall recorded from three plots in evergreen forest on Maracá by Scott *et al.* (1992). Its seasonality resembled that of the ever-

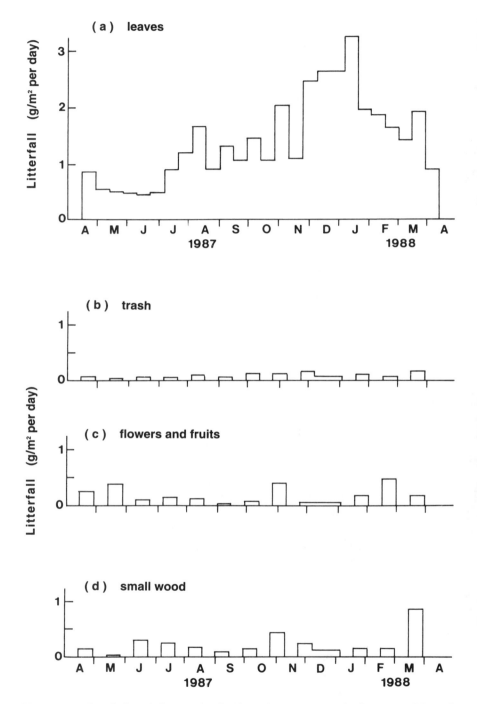

Figure 4.1 Small litterfall on a lowland semi-evergreen rain forest on Maracá. Leaf litter was sorted from all the collections; for alternate collections only, the remaining fraction was sorted into trash, flowers and fruits, and small wood. Data for the unsorted non-leaf fraction are not given.

Table 4.2 The mass (tonnes/ha) (±95 per cent CL) of small litter, estimated from nine 1 × 1 m quadrats on each of four sample dates, on the floor of a semi-evergreen forest on Maracá Island, Brazil (a). The annual means (with ranges in parentheses) of a parallel study (Scott *et al.* 1992) in three evergreen forest plots (b) are also shown.

date	leaves	small wood (< 2 cm)	flowers & fruits	total
(a)				
7 April 1987	3.39±0.84	0.99±0.29	0.22±0.17	4.60±1.06
17 June 1987	1.38±0.37	0.88±0.35	0.13±0.07	2.39±0.53
29 September 1987	0.97±0.51	0.91±0.47	0.07±0.05	1.95±0.77
5 January 1988	2.02±0.56	1.17±1.11	0.23±0.25	3.43±0.82
annual mean	1.94	0.99	0.16	3.09
(b)				
annual mean	2.14	1.78	0.61	4.63
	(1.84–2.27)	(1.63–2.05)	(0.35–0.87)	(4.27–4.92)

Table 4.3 The values of k_L, a coefficient calculated by dividing the mass of annual litterfall (Table 4.1) by the mean mass of the small-litter layer (Table 4.2) for a semi-evergreen forest on Maracá Island, Brazil (a). The mean k_L values (with ranges in parentheses) of a parallel study (Scott *et al.* 1992) in three evergreen forest plots are also shown (b).

litter fraction	leaves	small wood	flowers & fruits	total
(a)	2.65	0.79	3.94	2.22
(b)	2.94	0.76	2.00	2.01
	(2.69–3.26)	(0.65–0.84)	(1.37–2.77)	(1.93–2.07)

Table 4.4 The mass (tonnes/ha) (±SE, n = 9) of large woody litter of a range of size classes and the mass of the standing dead trees in a 50 × 50 m plot in a semi-evergreen forest on Maracá Island, Brazil. The mean values (with ranges in parentheses) for a parallel study (Scott *et al.* 1992) in three evergreen forest plots are also shown.

large woody litter diameter classes	semi-evergreen forest	evergreen forest
≥ 2–< 5 cm	0.28±0.08	0.71 (0.51–1.09)
≥ 5–< 10 cm	0.36±0.16	0.57 (0.04–0.94)
≥ 10 cm	5.09±4.31	2.38 (1.25–4.48)
standing dead trees (≥ 5 cm dbh)	2.96	0.98 (0.0–1.91)
total	8.68	5.08 (3.54–7.37)

Table 4.5 The concentrations (mg/g oven dry weight ± 95% CL) of nitrogen, phosphorus, potassium, calcium and magnesium in the small litterfall in semi-evergreen forest on Maracá Island, Brazil (a). (For the leaves n=25; for small wood, flowers and fruits, and trash n=13; for unsorted n=12). The mean values (with ranges in parentheses) of a parallel study (Scott *et al.* 1992) in three evergreen forest plots are also shown (b).

litterfall fraction	N	P	K	Ca	Mg
			elements		
(a)					
leaves	12.0±0.5	0.71±0.04	6.6±1.0	11.5±1.0	3.5±0.2
small wood (< 2 cm)	8.2±1.2	0.7±0.1	2.8±0.8	12.4±1.7	2.2±0.3
flowers & fruits	18.3±2.5	2.0±0.3	14.8±2.2	6.8±1.6	3.6±0.5
trash	17.5±1.9	1.6±0.2	7.1±1.2	12.3±1.0	3.0±0.2
unsorted	14.1±1.9	1.1±0.3	8.2±1.5	9.5±0.9	3.0±0.4
total	12.5±0.5	0.85±0.09	7.1±1.0	11.0±0.8	3.4±0.2
(b)					
leaves	12.6	0.58	4.7	7.4	2.7
	(12.3–12.7)	(0.55–0.61)	(4.1–5.2)	(6.4–7.9)	(2.6–2.9)
small wood (< 2 cm)	9.7	0.71	2.7	9.3	2.1
	(8.6–10.7)	(0.68–0.76)	(1.9–3.4)	(8.6–10.4)	(2.0–2.2)
flowers & fruits	14.6	1.30	10.7	4.8	2.6
	(12.9–17.3)	(1.26–1.43)	(10.1–11.4)	(4.6–5.2)	(2.5–2.8)
trash	19.3	1.12	6.1	6.3	2.6
	(18.9–19.9)	(1.00–1.34)	(5.6–7.0)	(2.8–8.3)	(2.3–2.7)
unsorted	12.8	0.67	5.4	6.9	1.9
	(12.1–13.9)	(0.62–0.74)	(5.1–5.6)	(6.4–7.4)	(1.8–2.0)
total	12.4	0.64	5.1	7.2	2.5
	(12.3–12.6)	(0.62–0.66)	(4.5–5.6)	(6.4–7.8)	(2.4–2.6)

green forest, however, and showed a peak fall in the dry season. A similar pattern of litterfall with a dry season peak has been recorded from Amazonian *terra firme* forests by Klinge & Rodrigues (1968a), Franken *et al.* (1979), Dantas & Phillipson (1989), and Luizão (1989). The peak litterfall in the dry season may be related to a period of water stress which is likely to be severe in the long Maracá dry season. However, peak litterfall has been reported during the wet season in Brazilian Atlantic forest (Jackson (1978).

Small-litter layer
The small-litter layer lies directly on the surface of the sandy soil. There is no surface root mat of the type often found elsewhere in Amazonia (e.g.

Table 4.6 The concentrations (mg/g oven dry weight ± S.E.) (*n* = 4) of nitrogen, phosphorus, potassium, calcium and magnesium in the small-litter layer on a plot in a semi-evergreen forest on Maracá Island, Brazil (a). The mean values with ranges in parentheses of a parallel study (D. A. Scott *et al.* 1992) in three evergreen forest plots are also shown (b).

litter fraction	N	elements P	K	Ca	Mg
(a)					
leaves	11.7 ± 0.1	0.76 ± 0.02	3.1 ± 0.8	12.1 ± 1.0	2.1 ± 0.4
small wood (< 2 cm)	7.5 ± 0.5	0.58 ± 0.02	0.8 ± 0.1	10.9 ± 1.0	1.0 ± 0.03
flowers & fruits	9.6 ± 0.8	0.70 ± 0.05	4.6 ± 2.2	5.5 ± 0.7	1.3 ± 0.2
total	10.2 ± 0.1	0.70 ± 0.02	2.5 ± 0.6	11.6 ± 0.5	1.7 ± 0.2
(b)					
leaves	12.6	0.47	2.1	7.4	2.2
	(12.0–12.9)	(0.45–0.49)	(1.8–2.2)	(6.6–8.1)	(2.1–2.4)
small wood (< 2 cm)	8.8	0.5	1.0	7.8	1.4
	(8.6–9.1)	(0.48–0.52)	(0.91–1.06)	(6.7–9.2)	(1.3–1.5)
flowers & fruits	9.2	0.80	3.1	3.5	1.3
	(7.4–11.0)	(0.75–0.83)	(1.9–4.6)	(3.1–3.7)	(1.0–1.6)
total	10.5	0.53	1.7	7.0	1.8
	(10.4–10.8)	(0.52–0.53)	(1.6–1.8)	(6.6–7.5)	(1.8–1.8)

Herrera *et al.* 1978). The estimated mean small-litter layer mass is 3.09 tonnes/ha which is less than that recorded for the evergreen forest (Table 4.2). There are few data on small-litter layer quantities for other Amazonian forests (Table 4.9) and the Maracá data are among the lower values published for lowland tropical forests elsewhere (Anderson & Swift 1983).

The use of the k_L quotient as proposed by Olsen (1963) is based on assumptions of simple exponential breakdown of litter in conditions where the amount of litter accumulated on the soil surface oscillates around some 'steady state' value. Thus, where k_L is greater than unity, the turnover of the small-litter layer occurs in a year or less. Some evidence (Bernhard-Reversat 1972; Edwards 1977) suggests that litter decomposition losses in tropical forests follow a linear model, while other evidence suggests that a double exponential model may be more appropriate (Wieder & Lang 1982; Luizão & Schubart 1987). As a result k_L estimates must be considered imperfect indicators of the turnover of the small-litter layer (Spain 1984). They remain, however, a basis for comparison with other published data. The decomposition quotient (k_L) value for total small litterfall of 2.2 (Table 4.3) is relatively high (Anderson & Swift 1983). The k_L value for

Table 4.7 Estimated rate of addition (kg/ha per year) of mineral elements in the small litterfall and their quantities (kg/ha) in the small-litter layer and in the soil in a semi-evergreen forest on Maracá Island, Brazil (a). Soil nitrogen and phosphorus are total amounts and soil potassium, calcium and magnesium refer to exchangeable quantities. The mean values with ranges in parentheses of a parallel study (Scott 1992) in three evergreen forest plots are also shown (b).

litter fraction	mineral elements				
	N	P	K	Ca	Mg
(a)					
small litterfall (x_1)	85.2	5.8	47.5	76.8	23.0
small-litter layer (y_1)	31.6	2.2	7.6	35.1	5.3
soil (top 10 cm)(z_1)	1633	256	98	169	83
quotient $(x_1)/(y_1)$	2.70	2.64	6.25	2.19	4.34
quotient $(x_1)/(z_1)$	0.052	0.023	0.48	0.45	0.28
(b)					
small litterfall (x_2)	118	6.7	48.5	63.7	23.8
	(114–120)	(6.3–7.1)	(46.0–55.0)	(62.1–71.1)	(21.8–25.6)
small-litter layer (y_2)	49.2	2.4	8.2	32.0	8.1
	(46–52)	(2.2–2.5)	(7.5–8.6)	(29.6–34.3)	(7.4–8.6)
soil (top 10 cm)(z_2)	578	78	36	60	28
	(570–603)	(72–81)	(28–40)	(50–80)	(24–36)
quotient $(x_2)/(y_2)$	2.40	2.79	5.91	1.99	2.94
quotient $(x_2)/(z_2)$	0.20	0.086	1.35	1.06	0.85

Table 4.8 Small litterfall (tonnes/ha per year) in some Amazonian forests.

locality	annual rainfall (mm)	total small litterfall	leaves	small wood	flowers & fruits	trash	authors
San Carlos, Venezuela	3600						
mixed forest		–	6.5	–	–	–	Medina & Cuevas (1989)
guaco forest		–	7.0	–	–	–	
tall *caatinga*		–	5.2	–	–	–	
low *caatinga*		–	2.1	–	–	–	
200 km NE of Belém	2600	8.04	–	–	–	–	Dantas & Phillipson (1989)
Manaus	1800	7.9	6.4	1.03	0.47	–	Franken *et al.* (1979)
San Carlos, Venezuela	3600						Jordan & Murphy (1982)
mixed forest		5.8	–	–	–	–	
caatinga		4.8	–	–	–	–	
Mocambo, Belém	2300	9.9	8.0	1.3	0.6	–	Klinge (1977)
Manaus	1800	7.3	5.6	1.3	0.4	–	Klinge & Rodrigues (1968a)
80 km N of Manaus (plateau)	2100	8.3	5.4	1.56	0.42	0.79	Luizão (1989)
80 km N of Manaus (valley)	2100	7.4	4.7	1.17	0.43	1.12	Luizão (1989)
Mocambo, Belém	2220	7.3	6.1	0.88	0.31	–	Silva & Lobo (1982)
Maracá (semi-evergreen)	1800	6.9	5.1	0.78	0.63	0.32	This study
Maracá (evergreen)	1800	9.3	6.3	1.34	1.21	0.42	Scott *et al.* (1992)

Table 4.9 Small-litter layer mass (tonnes/ha) and k_L in Amazonian *terra firme* forests.

locality	annual rainfall (mm)	total small litter layer	leaf litter layer	k_L	authors
Manaus	1800	7.2	4.0	1.5 (leaves) 1.1 (total)	Klinge (1973)
Maracá Island (semi-evergreen)	1800	3.1	1.9	2.7 (leaves) 2.2 (total)	This study
Maracá Island (evergreen)	1800	4.6	2.15	2.9 (leaves) 2.0 (total)	Scott *et al.* (1992)

leaf litter is less than, and k_L values for flowers and fruit and total small litter are higher than, those recorded in the evergreen plots. The litter turnover on Maracá seems to be generally rapid and the values exceed those recorded for other Amazonian forests (Klinge 1973; Franken *et al.* 1979).

Large wood and standing dead trees
The amount of large dead wood (8.68 tonnes/ha) in the Maracá semi-evergreen forest is low and similar to the values (3.5–7.5 tonnes/ha) found by Scott *et al.* (1992) for the evergreen forests (Table 4.4). In Central Amazonian *terra firme* forest near Manaus, Klinge (1973) reported 18.2 tonnes/ha of large trunks and branches on the forest floor with standing dead trees contributing a further 7.6 tonnes/ha. At San Carlos, Venezuela, in Amazonian heath forest (*caatinga*) on spodosols, Jordan & Murphy (1982) found 39 tonnes/ha of large dead wood. Proctor *et al.* (1983) reported large dead wood of 23.8–57.8 tonnes/ha on four lowland forests in Sarawak. John (1973), in mature secondary forest Ghana, found total large dead wood of 8.35 tonnes/ha, and the similarity of this value with those of the Maracá forests supports the view of Proctor & Miller (1993) that they may still be recovering from human disturbance.

Mineral element concentrations and accession in the small litter
The concentrations of elements in the small litterfall on the semi-evergreen forest were generally higher than those on the evergreen forest (Table 4.5). Both Maracá forests had low leaf litterfall nitrogen concentrations compared with other neotropical forests (Table 4.10) but the Maracá

Table 4.10 Mineral element concentrations (mg/g) in leaf litterfall in several lowland neotropical forests.

locality	N	P	K	Ca	Mg	authors
			mineral elements			
Manaus (*terra firme*)	15	0.26	2.1	4.8	1.8	Adis *et al.* (1979)
Mocambo, Belém (*terra firme*)	17	0.41	1.7	3.1	2.8	Klinge (1977)
Manaus (*terra firme*)	15	0.30	1.8	2.2	1.8	Klinge & Rodrigues (1968a, b)
80 km N of Manaus (*terra firme*: plateau)	18	0.20	1.5	3.8	1.8	Luizão (1989)
80 km N of Manaus (*terra firme*: valley)	14	0.30	3.0	7.7	2.1	Luizão (1989)
San Carlos, Venezuela mixed forest	16	0.32	2.4	1.7	0.7	Medina & Cuevas (1989)
guaco forest	12	0.26	1.3	1.8	0.9	
tall *caatinga*	7.0	0.50	2.1	7.7	3.1	
low *caatinga*	5.8	0.21	4.7	7.4	2.5	
São Paulo (secondary semi-deciduous)	22	1.1	4.8	11.6	2.4	Meguro *et al.* (1979)
Maracá (*terra firme*: semi-evergreen)	12	0.71	6.6	11.5	3.5	This study
Maracá (*terra firme*: evergreen)	13	0.58	4.7	7.4	2.7	Scott *et al.* (1992)

forests' concentrations of phosphorus, potassium, calcium and magnesium were high and are amongst the highest recorded from elsewhere (Proctor 1984). The rates of accession are, with the exception of calcium, lower on the semi-evergreen forest than on the evergreen forest (Table 4.7). For both Maracá forests the rates of mineral-element (except nitrogen) accession are high in comparison with other neotropical forests (Table 4.11) and with those elsewhere (Proctor 1984). The high mineral-element quotients (Table 4.7) show high rates of turnover in both Maracá forests. The semi-evergreen forest has lower quotients of litterfall accession/soil content (Table 4.7) which reinforces the conclusion (Thompson *et al.*, this volume) that this forest is better supplied with soil nutrients than the evergreen forest. High nutrient concentrations (including nitrogen) and accession rates are also found in the litterfall of a 'semi-deciduous' secondary forest near São Paulo, Brazil (Meguro *et al.* 1979). The work on litterfall thus supports the view of Furley *et al.* (1988) and Ratter *et al.* (1973, 1978) that the degree of forest deciduousness in the more seasonal areas of Brazil is related to soil nutrient supply.

Table 4.11   Mineral element accession (kg/ha/yr) in total small litterfall in several lowland neotropical forests.

| | mineral element | | | | | |
locality	N	P	K	Ca	Mg	authors
200 km north-east of						
Belém (*terra firme*)	115.0	3.6	28.5	114.5	15.9	Dantas & Phillipson (1989)
Manaus (riverine)	73.8	1.4	21.1	20.5	1.1	Franken *et al.* (1979)
Panama (mean of 2 sites)	–	9.4	29.0	256.0	34.0	Golley *et al.* (1975)
Mocambo, Belém						
(*terra firme*)	156.5	4.1	17.0	32.8	26.8	Klinge (1977)
Manaus (*terra firme*)	105.6	2.1	12.7	18.3	12.6	Klinge & Rodrigues (1968a, b)
80 km N of Manaus						
(*terra firme*: plateau)	151.0	3.1	15.0	36.7	13.8	Luizão (1989)
80 km N of Manaus						
(*terra firme*: valley)	109.0	3.7	22.2	58.2	14.0	Luizão (1989)
São Paulo (semi-						
deciduous secondary	186	9.4	38	104	18	Meguro *et al.* (1979)
forest)						
Maracá (*terra firme*:						
semi-evergreen)	85.2	5.8	47.5	76.8	23.0	This study
Maracá (*terra firme*:						
evergreen)	117.9	6.7	48.5	63.7	23.8	Scott *et al.* (1992)

Acknowledgements

The acknowledgements in J. Thompson *et al.* (this volume) apply here.

References

Adis, J., Furch, K. & Irmler, U. (1979), Litter production of a Central-Amazonian black water inundation forest, *Tropical Ecology*, 20, 236–45.

Allen, S. E., Grimshaw, H. M., Parkinson, J. A. & Quarmby, C. (1974), *Chemical Analysis of Ecological Materials*, Oxford, Blackwell Scientific Publications.

Anderson, J. M. & Swift, M. J. (1983), Decomposition in tropical forests, in Sutton, S. L., Whitmore, T. C. & Chadwick, A. C. (eds.), *Tropical Rain Forest: Ecology and Management*. Oxford, Blackwell Scientific Publications, 287–309.

Bernhard-Reversat, F. (1972), Decomposition de la litière de feuilles en forêt ombrophile de basse Côte-d'Ivoire, *Oecologia Plantarum*, 7, 279–300.

Dantas, M. & Phillipson, J. (1989), Litterfall and litter nutrient content in primary and secondary Amazonian 'terra firme' rain forest, *Journal of Tropical Ecology*, 5, 27–36.

Dawkins, H. C. (1961), Estimating total volume of some Caribbean trees, *Caribbean Forester*, 22, 62–3.

Dawkins, H. C. (1963), *The Productivity of Tropical High Forest Trees and their Reaction to Controllable Environment*, D.Phil. thesis, Oxford University.

Edwards, P. J. (1977), Studies of mineral cycling in a montane rain forest in New Guinea II. The production and disappearance of litter, *Journal of Ecology*, 65, 971–92.

Edwards, P. J. (1982), Studies of mineral cycling in a montane rain forest in New Guinea V. Rates of cycling in throughfall and litterfall, *Journal of Ecology*, 70, 807–27.

Franken, M., Irmler, U. & Klinge, H. (1979), Litterfall in inundation, riverine and terra firme forests of central Amazonia, *Tropical Ecology*, 20, 225–35.

Furley, P. A., Ratter, J. A. & Gifford, D. R. (1988), Observations on the vegetation of eastern Mato Grosso, Brazil III. The woody vegetation and soils of the Morro de Fumaca, Torixoreu, *Proceedings of the Royal Society of London, B, 235*, 259–80.

Golley, F. B., McGinnis, J. T., Clements, R. G., Child, G. I. & Duever, M. J. (1975), *Mineral Cycling in a Tropical Moist Forest Ecosystem*, Georgia, University of Georgia Press.

Herrera, R., Jordan, C. F., Klinge, H. & Medina, E. (1978), Amazon ecosystems: their structure and functioning with particular emphasis on nutrients, *Interciencia*, 3, 223–32.

Jackson, J. F. (1978), Seasonality of flowering and leaf-fall in a Brazilian subtropical lower montane moist forest, *Biotropica*, 10, 38–42.

John, D. M. (1973), Accumulation and decay of litter and net production of forest in tropical West Africa, *Oikos*, 24, 430–5.

Jordan, C. F. & Murphy, P. G. (1982), Productivity and morality of two forest types in the Amazon Territory of Venezuela, in *Nutrient Dynamics of a Tropical Rain Forest Ecosystem and Changes in the Nutrient cycle due to Cutting and Burning*, Annual Report to U. S. National Science Foundation, Institute of Ecology, University of Georgia, USA, 122–66.

Klinge, H. (1973), Biomasa y materia organica del suelo en el ecosistema de la pluviselva centroamazonica, *Acta Cientifica Venezolana*, 24, 174–81.

Klinge, H. (1977), Fine litter production and nutrient return to the soil in three natural forest stands of eastern Amazonia, *Geo-Eco-Trop*, 1, 159–67.

Klinge, H. & Rodrigues, W. A. (1968a), Litter production in an area of Amazonian *terra firme* forest. Part I. Litterfall, organic carbon and total nitrogen contents of litter, *Amazoniana*, 1, 287–302.

Klinge, H. & Rodrigues, W. A. (1968b), Litter production in an area of Amazonian *terra firme* forest. Part II. Mineral nutrient content of the litter, *Amazoniana*, 1, 303–10.

Luizão, F. J. (1989), Litter production and mineral element input to the forest floor in a central Amazonian forest, *Geo Journal*, 19, 407–17.

Luizão, F. J. & Schubart, H. O. R. (1987), Litter production and decomposition in a terra-firme forest of Central Amazonia, *Experientia*, 43, 259–65.

Medina, E. & Cuevas, E. (1989), Patterns of nutrient accumulation and release in Amazonian forests of the upper Rio Negro basin, in Proctor, J. (ed.), *Mineral Nutrients in Tropical Forest and Savanna Ecosystems*, Oxford, Blackwell Scientific Publications, 217–40.

Meguro, M., Vinueza, G. N. & Delitti, W. B. C. (1979), Ciclagem de nutrientes minerais na mata mesófila secundaria – São Paulo. I – Produção e conteúdo de nutrientes minerais no folhedo, *Boletim de Botânica, Universidade de São Paulo*, 7, 11–31.

Olsen, J. S. (1963), Energy storage and the balance of producers and decomposers in ecological systems, *Ecology*, 44, 322–32.

Proctor, J. (1983), Tropical forest litterfall I. Problems of data comparison, in Sutton, S. L., Whitmore, T. C. & Chadwick, A. C. (eds.), *Tropical Rain Forest Ecology and Management*, Oxford, Blackwell Scientific Publications, 267–73.

Proctor, J. (1984), Tropical forest litterfall II. The data set, in Sutton, S. L., Whitmore, T. C. & Chadwick, A. C. (eds.), *Tropical Rain Forest: The Leeds Symposium*, Leeds, Leeds Philosophical and Literary Society, 83–113.

Proctor, J., Anderson, J. A. M., Fogden, S. C. L. & Vallack, H. W. (1983), Ecological studies in four contrasting lowland rain forests in Gunung Mulu National Park, Sarawak. II. Litterfall, litter standing crop and preliminary observations on herbivory, *Journal of Ecology*, 71, 261–83.

Proctor, J. & Miller, R. P. (1994), Human occupation on Maracá Island: preliminary notes, in Ratter, J. A. & Milliken, W. (eds.), *Maracá: Ecology, of an Amazonian Rain Forest*, Manchester, Manchester University Press.

Ratter, J. A., Askew, G. P., Montgomery, R. F. & Gifford, D. R. (1978), Observations of forests of some mesotrophic soils in central Brazil, *Revista Brasileira de Botânica*, 1, 47–58.

Ratter, J. A., Richards, P. W., Argent, G. & Gifford, D. R. (1973), Observations on the vegetation of north-eastern Mato Grosso I. The woody vegetation types of the *Xavantina–Cachimbo* Expedition area, *Philosophical Transactions of the Royal Society of London*, B, 266, 449–92.

Scott, D. A., Proctor, J. & Thompson, J. (1992), Ecological studies on a lowland evergreen rain forest on Maracá Island, Roraima, Brazil. II. Litter and nutrient cycling, *Journal of Ecology*, 80, 705–17.

Silva, M. F. F. & Lobo, M. G. A. (1982), Nota sobre deposiçâo de matéria orgânica em floresta de *terra firme, várzea* e *igapó*, *Boletim do Museu Paranaense Emilió Goeldi Botânica*, 66, 1–13.

Spain, A. V. (1984), Litterfall and the standing crop of litter in three tropical Australian rainforests, *Journal of Ecology*, 72, 947–61.

Wieder, R. K. & Lang, G. E. (1982), A critique of the analytical methods used in examining decomposition data obtained from litterbags, *Ecology*, 63, 1636–42.

5 *Robert H. Marrs, Jill Thompson, Duncan A. Scott and John Proctor*

Nitrogen mineralization and nitrification in *terra firme* forest and savanna soils on Maracá Island

Introduction

The breakdown of soil organic nitrogen to NH_4-N (nitrogen mineralization), and its subsequent transformation to NO_3-N (nitrification), are key processes in most ecosystems. Both processes have been studied intensively in tropical rain forests, where the effects of altitude (Tanner 1977; Vitousek *et al.* 1983; Marrs *et al.* 1988), successional age (Robertson 1984), and some management practices (Matson *et al.* 1987) have been investigated. By comparison, less information is available about soil nitrogen transfers in *terra firme* rain forest and particularly in the transition zone between such forest and savanna.

In this paper we report the results from an investigation where soil nitrogen mineralization and nitrification rates were measured at different times of the year on Maracá Island in Brazil. Measurements were made in (1) *terra firme* forest cut at two different scales, the largest simulating the effect of forest cutting, and smaller areas simulating forest gaps, and (2) the different plant communities along a forest–savanna transect. In addition, the effects of soil nutrient resource limitation on both nitrogen mineralization and nitrification in *terra firme* forest and savanna soils were compared by experimental nutrient additions.

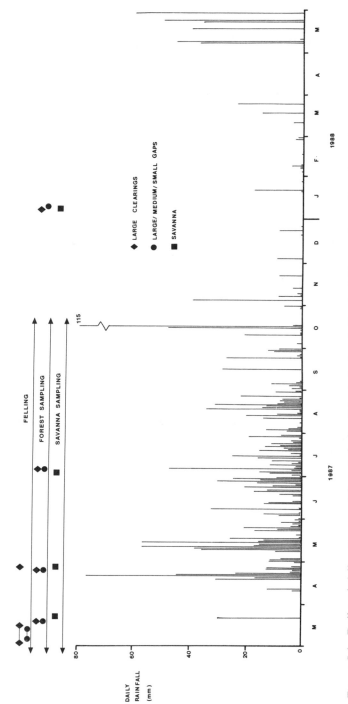

Figure 5.1 Daily rainfall pattern on Maracá during this study in relation to felling and sampling dates. Accurate measurements of rainfall started on 20 March 1987, but rain was noted on six days between 21 February and 20 March: 21 February – short showers; 12 March – heavy rain all night; 15 March – heavy rain all night; 16 March – heavy rain in morning; 17 March – showers; 19 March – showers in morning (J. A. Ratter, personal communication, 1987).

Methods

Forest regeneration study
Two series of replicated plots were set up to study the effects of the scale
of gap creation on soil nitrogen transformations. The first study compared
the effects of creating relatively large gaps (2500 sq m) with undisturbed
'control' plots, and the second investigated the effects of gap sizes (smaller
than 500 sq m) approximating those created naturally by the death of
individual trees or small groups of trees. All forest plots were situated on
soils classified as ultisols (Nortcliff & Robison 1989).

(1) *Felled* v. *undisturbed forest plots*   Six plots each of 50 m × 50 m were
marked out in *terra firme* forest near the Maracá research station in March
1987. Three of these plots were randomly selected to be felled; two were
felled between 8 and 16 March 1987, and the remaining plot was felled
between 23 and 27 April 1987. All plots were gridded into twenty-five
10 m × 10 m sub-plots, and on each sampling occasion soil samples were
collected from random positions within ten sub-plots.

(2) *Gap-size study*   Between 14 and 17 March 1987 nine gaps were created by felling near the first study area; three replicate gaps were created
in each of three size classes (small = 30–50 sq m; medium = 100–200 sq m;
large = 300–400 sq m). On each sampling occasion four soil samples were
collected from each gap, two from the centre and one from each edge
along a north–south transect.

Forest–savanna boundary study
Two 10 m × 10 m plots were placed in each of seven vegetation types along
a 300 m forest–savanna–forest transect near Casa Santa Rosa, approximately 4 km north of the forest study plots. The soils in this area were
a complex of ultisols and oxisols, with the oxisols showing signs of waterlogging (Nortcliff & Robinson 1989). The vegetation types studied were
(in sequence from the southern Maracá end): (1) *terra firme* forest, (2)
forest/scrub transition, (3) scrub, (4) savanna, (5) scrub, (6) forest/scrub
transition, and (7) *terra firme* forest. On each sampling occasion two soil
samples were collected from each of the plots.

Soils collection and analysis
Soils were collected (0–10 cm depth) from all forest and savanna plots at
four times during the 1987/88 season; the four sampling times were chosen
to reflect the different seasonal rainfall patterns on Maracá Island, and the
relationship between felling/sampling dates and the rainfall distribution is
shown in Figure 5.1. The sampling dates were:

(1)   16–21 March 1987: transition between dry and wet season. This was the starting point for all soil studies. At this time only two of the large 2500 sq m felled plots had been felled, and the remaining four plots were sampled as undisturbed plots.

(2)   22–25 April: early wet season and one month after the main fellings. It was hoped to detect initial flushes in nitrogen supply brought about by both increases in moisture supply and the effects of felling. Again at this point only two of the large 2500 sq m felled plots were available.

(3)   29 June–2 July: mid-wet season.

(4)   4–6 January: mid-dry season

All soil samples were separated into three fractions:

Fraction 1 – *c*. 100 g air-dried, sieved to pass a 2 mm screen and shipped to Britain for physico-chemical analysis; the percentage moisture content was also determined during air drying.

Fraction 2 – 5 g fresh soil extracted in 25 ml 1M KCl, filtered, a biocide added and the solutions shipped to Britain for analysis.

Fraction 3 – *c*. 50 g fresh soil incubated in a polythene bag (Robertson 1984; Marrs *et al*. 1988) in the non-air-conditioned laboratory on Maracá for 30 days. After incubation a 5 g sub-sample was treated in the same way as Fraction 2.

Assessment of the effects of added nutrients on nitrogen mineralization and nitrification in forest and savanna soils
Bulk samples (*c*. 1 kg) of surface soil (0–10 cm depth) were collected towards the end of the wet season (29 and 30 September 1987) from four randomly allocated positions in both *terra firme* forest and savanna. Three sub-samples of these bulk samples were taken and each treated in the same way as Fractions 1–2 above. Sub-samples (50 g) were then weighed into polythene bags, and randomly allocated one of twelve treatment combinations (six nutrients × two NH_4-N amendments in factorial combination). The nutrient additions were modified from those of Robertson (1984) and Marrs *et al*. (1988), and were as follows:

   (1)   nutrient additions
         (i)   no nutrient addition, 6 ml deionized water only
         (ii)   + 5 mg P per kg wet soil as NaH_2PO_4
         (iii)   + 50 mg K per kg wet soil as KCl
         (iv)   + 200 mg Ca per kg wet soil as $CaSO_4$
         (v)   + 200 mg Ca per kg wet soil as $CaCO_3$
         (vi)   + 176 mg SO_4 per kg wet soil as Na_2SO_4 (a contrast with $CaSO_4$)
   (2) NH_4-N additions, the substrate for nitrification

(i) none

(ii) + 100 mg NH_4-N per kg wet soil as NH_4Cl.

All treatment combinations were added either in 6 ml solution or in addition to 6 ml deionized water. These soils were then incubated for 30 days when three separate 5 g sub-samples were extracted in the same way as Fraction 3 above.

Chemical analysis

A biocide was added to all potassium chloride extracts to retard microbial action: either 0.1 ml of formalin was added to the 25 ml extract, or 1 μg/ml $HgCl_2$ was included in the extracting solution. In Britain the NH_4-N and NO_3-N concentrations in the potassium chloride extracts were determined. When $HgCl_2$ was added, direct estimates of both NH_4-N and NO_3-N concentrations were made using automated colorimetry (Allen *et al.* 1974). Where formalin was added the extracts were unsuitable for colorimetry, because of interference with colour development. Therefore, steam distillation of the extracts followed by titration was used to estimate both the NH_4-N and NH_4-N plus NO_3-N concentrations, with the NO_3-N concentration being estimated by difference (Allen *et al.* 1974). When this method was used, extracts taken from within each replicate plot had to be pooled, thus reducing estimates of within-plot errors. Where possible, samples were pooled from four and ten individual samples into two and three pooled samples respectively, and statistical analysis done on the mean values.

Mineralization rates (expressed on an air-dried basis) were determined as incubated mineral nitrogen (NH_4-N and NO_3-N) less initial mineral nitrogen, and nitrification N rates incubated less initial NO_3-N (Robertson & Vitousek 1981; Robertson 1984; Marrs *et al.* 1988). In all incubations there was no appreciable loss of water.

Analysis of variance, covariance and regressions were done on both original and appropriately transformed data using the GLM procedure of SAS (SAS, 1985).

Results

Effects of felling on soil nitrogen transformation in forest soils
(Table 5.1)

Nitrogen mineralization and nitrification rates were at a maximum at the start of the study in the dry–wet season transition period. The values declined slightly in the wet season, and were lowest in the dry season. Moreover, there were no significant differences in either rate between the felled and undisturbed 'control' plots at any time, although at the start of the study the mean rates in the undisturbed plots were double those in the felled plots. The lack of statistical significance of this result at $P < 0.05$

The rainforest edge

Table 5.1 A comparison of nitrogen mineralization and nitrification rates in felled and undisturbed forest plots at five times of the year; means with LSD (*P* < 0.05) values in parentheses are presented.

time of year	treatment	mineralization rate (µg N/g/30d)	nitrification rate (µg N/g/30d)
dry–wet season transition (March '87)	undisturbed	20.5	17.2
	felled	10.9	9.5
		(16.3)	(14.0)
early wet season (April '87)	undisturbed	11.5	11.2
	felled	13.2	12.7
		(2.3)	(2.0)
mid–wet season (June–July '87)	undisturbed	8.5	10.0
	felled	11.0	12.7
		(7.4)	(3.2)
mid–dry season (January '88)	undisturbed	4.9	3.0
	felled	3.9	2.0
		(3.1)	(3.3)

reflects the fact that only two felled plots were available, plus the large variability in the undisturbed plots at this time.

At all times and in all plots the nitrification rates were highly correlated with the mineralization rates (r > 0.746, *P* < 0.001), and were in the same order of magnitude.

Effects of different gap size and position within gaps on nitrogen transformations in forest soils (Table 5.2)
The seasonal pattern and absolute values for both mineralization and nitrification were similar to undisturbed 'control' plots, with maxima in the dry–wet transition period and minima in the dry season. No significant differences were found at any time between (1) small, medium or large

Table 5.2 A comparison of (a) nitrogen mineralization and (b) nitrification rates (both µg/g/30d) in different positions within newly-created gaps of different sizes with undisturbed 'control' plots at four times of the year. Means (n = 3) are presented with LSD (*P* < 0.05) values for comparisons between gap size classes and positions, and standard errors for comparison with the undisturbed means.

gap size class	gap position	dry–wet season transition (March '87)	early wet season (April '87)	mid–wet season (June–July '87)	mid–dry season (January '88)
(a) mineralization rate					
small	edge	14.1	–	10.9	4.8
	centre	16.8	8.0	8.2	3.8
medium	edge	18.2	12.7	10.1	4.5
	centre	14.4	15.4	8.6	3.0
large	edge	19.7	12.5	9.7	3.2
	centre	21.7	19.2	11.3	2.8
LSD		10.5	11.8	5.6	2.9
(SE)		(3.2)	(3.6)	(1.7)	(0.9)
undisturbed 'control' (SE)		20.5 (3.9)	11.5 (0.5)	8.5 (1.9)	4.9 (0.8)
(b) Nitrification rate					
small	edge	14.6	–	11.8	4.7
	centre	20.3	9.5	9.4	3.7
medium	edge	18.9	12.3	11.7	4.4
	centre	14.2	12.7	8.2	3.5
large	edge	20.2	11.2	11.7	3.8
	centre	22.2	17.3	12.9	3.5
LSD		9.6	1.4	6.0	2.5
(SE)		(2.9)	(0.4)	(1.8)	(0.8)
undisturbed 'control' (SE)		17.2 (3.2)	11.2 (0.4)	10.0 (1.3)	3.0 (0.8)

Table 5.3　Regression equations and their significance (ns = $P > 0.05$) between both (a) nitrogen mineralization and (b) nitrification rates and gap size. The regression equation fitted was N parameter = A + B* $\sqrt{\text{gapsize}}$, with the undisturbed plots assigned a gap size of zero.

| | time of year | | | |
	dry–wet season transition (March '87)	early wet season (April '87)	mid–wet season (June–July '87)	mid–dry season (January '88)
(a) Mineralization rate				
constant (A)	19.5	11.8	9.1	4.2
coefficient (B)	−0.15	0.05	0.04	−0.01
F value	2.49	1.26	1.61	0.38
significance	ns	ns	ns	ns
r^2	0.1846	0.1116	0.1103	0.0285
(b) Nitrification rate				
constant (A)	18.5	11.3	10.4	3.9
coefficient (B)	−0.13	0.04	0.05	−0.04
F value	2.41	0.94	3.05	2.73
significance	ns	ns	ns	ns
r^2	0.1799	0.0858	0.1901	0.1222

gaps, (2) the centre or edge of the gaps, and (3) the interaction of gap size and position.

The relationship between gap size and soil nitrogen transformations in forest soils
As no significant effects of gap creation were detected in either the large felling or the gap experiments using analysis of variance, regressions of both nitrogen mineralization and nitrification rate against gap size were calculated using the combined data from both studies (note that in this analysis the undisturbed 'control' plots were assigned a gap size of zero). The equations (Table 5.3) confirm that creating gaps had little impact on soil nitrogen mineralization and nitrification rates. Analysis of covariance of the data from all sampling dates showed significant ($P < 0.001$) differences between the coefficients of the linear equations fitted for each sampling occasion (mineralization rates F = 33.02, nitrification F = 39.63), confirming the significance of the seasonal effects noted earlier. Gap size had no significant effect.

Changes in soil nitrogen transformations along the forest–savanna transect (Figure 5.2)

Rates of nitrogen mineralization and nitrification in the *terra firme* forest at the southern end of the transect were similar to those found in the forest studies described earlier in this paper, and showed similar seasonal changes. However, at the northern end of the transect, where the forest was more deciduous, the rates (especially mineralization) were much higher in both the scrub and forest zones during both the dry–wet transition period and the dry season when rates were more than double those found elsewhere (40 compared with 20 µg N/g over 30 d mineralized in other forest plots; see Table 5.1). As the vegetation changed towards savanna, there was a reduction in both mineralization and nitrification rates at all times. Indeed, during the wet season (both early and middle) the rates in the scrub and savanna plots were negative, i.e. there was net immobilization of inorganic nitrogen.

The relationship between soil nitrogen transformations and soil moisture content (Table 5.4)

In the forest soils the moisture content ranged between 5 and 12 per cent in the dry–wet transition period and all wet season samples, but in the dry season this was reduced to between 0.5 and 3 per cent. In the savanna study similar values were found in the forest and transition zones, but the scrub and savanna soils had greater moisture contents (15–22 per cent) at the time of sampling during the wet season. At some points during the wet season, parts of the savanna were flooded and moisture contents may have been greater than these measured values.

In the forest soils a significant correlation was found only in the dry season when both nitrogen mineralization and nitrification were significantly greater at high soil moisture contents. In the savanna study a significant correlation was found only in the wet season where both rates were lower at high moisture contents, indicating that highest rates were found in the driest soils. This conclusion was confirmed by the positive correlation found between mineralization rate and the distance of the water table below the soil surface ($r = 0.5863$, $P < 0.01$).

Effects of added nutrient additions on nitrogen mineralization and nitrification rates in forest and savanna soils

No significant differences were found in inorganic nitrogen concentrations between woodland and savanna soils prior to incubation (*terra firme* forest = 1.1 ± 0.5 µg NH_4-N/g; 1.4 ± 1.1 µg NO_3-N/g: savanna = 0.8 ± 0.3 µg NH_4-N/g; 1.2 ± 1.0 µg NO_3-N/g).

After incubation, significant differences in mineralization rates were found between (1) nutrient additions, (2) NH_4-N additions, and (3) their interaction. No differences were found, however, between habitat type

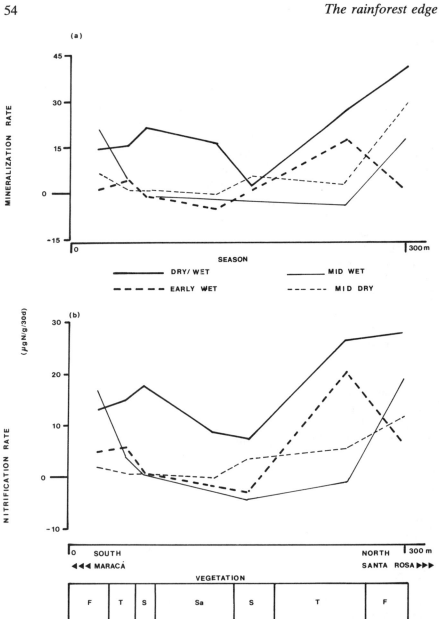

Figure 5.2 Mineralization and nitrification rates in various vegetation types along a forest–savanna–forest transect; F = Forest, T = transition zone between forest and scrub; S = scrub, and Sa = savanna.

Table 5.4 Correlation coefficients between nitrogen mineralization and nitrification rate (fresh weight basis) and moisture content in both forest and savanna studies; * = $P < 0.05$; ** = $P < 0.01$; *** = $P < 0.001$, n = 20).

	time of year			
	dry–wet season transition	early wet season	mid–wet season	mid–dry season
	(March '87)	(April '87)	(June–July '87)	(January '88)
forest cutting study				
nitrogen-mineralization rate	0.0879	0.0594	0.3771	0.5219**
nitrification rate	−0.1675	0.1838	0.3410	0.7162***
savanna study				
nitrogen-mineralization rate	−0.3168	−0.1465	−0.5178*	−0.0165
nitrification rate	−0.2992	−0.2850	−0.5898*	0.0764

(woodland *v.* savanna) and its interaction with any other treatment. The important effects on mineralization rate were (Figure 5.3):

(1) Where no NH_4-N was given, a significant increase in mineralization rate was found only where $CaSO_4$ and $CaCO_3$ were added. Although other elements increased mineralization compared to controls, these increases were not significant ($P < 0.05$).

(2) Where the substrate for nitrification (NH_4-N) was added, there was immobilization of the substrate in all treatments, because less than 100 μg N/g was recovered. Immobilization of 40 per cent of the added NH_4-N occurred in most treatments, but where $CaCO_3$ was also added, a 62 per cent immobilization was found. The greater immobilization with $CaCO_3$ implies that soil pH rather than calcium *per se* is a major factor limiting soil microbial activity.

In contrast to the mineralization data, differences in nitrification rates were found between forest and savanna soils. In the forest, where no NH_4-N was given and where phosphorus, potassium, $CaCO_3$ and $CaSO_4$ were also added, nitrification rates were similar to mineralization rates. Where the substrate for nitrification was also added in combination with phosphorus, potassium, $CaSO_4$ and Na_2SO_4, nitrification rates were not significantly different from controls, but where $CaCO_3$ was added, the nitrification rate was similar to that of mineralization.

In the savanna, nitrification rates were negligible (between −1.2 and

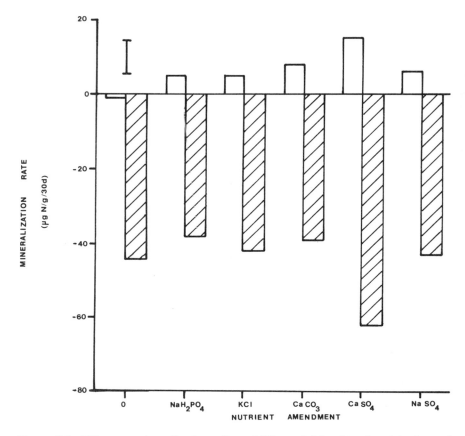

Figure 5.3 Nitrogen mineralization after addition of (a) mineral nutrients, and (b) NH_4-N (– = unhatched; + = hatched); as no significant differences were found between forest and savanna soils pooled means (N = 8) plus LSD ($P < 0.05$) are presented.

3.0 µg N per g over 30 days – LSD = 6.1 µg N per g over 30 days) in all treatments.

Discussion

The rates of soil nitrogen mineralization and nitrification in the *terra firme* forests on Maracá Island are generally lower than other lowland rain forests (Table 5.5), with maximum rates in March 1987 of 9–40 µg N/g over 30 days compared to 40–146 µg N/g over 30 days in Costa Rica, although they overlap with ranges reported for Brazil and Panama (Table 5.5). Moreover, the Maracá data must be viewed in a seasonal context, with these maximum rates being found only at one point in the year, during the

Table 5.5 A comparison of soil–nitrogen mineralization in *terra firme* forest on Maracá with values from lowland forests elsewhere. All data have been converted to µg N/g/30d assuming linearity through time.

country	description	mineralization rate	reference
Costa Rica	La Selva	40–81	Vitousek & Denslow 1986
" "	La Selva	56–83	Vitousek & Matson 1987
" "	La Selva	81	Marrs *et al.* 1988
Costa Rica	Turrialba	57–146	Vitousek & Matson 1987
Panama	*terra firme*	17–41	Vitousek & Matson 1987
Brazil	–	26–34	Vitousek & Matson 1987
Venezuela	Oxisol	14	Montagnini & Buschbacher 1989
Venezuela	Ultisol	2	Montagnini & Buschbacher 1989
Brazil	Maracá range in dry–wet transition	9–40	This paper

transition between the dry and wet season, with much lower levels at other times. In the few examples where seasonal data are available (Costa Rica: Vitousek & Denslow 1986; Matson *et al.* 1987) some small fluctuations were detected (Figure 5.4), but they were smaller than those found on Maracá, and there were no obvious correlations with season. The marked seasonal changes found in the *terra firme* forest on Maracá are possibly related to the pronounced wet and dry season cycle, which is much less evident at the Costa Rican sites studied. Marked seasonal fluctuations in mineralization and nitrification rates have, however, been found in other dry seasonal forests/savanna studies in India (Singh *et al.* 1989), but in this study nitrogen transfers were greater in the rainy season and lower in the dry season. In contrast, on Maracá the highest rates were found in the transition between dry and wet seasons.

At the point of maximum mineralization in the transition period between the dry and wet seasons, there was an accumulation of organic matter during the dry season (Scott 1988, unpublished), which was available for rapid decomposition when soil moisture supply increased as the rains started. We can hypothesize that, as the season becomes wetter, nitrogen mineralization declines, perhaps because of a reduced organic nitrogen substrate or a change in the carbon – nitrogen ratio (Swift *et al.*

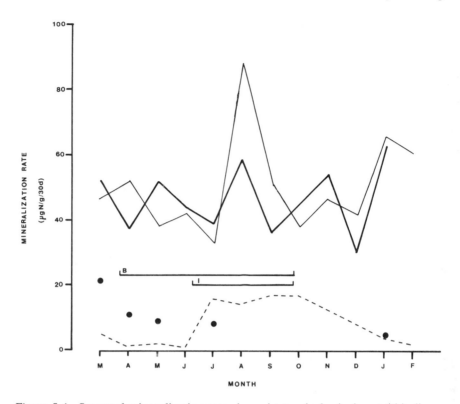

Figure 5.4 Seasonal mineralization rates in moist tropical rain forest (thin lines – Costa Rica, Vitousek & Denslow 1986; thick lines – Costa Rica, Matson *et al.* 1987 and dry seasonal forest (dotted lines – India, Singh *et al.* 1989; circles – Maracá Island, Brazil, present study). The approximate lengths of the rainy season for the Indian (I) and Brazilian (B) studies are also shown.

1979), and reaches a minimum during the dry season, where moisture is probably the limiting factor. This latter hypothesis is confirmed by the significant positive correlation between moisture content and nitrogen mineralization in forest soils during the dry season, which suggests that in critical dry periods mineralization is faster in areas which remain slightly moister. However, a more detailed investigation on the wet–dry transition period is required with more intensive sampling to test this hypothesis further.

The high correlation between nitrification and mineralization rate found in both the *terra firme* forest felling and the forest–savanna study implies that NO_3-N is the form most likely to be available for plant uptake. Similar results were obtained from a successional series of rain forest plots at La Selva in Costa Rica (Robertson 1984). Nitrification rate under natural forest conditions appears, therefore, to be determined mainly by its substrate, i.e. by the NH_4-N produced during mineralization. This hypothesis was confirmed for the Costa Rican soils by Robertson (1984), who amended forest soils with NH_4-N, and showed that it was rapidly converted to the NO_3-N form.

There are clear implications from these results for the regeneration of *terra firme* forest on Maracá. First, the nitrogen supply from soil sources is lower than other rain forests, therefore productivity might be restricted. Second, the low nitrogen supply might be a selective force favouring leguminous species which have root nodules capable of fixing atmospheric nitrogen. Third, it is possible that mineralization of soil nitrogen is a minor pathway for nitrogen cycling in these forests, and the main fluxes from decomposers occurs either in the surface litter layer or direct through mycorrhizae (Jordan 1985).

Forest cutting/gap study
The effect of cutting at any scale up to 2500 sq m on nitrogen mineralization were slight. These conclusions are in agreement with those of Vitousek & Denslow's study (1986) of natural gaps two months to two years old in Costa Rican rain forests. However, these authors did not sample gaps immediately after felling and they suggested that they had perhaps missed a significant burst of nitrogen mineralization immediately after gap creation. Moreover, they speculated that detection of elevated levels in the gaps might have been masked by the very high background rates found in their sample area. The results from Maracá do not support either suggestion as the *terra firme* forest had low background rates, and no increases were found either immediately (within one week) or one month after cutting. These conclusions suggest that gap creation, whether by natural means or by cutting, has little effect on soil nitrogen processes. However, where cut and slash has been burnt in forests after cutting, two- to threefold increases in nitrogen mineralization have been reported (Jordan *et al.* 1983; Matson *et al.* 1987). Further experiments on gap creation which include a burning treatment are clearly required.

Forest–savanna transition study
In the forest–savanna study both nitrogen mineralization and nitrification were generally lower in the scrub and savanna soils, during the wet and dry seasons. Indeed, in the wet season negative rates were found indicating immobilization of plant-available nitrogen by soil micro-organisms. Moreover, there was a clear negative correlation between mineralization and moisture content during the wet season, suggesting that rates were reduced by the seasonal waterlogging (Thompson & Scott, unpublished). These seasonal effects may not be typical of all forest–savanna systems, because Singh *et al.* (1989) found higher nitrification rates in the wet

season and low rates in the dry season, with an implication that moisture was a controlling factor. On Maracá, however, it appears that rates were limited in both wet and dry season, and the main mineralization and nitrification phase was in the transition period between dry and wet seasons. Clearly the discrepancy between these two studies may be the differing amounts and distributions of rainfall.

The low rates in the savanna soil are typical of early secondary successions in tropical rain forests (Robertson 1984), and suggest that shrubs and tree species colonizing the savanna must either be able to subsist on a low nitrogen supply, i.e. with a low Relative Growth Rate (RGR), or be adapted to obtain their nitrogen from other sources, e.g. by symbiotic nitrogen fixation, or efficient mycorrhizal activity. However, leguminous trees form only a small proportion of the basal area in the study area (Proctor, 1988, unpublished).

Effects of added nutrients on soil mineralization and nitrification in forest and savanna
The nutrient amendment studies showed that where no NH_4-N was given, mineralization was significantly increased by $CaSO_4$ or $CaCO_3$ and no other element, implying that the calcium status in these highly weathered and leached soils limits microbial breakdown of organic matter. Where NH_4-N was also given, 40 per cent immobilization of the spike occurred in all treatments except where $CaCO_3$ was added and where 60 per cent immobilization was found. This result implies that immobilization of added NH_4-N is restricted by the low pH. These data are in agreement with those of Robertson (1984), who found immobilization of NH_4-N, and increased mineralization after $CaCO_3$ addition, in late-successional forest plots in Costa Rica. Marrs *et al.* (1988), on the other hand, found NH_4-N stimulated mineralization (i.e. a recovery of more than 100 per cent) at low and high altitudes (100 and 2600 m), but not at medium altitudes (1500 m) in mature forest in Costa Rica. Moreover, responses to calcium addition were also found to differ with altitude; at low and medium altitudes a response to $CaCO_3$ (pH effect) occurred, but there was a response to $CaSO_4$ at an altitude of 2600 m.

For nitrification, there were important differences between forest and savanna, with negligible nitrification in savanna soils in any treatment. In the forest soils where no NH_4-N was given nitrification rates were similar to mineralization rates. However, where the substrate for nitrification was also given, nitrification remained at low levels, except where $CaCO_3$ was also supplied, indicating a pH rather than a calcium substrate limitation. It is possible that this result is brought about by low population growth rates of nitrifying organisms as a result of the acid conditions. These data conflict with Robertson's, where over 50 per cent of NH_4-N additions were nitrified, and even in the oldest seral stage, where immobilization was greatest, all of the inorganic nitrogen fraction was in the NO_3-N form. Moreover, he also showed that $CaCO_3$ suppressed nitrification in the oldest stands.

Clearly, it is impossible to generalize on the constraints controlling soil nitrogen cycling in tropical forest and savanna soils, as the supply of different nutrients has been found to stimulate mineralization and nitrification in some ecosystems and have opposite effects in others. More detailed information is needed on the interaction of different nutrients on soil nitrogen processes in a wide range of tropical soils.

The high rates of immobilization of NH_4-N found in this study on Maracá Island may be an important nutrient conservation mechanism. Any NH_4-N inputs which reach the upper soil layers, whether from fertilizer addition, animal excreta, cut vegetation residues or leachates, are likely to be rapidly immobilized in soil organic matter, thus preventing further loss. However, liming these soils may enhance immobilization, but would also stimulate nitrification, and perhaps leaching losses of NO_3-N, although leaching losses will depend on the abundance of variable charge clays in these soils, which may help to conserve NO_3-N (reviewed Robertson 1989).

Acknowledgements

This work was funded by the Royal Geographical Society, the Overseas Development Agency and the Natural Environment Research Council. We are grateful to SEMA for facilities provided on Maracá and the staff of INPA for advice and critical discussion.

References

Allen, S. E., Grimshaw, H. M., Parkinson, J. A. & Quarmby, C. (1974), *Chemical Analysis of Ecological Materials*, Oxford, Blackwell Scientific Publications.

Jordan, C. F. (1985), *Nutrient Cycling in Tropical Forest Ecosystems*, New York, John Wiley.

Jordan, C. F., Caskey, W., Escalante, G., Herrera, R., Montagnini, F., Todd, R. & Uhl, C. (1983), Nitrogen dynamics during conversion of primary Amazonian rainforest to slash and burn agriculture, *Oikos*, 40, 131–9.

Marrs, R. H., Proctor, J., Heaney, A. & Mountford, M. D. (1988), Changes in soil nitrogen-mineralization along an altitudinal transect in tropical rain forest in Costa Rica, *Journal of Ecology*, 76, 466–82.

Matson, P. A., Vitousek. P. M., Ewel, J. J., Mazzarino, M. J. & Robertson, G. P. (1987), Nitrogen transformations following tropical forest felling and burning on a volcanic soil, *Ecology*, 68, 491–502.

Milliken, W. & Ratter, J. A. (1989), *The Vegetation of the Ilha de Maracá*, Edinburgh, Royal Botanic Garden.

Montagnini, F. & Buschbacher, R. (1989), Nitrification rates in two undisturbed tropical rain forests and three slash-and-burn sites of the Venezuelan Amazon, *Biotropica*, 21, 9–14.

Nortcliff, S. & Robison, D. (1989), *The Soils and Geomorphology of the Ilha de Maracá, Roraima*, London, Royal Geographical Society.

Robertson, G. P. (1984), Nitrification and nitrogen mineralization in a lowland rainforest succession in Costa Rica, Central America, *Oecologia*, 61, 99–104.

Robertson, G. P. (1989), Nitrification and denitrification in humid tropical ecosystems: potential controls on nitrogen retention, in Proctor, J. (ed.), *Mineral Nutrients in Tropical Forest and Savanna Ecosystems*, Oxford, Blackwell Scientific Publications, 55–69.

Robertson, G. P. & Vitousek, P. M. (1981), Nitrification potentials in primary and secondary succession, *Ecology*, 62, 376–86.

SAS (1985), *SAS Users Guide: Statistics, Version 5 edition*, SAS Institute Inc., Cary, N.C.

Singh, J. S., Raghubanshi, A. S., Singh, R. S. & Srivastave, S. C. (1989), Microbial biomass acts as a source of nutrients in dry tropical savanna, *Nature, London*, 338, 499–500.

Swift, M. J., Heal, O. W. & Anderson, J. M. (1979), *Decomposition in terrestrial ecosystems*, Oxford Blackwell Scientific Publications.

Tanner, E. V. J. (1977), Four montane rain forests of Jamaica: a quantitative characterization of the floristics, the soils and the foliar mineral levels, and a discussion of their interrelations, *Journal of Ecology*, 65, 883–918.

Vitousek, P. M. & Denslow, J. S. (1986), Nitrogen and phosphorus availability in treefall gaps of a lowland tropical rainforest, *Journal of Ecology*, 74, 1167–78.

Vitousek, P. M. & Matson, P. A. (1987), Nitrogen transformations in tropical forest soils, *Soil Biology & Biochemistry*, 20, 361–7.

Vitousek, P. M., Van Kleve, K., Balakrichnan, N. & Mueller-Dombois, D. (1983), Soil development and nitrogen turnover in montane rainforest soils on Hawaii, *Biotropica*, 15, 268–74.

Soil nutrients and organic matter in forest and savanna habitats on Maracá Island

Introduction

The interaction of climate, soils, hydrology and man in influencing the nature of tropical vegetation, and the form and location of boundaries between different tropical vegetation types, have attracted scientific enquiry for many decades. The complexity of these systems has meant that most of these studies have simply described their various compartments. Experimental approaches, even in complicated environmental and ecological systems, offer an opportunity to test theories based on description and to develop new ones. Several such experimental approaches were adopted to study aspects of tropical rainforest ecology and dynamics on Maracá Island, Roraima, northern Brazil.

In northern Brazil and southern Venezuela, the current boundary between *terra firme* forest and savanna is thought to be determined by a combination of climatic limitations for forest growth and the advance of agricultural development. Interdigitation of forest and savanna to the west in south-west Venezuela is described by Eden (1974). He suggests that islands of savanna in the region are relics of a more widespread savanna which existed under previously drier conditions and that present-day savanna fragments have been maintained by burning. In northern Roraima both on, and in the vicinity of, Maracá Island, soil and vegetation studies have been used by Furley & Ratter (1990) and Thompson *et al.* (1991) to suggest that current locations of some forest–savanna boundaries are determined, at least in part, by soil hydrological conditions.

Currently quoted high rates of deforestation in the Amazon basin and the opening up of new lands for agricultural cultivation mean that an understanding of tropical soil characteristics and their alteration by forest clearance is particularly important. In regions close to the current forest–savanna boundary, it is also necessary for understanding whether contemporary savannas are advancing into the forest or vice versa. A plethora of soil research worldwide supports the view that deforestation detrimentally alters the soil as a substrate for plant growth. In both agricultural cultivation after deforestation, and savanna invasion after deforestation, success will be equated with the relative abilities of tree seedlings and crops or grass to colonise the resultant soils. These types of questions on vegetation regeneration after forest clearance are the subject of a parallel study carried out on Maracá Island by a team of researchers led by Dr John Proctor of Stirling University. Soil physical properties are severely altered by deforestation techniques, particularly those practices which involve heavy mechanical clearance, such as bulldozing (Seubert *et al.* 1977; Dias & Nortcliff 1985). Altered soil properties include increased soil compaction and bulk density, loss of structural stability and reduced infiltration capacity. The quite substantial differences between manual and mechanical clearance techniques reported by Seubert *et al.* (1977) suggest that alteration of soil physical properties is caused by the clearance procedure. In the case of soil chemical properties, such as the alteration of nutrient status, changes, particularly nutrient losses, are controlled mainly by tree canopy removal and resultant alteration of hydrological processes rather than by the clearance technique *per se*.

According to Sanchez & Salinas (1981), as much as 90–95 per cent of the acid soils of tropical America (23° S–23° N) suffer from nitrogen and phophorus deficiency, with more than 60 per cent of these soils suffering from deficiencies in potassium, sulphur, calcium & magnesium. With this inheritance of soil acidity and infertility, further nutrient losses simply exacerbate an existing problem. Some attention should be paid, not only to remedial action for the restoration of already degraded soils caused by forest clearance, but initially to the prevention of severe soil nutrient losses when trees, and their protective canopy, are removed.

In this paper, the aim is to review some of the results of work on the background characterisation of the soils, soil surface litter, nutrients and organic matter decomposition of *terra firme* forest and savanna habitats on Maracá Island, and to examine soil erosion and nutrient losses after experimental clearing of the forest. In the first section of the paper, the results of soil chemical analyses published by several participants in the Maracá Rainforest Project are summarised and compared to data published for other, similar vegetation habitats in South America. The second section of the paper discusses the experimental work which was designed to aid our understanding of the role of hydrological processes in controlling soil fertility and nutrient dynamics, particularly after differential forest clearance.

Field sites and methods

For the experimental work described in the second half of the paper, several locations on Maracá Island, within 5 km of the ecological research station, at the eastern end of the island, were selected for examination of soil hydrology, soil chemistry, soil erosion and litter decomposition studies in *terra firme* forest, savanna and campo habitats. Firstly, for the location of experimentally cleared forest plots, sites were chosen in the *terra firme* forest at a location about 2 km north east of the station, on a gently north-easterly facing slope. Milliken & Ratter (1989) describe this type of *terra firme* forest as relatively low in species diversity by Amazonian standards, dominated by *Pradosia surinamensis, Licania kunthiana* and *Tetragastris panamensis,* with an understorey which included the palms *Maximiliana maripa* and *Astrocaryum aculeatum.* The canopy height was around 25–30 m in the vicinity of the experimental plots for this study. The ground storey consisted primarily of *Marantacea* and *Bromeliacea.* Savanna and campo habitats were studied in the Santa Rosa region at the eastern end of the island, about 5 km north-north-east of the station. In this region, small areas of poor, low grass/sedge savanna, of the type described as *campo limpo* by Sarmiento (1983), are surrounded by savanna with low trees, around 5 m in height, primarily *Curatella americana* and *Byrsonima crassifolia,* representing the *campo sujo* of Sarmiento (1983). Campo areas in the Santa Rosa region show distinctly wet regions with tall grass/sedge groundstorey of around 1 m tall, and drier regions with rather shorter, more open grass/sedge swards of around 40–50 cm height. The main soil type of the *terra firme* forest in the region of the ecological station is a coarse-textured, nutrient-poor and quartzitic *Podzolico amarelo* (Nortcliff & Robison 1989). These soils have only a very thin surface layer of organic matter, and frequently show no evidence of any surface root mat which is so characteristic of rain forest sites elsewhere in Amazonia. As much as 25–30 per cent of the ground surface was unvegetated and covered with leaf litter. The soil of the Santa Rosa savanna region is described by Nortcliff & Robison (1989) as a nutrient-poor *Latossolo amarelo* with a less coarse and silty texture. In the short grass/sedge savanna, around 25 per cent of the soil surface was unvegetated. In these places, growth of a thin film of algae, during the wet season when the soil was saturated, produced a superficial, black organic layer.

Sites in the Santa Rosa region were used to carry out background characterisation of soil nutrient status in different vegetation types. The study was carried out in five habitats previously identified, and in which the vegetation had been described, by Ferraz (personal communication, 1987), Furley (personal communication, 1987) and Milliken & Ratter (1989). They were described as: *terra firme* forest (F), low grass savanna (S), dry campo (DC), wet campo (WC) and in the transition zone between forest and savanna (B).

Habitat soil studies – field sites and methods
Twelve replicate surface soil samples were taken from the top 10 cm of each of the five Santa Rosa habitats listed above: F, S, DC, WC and B, and

used for chemical and biological analyses. In two field plots in each habitat, soil samples were also taken down the profile to a depth of 120 cm, or more shallow, depending on the depth of the water table, and used for the determination of pH, loss-on-ignition, organic carbon by a Walkley Black technique (Black 1965) and total nitrogen content by micro-kjeldhal digestion followed by colorimetric analysis (Crooke & Simpson 1972). Carbon–nitrogen ratios were calculated for all profiles. 'Available' ammonium and nitrate nitrogen were analysed in potassium chloride extracts of fresh soil samples, using six replicates from the top 5 cm soil of each plot. A series of soil biological characteristics, including microbial biomass, root biomass, soil respiration, potential ammonification and nitrification, microbially immobilised nitrogen and the numbers and diversity of soil mesofauna are reported by Ross *et al.* (1992) for surface soil samples in the same habitats listed above.

Experimental forest clearings
Three treatment plots, each 15 m × 20 m, were set up on each of three slope transects, representing virgin *terra firme* forest, partial forest clearance and total forest clearance. On each transect, the three plots represented top of slope, midslope and foot of slope locations (Figure 6.1), with maximum midslope angles of 12–13°. Total clearance completely removed all trees, vegetation, and leaf litter at the soil surface. During partial clearance, all trees were cut and vegetation removed above 1.5 m, but below this, all vegetation and leaf litter were retained. Treatment plots were created in May 1987, at the beginning of the wet season in northern Roraima.

Instruments for monitoring surface runoff and soil hydrology (Nortcliff *et al.* 1990), and a series of experiments for studying soil erosion, leaf litter decomposition and soil nutrient status, were located within each of the nine treatment plots. Slope/soil conditions, rainfall, soil hydrology and soil erosion results for the period from March to November 1987 are reported in detail in Nortcliff *et al.* (1990). The losses of soil nutrients in eroded sediments from each treatment are reported in the present study for a one-month period during the wet season, from July to August 1987.

Runoff waters and eroded sediments were collected in 2 m × 5 m gerlach troughs at the foot of each plot. Volumes of runoff waters and masses of eroded mineral sediments, leaf litter and particulate organic matter were collected and measured every two days during May to October 1987. Three fractions of accumulated eroded sediments (two mineral fractions, > 500 µm, < 500 µm, and particulate organic matter > 500 m) were measured every fortnight for three months during July to September. Mineral fractions were separated using wet sieving, while particulate organic matter was separated from mineral material by hand.

Decomposition of soil surface leaf litter was examined by measuring

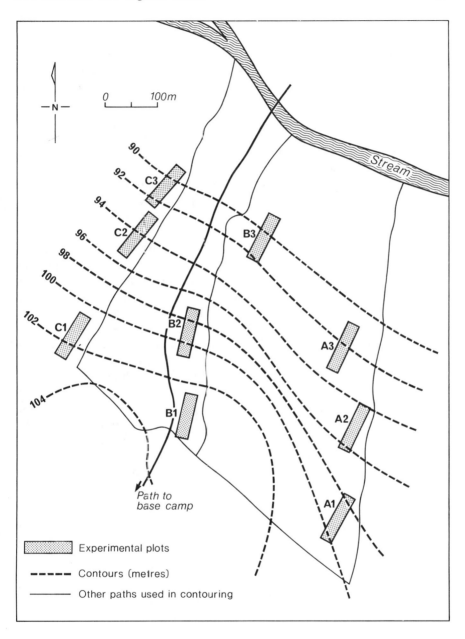

Figure 6.1 Forest experimental clearance plots on Maracá Island, showing top (1), mid (2) and foot (3) of slope locations of forest (A), partially (B) and totally cleared (C) plots.

weight loss in leaf litter bags (Ross 1992). Weight loss of leaf litter in nylon mesh bags was determined for two forest tree species over a period of three months. The tree species chosen, *Tetragastris* sp. and *Ecclinusa* sp., are very common trees in the *terra firme* forest of the eastern part of Maracá Island. Leaves were collected in June before abscission, gently washed, then air dried. Nylon mesh bags, 20 cm × 15 cm, were constructed, containing approximately 4–5 g of air-dried leaf material. The mesh size used was 2 mm, with larger holes, 4 mm in diameter, pierced in the top surface of each bag to ease entry of larger soil mesofauna. The litter bags were placed in random locations on the soil surface in each of the totally cleared, partially cleared and forest plots. Litter bags were sampled after 30, 60 and 90 days and the dry weights of remaining litter determined.

Laboratory analytical methods
Soil and leaf litter samples were oven-dried at 105 °C, packed and returned to England for total chemical analysis. Total nitrogen, phosphorus, potassium, sodium, calcium and magnesium were determined in each of the sediment fractions after micro-digestion (Allen 1989). Total nitrogen and phosphorus in solution were determined colorimetrically by the techniques of Crooke & Simpson (1972) and Murphy & Riley (1965) respectively. Total potassium and sodium in solution were determined directly by atomic emission, while total calcium and magnesium were determined by atomic absorption spectrophotometry after the addition of lanthanum chloride releasing agent.

Extractable ammonium and nitrate nitrogen was determined in the field using a DREL portable environmental laboratory manufactured by the HACH Chemical Company, USA. These methods were subsequently calibrated using the standard laboratory colorimetric methods of Crooke & Simpson (1972) for ammonium and Henriksen & Selmer-Olsen (1970) for nitrate.

Results and discussion

(a) Soil nutrient characterisation of Maracá habitats
A summary of a few key soil analytical results from this and contemporary studies on Maracá Island are given in Table 6.1. Only four major soil groups were represented on Maracá Island in the reconnaissance work of Nortcliff & Robison (1989). For the limited chemical soil data represented in Table 6.1, there are few major differences between soil types; the main difference, as would be expected, is in lower pH, cation exchange capacity and in exchangeable calcium and magnesium in podzolic soils described as *distrofico* (nutrient-poor) compared to those described as *eutrofico* (nutrient-rich). Soils described by Nortcliff & Robison (1989) as *Latossolo amarelo distrofico* include those characteristic of the Santa Rosa region,

Table 6.1 Summary of basic soil characteristics of Maracá Island, northern Roraima. (ND = not determined.)

Soil types	pH		% org. C		% tot. N		% tot. P		CEC (meq/100g)		particle size	author
	Mean	Range	Mean	Range	Mean	Range	Mean	Range	Mean	Range		
Maracá overall												
Podzolico distrofico (arenoso)	5.046	4.4–5.74	ND		0.035	0–0.095	0.058	0.032–0.139	4.91	2.01–10.14	ND	Nortcliff and Robison (1989)
Podzolico distrofico (argilosa)	5.064	3.64–6.97	ND		0.083	0.0003–0.251	0.115	0.008–0.368	9.07	5.0–12.5	ND	''
Podzolico eutrofico	5.892	5.38–6.54	ND		0.116	0–0.239	0.167	0.059–0.336	18.29	10.93–22.36	ND	
Latossolo distrofico	4.751	3.93–5.43	ND		0.092	0.009–0.251	0.198	0.086–0.384	4.64	2.64–6.47	ND	''
Santa Rosa soils (all vegetation types)	5.528	4.7–8.0	1.129	1–2.25	ND		ND		2.34	0.32–8.76	ND	Furley (1989)
''	4.66	4.3–5.3	ND		0.85	0.27–2.4	0.086	0.007–0.31	0.99	0.15–1.55	% sand 20.1–88.4 % silt 1.0–49.6 % clay 9.1–39.7	Thompson et al. (1991)
''	4.125	3.9–4.5	1.76	0.63–4.38	0.050	0.033–0.104	ND		ND		ND	Ross et al. (1992)

for which data in Table 6.1 have also been gleaned from Furley (1989), Thompson *et al.* (1991) and Ross *et al.* (1992). The soil data of Furley and of Thompson *et al.* are from soils sampled from the same vegetation transect across savanna and *terra firme* forest at Santa Rosa; the data of Ross *et al.* are from sites about 1 km to the east. Despite Nortcliff & Robison's description of these soils as *argiloso*, the data of Thompson *et al.* suggest that these soils are predominantly sandy in texture. They also have significant amounts of mobilisable iron and aluminium sesquioxides, which give distinct ochreous coloration to subsurface soil horizons in relation to the rise and fall of the groundwater table. The role of the groundwater table in affecting vegetation growth, and as a control on the location of the forest–savanna boundary, is debated by Furley & Ratter (1990) and Thompson *et al.* (1991).

It is clear in the habitat soil characterisation studies reported here and biological analyses reported by Ross *et al.* (1992) that the groundwater table effectively controls soil chemistry, soil biology and soil biochemical processes. Sites described as wet campo (WC) showed highest water table levels at all times of the year, and were frequently flooded during the wet season. Ross *et al.* (1992) showed highly significant differences in gravimetric moisture contents in the surface 5 cm of soil, with higher values in wet campo, declining in dry campo and savanna to lowest moisture contents in *terra firme* forest. These soil hydrology differences result in relatively high organic carbon contents and total soil nitrogen in the top 5 cm of soil in wet campo. Lowest organic carbon contents in surface soil were found in *terra firme* forest. This is a little unexpected, since we might expect that the larger litter influx would result in higher organic matter contents, and maybe even a measurable depth of surface leaf litter. Neither of these occur in the *terra firme* forest close to the Santa Rosa savanna. The distribution of organic carbon and total nitrogen down the profile in each of the five habitats is illustrated in Figure 6.2(a) and (b). All profiles show highest percentage of organic carbon contents in the top 5 cm. Surface soil values are generally greater than 0.6 per cent, with highest values up to 2.1 per cent in wet campo. The general trend for percentage organic carbon in surface soils appears to show higher values in the zones where the water table is nearer to the soil surface, such as in the wet campo. This result reflects slower decomposition rates under wet and waterlogged conditions. In all habitats apart from the forest, subsurface horizons of soil profiles show a very dramatic decline in percentage organic carbon below 5 cm. Values decline to around 0.2–0.4 per cent at 30 cm in all profiles. Total soil nitrogen contents in all four habitats are generally low. Values of total nitrogen in surface soils (top 5 cm) range from 100–120 mg/100 g, with higher values again at the wetter end of the transect, in the wet campo. The downprofile pattern of decline in total nitrogen with depth is very similar to the decline in percentage organic carbon with depth. All profiles show total nitrogen values of around 15–30 mg/100 g at a depth of 30 cm.

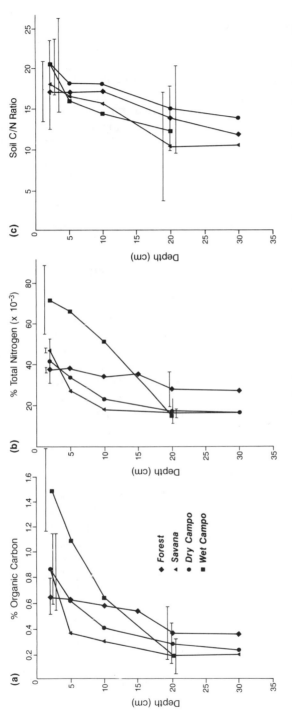

Figure 6.2 Soil profile: Carbon, Nitrogen and C/N ratios in forest, savanna, dry campo and wet campo habitats in the Santa Rosa region of Maracá Island.

The less steep declines in soil organic carbon and nitrogen with depth downprofile in *terra firme* forest may indicate more active mixing of soil by soil organisms, perhaps in relation to more clement (less waterlogged) soil conditions found in the more open savanna and campo habitats in the wet season (see Thompson *et al.* 1991, for groundwater table levels in these habitats through wet and dry seasons).

Carbon–nitrogen ratios are frequently useful for interpretation of nutrient and decomposition status of the soil. During aerobic respiration of soil decomposer organisms, oxidised carbon is evolved as carbon dioxide and lost from the soil. At the same time, decomposer organisms use, or immobilise, the nitrogen that they mineralise from organic matter to incorporate into their own tissues. These processes act to reduce high carbon–nitrogen ratios through time as carbon is lost and nitrogen is retained. Thus agricultural soils with conditions ideal for decomposition and nutrient mineralisation, tend to have carbon–nitrogen ratios of around 8–12. The pattern of carbon–nitrogen ratio downprofile is similar for all five habitats (Figure 6.2(c)). Again, highest values are found in the top 5 cm of soil, with most values lying between 15 and 20. These generally high ratios indicate rather incomplete organic matter decomposition.

In other forest and savanna soils in Amazonia, carbon–nitrogen ratios are generally similar to those found in Maracá soils, with savanna soils in the mainland region around Maracá, reported by Eden *et al.* (1990), showing values averaging 18.625; values for southern Venezuelan forests and savannas varying from 11.7 to 15.5 and from 15 to 17.5 respectively (Eden 1974); and for *terra firme* forest in Surinam, values of 13–15 for topsoils (Poels 1987), while Herrera (1979) quotes carbon–nitrogen values of around 35 for the particularly nutrient-poor *caatinga* forests at San Carlos in southern Venezuela.

(b) Experimental forest clearings
After the tree canopy and vegetation understorey are removed, the last line of protection for the soil is the surface leaf litter. The very simple leaf litter decomposition studies carried out in the experimental clearings on Maracá were designed to give an idea of changing soil protection over time after clearance. A second aim was to study litter comminution, which provides organic matter particles for transport.

The magnitude of weight loss observed in both *Tetragastris* and *Ecclinusa* leaf litter is similar over a three-month period, at around 40 per cent, with no significant differences between slope locations and clearance treatments (Figure 6.3). The leaves, however, visibly decompose differently. The sclerophyllous *Tetragastris* leaves become very brittle on drying and comminute easily, resulting in quite fine fragments of organic matter. Weight loss in the *Ecclinusa* litter appears to be more due to microbial attack (catabolism) than to comminution, and the leaves retain their intact shape

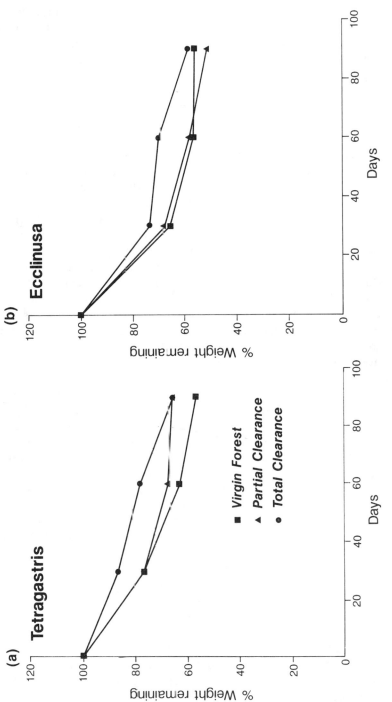

Figure 6.3 Percentage weight remaining in leaf litter bags at 30, 60 and 90 days for *Tetragastris* and *Ecclinusa* leaves, in experimental forest clearance plots, Maracá. (Means of top, mid and foot-of-slope locations.)

longer. Soil protection would clearly be enhanced by larger amounts of leaf litter characterised by the decomposition processes exhibited by *Ecclinusa*. Large amounts of easily comminuted litter would afford much less soil protection and would produce more easily transported organic matter fragments, with associated nutrient losses.

The magnitude of water runoff and sediment erosion after total and partial clearance of the forest have been reported by Ross *et al.* (1990). Total vegetation clearance was found to result in substantial sediment loss, particularly on steeper midslope locations at an angle of 13° (Figure 6.4). It is invalid to calculate annual soil loss rates from data collected over fortnightly periods during the wet season. However, to allow comparison with rates reported in other studies, Maracá monthly rates have been multiplied by three and published annual rates divided by four, to achieve three-month averages. Compared to values published elsewhere for tropical systems (Table 6.2), soil losses from completely cleared plots are rather high, at least as high as those on steeper deforested slopes (25–45°) in Mexico (Maass *et al.* 1988). Even erosion rates measured under forest cover on Maracá Island are higher than rates measured under intact forest elsewhere. Several characteristics of Maracá soils may be responsible for these high rates. Soils in the vicinity of the experimental clearance plots had very little surface leaf litter, and no clear root mat, with very little soil organic matter. The soils showed little structure and were rather poorly consolidated, facilitating particle detachment.

Although overall rates of organic matter loss in soil erosion appear to be small when expressed on a weight basis, as in Figure 6.4, the very low mass-to-volume ratio of leaf litter and litter fragments belies the importance of this loss for these coarse-textured Maracá soils, in which organic matter provides nutrition, structural stability and moisture retention.

Nutrient contents of eroded soil materials are illustrated in Figure 6.5. Again, the highest nutrient losses occur in midslope locations after total forest clearance. As much as 2.2 kg N/ha, 0.45 kg P/ha and 4 kg K/ha can be eroded from cleared forest plots in one month of the rainy season. If the same rationale as above is used to calculate amounts of eroded nutrients in a three-month period, the loss of nitrogen and phosphorus by soil erosion is of the same order of magnitude as rates reported by Maass *et al.* (1988) for cleared and cultivated steep slopes in Mexico (Table 6.3). In the Mexico study, as seen in the Maracá erosion experiments, a covering of soil surface litter, in the form of imported forest leaves, providing a mulch, was very valuable in reducing soil erosion and retaining nutrients on site.

As with sediment loss in the Maracá erosion experiments, Figure 6.5 shows a similarity in losses of nitrogen and phosphorus from forest and partially cleared plots, with almost four times higher nitrogen and phosphorus losses from the totally cleared plots.

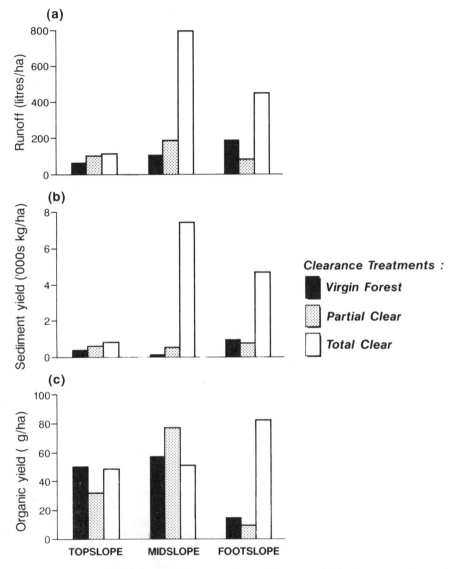

Figure 6.4 Runoff, mineral sediment and organic matter yields from experimental forest clearance plots for one month (10.7.87–12.8.87), calculated in litres, kilograms and grams per hectare respectively.

Table 6.2 Rates of soil erosion measured in different tropical ecosystems and agricultural systems. (All values are in tonnes per ha for a three-month period.)

location	land use	t/ha	author
West Africa	forest/savanna	0.0125–0.3	Roose & Lelong (1976)
S. W. Africa	cleared forest (manual)	0.625	Lal (1981)
	cleared forest (mechanical)	3.45	
	no tillage	1.625	
	with tillage	3.025	
South Africa	natural savanna	0.025	Haylett (1960)
	pasture	0.125	
	uncropped (bare)	1–3.25	
	maize crop (rows)	1–2.75	
Tanzania	evergreen forest		
	(12° slope)	0.01	Lungren (1980)
	(24° slope)	0.025	
Kenya	mixed agriculture & forestry catchment	0.02–48.8	Dunne (1977)
Java	natural rain forest	0.008–1.55	Weirsum (1985)
	tree crops (clean weeded)	0.3–45.73	
Puerto Rico		0.1125–0.75	Smith & Staney (1965)
Mexico	buffel grass	5.5–24	Maass et al. (1988)
	guinea grass	3.5–12.5	
	maize	9.5–25	
	mulched	1.5–1.8	
	rain forest	< 0.05	
Maraca	*terra firme* forest	1.2–2.85	Ross et al. (1990)
	partial clear	1.8–2.25	
	total clear	2.4–22.2	

The order in which nutrients are lost in eroded soil follows the sequence: Ca > N > K > P = Na > Mg for forest sites, Ca > N > K > Na > P > Mg for partially cleared sites, and N > K > Ca > P > Mg > Na for totally cleared sites. The fact that nitrogen and calcium are lost in the highest quantities is an important result for understanding the rapid impoverishment of tropical forest soils subjected to clearance for either shifting cultivation or for pasture. Ross (1992) showed that eroded organic matter is the main form of loss of nitrogen, phosphorus, calcium and magnesium, with as much as 80 per cent of both nitrogen and magnesium lost in this way. For sustaining soil fertility, research into new soil and agricultural management methods for retaining soil organic matter *in situ* after forest clearance is a top priority.

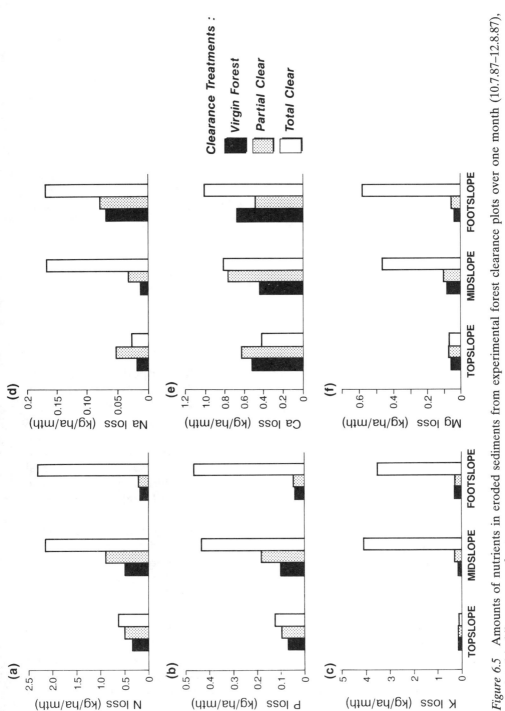

Figure 6.5 Amounts of nutrients in eroded sediments from experimental forest clearance plots over one month (10.7.87–12.8.87), calculated in kilograms per hectare.

Table 6.3 Comparison of nitrogen and phosphorus losses in eroded soil in experimental clearance plots on Maracá with those in agroforestry systems in Mexico (Maass *et al.* 1988). (All values are calculated for a three-month period.)

treatment	eroded nutrients (kg/ha over 3 months)	
	tot. N	tot. P
Mexico:		
(all 25–45° slopes)		
buffel grass[1]	20.5	2.8
guinea grass[1]	11.15	1.4
row maize[1]	17.1	2.2
forest litter (mulch)[1]	2.6	0.35
Maracá:		
(all 13° slopes)		
virgin *terra firme* forest	2.15	0.27
partially cleared	2.84	0.3
totally cleared	7.92	1.32

[1] Maass *et al.* (1988)

In terms of the processes operating during the transport of leaf litter and litter fragments during surface wash, the work by van Zon (1980) in oak woodlands in Luxembourg is particularly relevant. He found that substantial sediment was transported as mineral particles plastered to transported leaf surfaces and also that litter became entrained and encorporated into the surface soil over time due to sediment erosion and deposition. Both processes were frequently seen in operation in the Maracá experimental forest clearance plots, particularly on steeper, midslope locations. These processes made separation of eroded mineral and organic matter very difficult.

Very few studies in tropical environments have examined organic matter and nutrient losses in eroded soil. Lungren (1980) compared the inorganic and organic components of soil loss from organic-rich soils under evergreen rainforest sites and agricultural sites in Tanzania. He found very high organic matter losses, amounting to 70.5–77.4 per cent of all soil losses under forest and 50–76 per cent under agriculture. Although the organic matter losses in the Maracá plots were never more than 1 per cent, the soils were particularly sandy and lacking in humic matter. Lungren (1980) did not measure nutrient losses in eroded organic matter, but, considering the proportions of nutrient discovered in the Maracá study which are lost in organic form, it is suspected that very large organic nutrient losses were occurring in Tanzania.

Apart from providing organic substrates for nutrient cycling to crops after forest removal, leaf litter influx to the soil surface protects the soil from the energetic impact of raindrops. Herrera *et al.* (1978) suggested that the geometric arrangement of leaves on the forest floor protects the soil, preventing particle detachment and increasing infiltration. Since leaves and leaf fragments lie at various angles to one another, the percolation of water through the litter layer is rapid, thus minimising the residence time when water can be in contact with potentially leachable nutrients. Surface soil litter thus also acts to conserve nutrients.

Inorganic nitrogen, measured during the wet season in fresh potassium chloride extracts of the soils of forest and experimentally cleared plots, is given in Figure 6.6. Measurement were made ten weeks after the plots were cleared. Amounts of inorganic nitrogen in both soils of virgin forest and in cleared plots are very variable, with generally higher levels of nitrate than ammonium in surface soils. Rather surprisingly, forest and totally cleared plots show very similar NH_4-N and NO_3-N contents at all three depths in the soil profile. Partially cleared plots show slightly higher values of both NH_4-N and NO_3-N in the surface 5 cm of soil and at a depth of 25 cm. The decline in nitrate nitrogen with depth in all three treatments is expected, as organic matter contents decrease and since nitrate is particularly mobile and easily leached. Studies of nitrification by Marrs *et al.* (1991) and Ross *et al.* (1992) have shown that nitrification capacities in these soils are generally lower than rates found in other rain forests in tropical America. It is not clear why there should be an apparent increase in ammonium nitrogen at a depth of 25 cm in partially cleared plots. Since soil cation exchange capacities are generally very low, significant NH_4-N retention seems rather unlikely, although higher cation exchange capacity at a depth of 25 cm may account for apparent NH_4-N increases at that depth. It would appear that the most likely causes of differences in inorganic nitrogen, particularly nitrate, in the soil after clearing would be the relative magnitudes of increased leaching due to canopy removal on totally cleared sites, compared to intact root systems for nitrogen uptake on both forest and partial plots. The simple measurements made in this study cannot answer these questions, since both processes would maintain very low levels of inorganic nitrogen in the soil. It is useful to compare soil NH_4-N and NO_3-N in experimentally cleared plots to values of 4 µg NH_4-N/g and 1.26 µg NO_3-N/g for NO_3-N in *terra firme* forest and values of 4.01–8.1 µg NH_4-N/g and 0.03–0.73 µg NO_3-N/g for savanna and campo habitats (Ross *et al.* 1992). These comparisons show the greater amounts of soil ammonium than soil nitrate which are typical of wet and waterlogged savannas.

At San Carlos in Venezuela, inorganic nitrogen losses through soil leaching are reported by Jordan (1989) for experimental clearings of *terra firme* forest on an oxisol. Clearings were either cultivated or allowed to regenerate to secondary forest. After three and a half years, cultivated

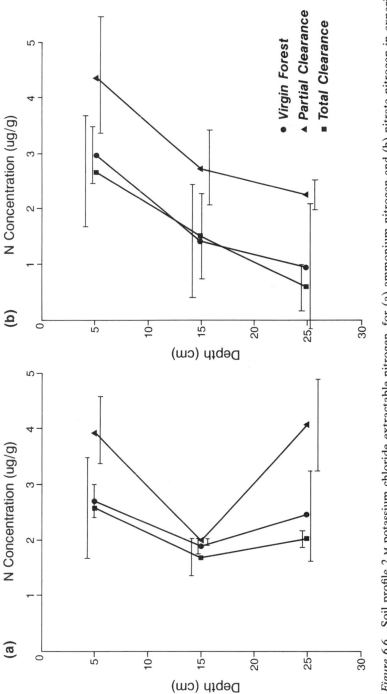

Figure 6.6 Soil profile 2 M potassium chloride extractable nitrogen, for (a) ammonium nitrogen and (b) nitrate nitrogen in experimental forest clearance plots, measured eleven weeks after the vegetation was removed. (Standard deviation bars are indicated.)

Table 6.4 Comparison of nutrient losses in eroded soil material (Maracá) with nutrient losses in throughflow and overland flow (Bahia: de Oliveira Leite 1985).

site	nutrient loss (kg/ha over 3 months)					
	N	P	K	Na	Ca	Mg
throughflow + overland flow (Bahia)[1]	5.48	0.45	4.23	5.88	21.4	4.55
erosion (Maracá, totally cleared plots)	7.92	1.32	12.6	0.51	3.03	1.79

[1] de Oliveira Leite (1985)

plots were abandoned. In forest soils prior to clearance NH_4-N concentrations in leachate from below 12 cm in the soil averaged 1–2 mg per litre, while NO_3-N concentrations averaged 0.5–0.9 mg per litre. Immediately after forest clearance and before burning, there was a steep rise in nitrate leachate concentration, followed by a further steep rise in both ammonium and nitrate concentrations after the fire. For three years after clearance, both nitrate and ammonium leachate concentrations were high (up to 7 mg NH_4-N per litre and 5 mg NO_3-N per litre) in both cultivated plots and forest succession plots. Inorganic nitrogen concentrations in soil leachates from the clearance plots fell to virtually zero after three years. Jordan (1989) notes that losses in leachates were higher than incoming nitrogen in rainfall and that denitrification losses were higher than soil nitrogen fixation. Under these conditions, plots become progressively denuded of nutrients. This, and other studies, indicate the relative importance of nutrient losses in both runoff, leachate and drainage waters. De Oliveira Leite (1985) for example, working in cacao plantations in Bahia, Brazil, found nutrient losses in interflow and overland flow amounting to as much as 22.1 kg N/ha per year and 85.8 kg Ca/ha per year. Comparing the amounts of nutrients lost in soil erosion in totally cleared forest plots on Maracá Island with amounts lost in throughflow and overland flow in the Bahia study (Table 6.4), it is surprising to see the magnitude of loss for all elements in water flow. Even if the cacao plantations had been fertilised, high values of sodium, calcium and magnesium are unusual in the light of low values of nitrogen and phosphorus loss. Three vital plant nutrients, nitrogen, phosphorus and potassium, are lost in higher amounts in eroded soil material rather than in drainage waters.

In Table 6.5, input and output nutrient data for *terra firme* forest at San Carlos in Venezuela (Herrera 1979) are compared to nutrient losses measured in erosion experiments at Maracá. Combined quantities of nitrogen

The rainforest edge

Table 6.5 Comparison of nutrient budgets for *terra firme* forest at San Carlos, Venezuela, (Herrera 1979) and on midslope locatians on Maracá Island. (All values = kg/ha over 3 months).

	N	P	K
San Carlos:			
rainfall input[1]	5.3	4.2	4.2
throughfall input[1]	6.3	1.4	7.4
vegetation uptake[1]	68.3	2.2	32.4
leaching[1]	3.8	5.3	6.5
stream discharge[1]	2.05	4.0	0.9
Maracá:			
(i) erosion:			
terra firme forest	2.15	0.27	0.54
partially cleared	2.84	0.30	0.81
totally cleared	7.92	1.32	12.6
(ii) runoff:			
terra firme forest	0.21	0.017	0.38
partially cleared	0.42	0.021	0.37
totally cleared	1.52	0.09	4.16

[1] Herrera (1979)

and potassium in runoff waters and eroded sediments for totally cleared plots exceed all throughfall nutrient inputs at San Carlos. This suggests that soil nutrient replenishment after forest clearance can only occur once water runoff and soil erosion have been substantially reduced by weed invasion and secondary forest regeneration, which stabilise the soil.

Sediment nitrogen, phosphorus and potassium losses in the erosion experiments were five, fourteen and three times higher than respective nutrient losses in runoff waters. It is clear from the magnitude of Maracá chemical erosion results that nutrient losses in runoff and soil erosion should be accounted in the future nutrient budgets calculated for tropical deforestation studies and in estimations of subsequent soil degradation. We can conclude, as have other authors in other deforestation studies, including Jordan (1989), that forest disturbance causes initial increases in measurable soil nutrients immediately after clearance, followed by severe nutrient declines over the longer period (e.g. Serrão *et al.* 1979; Sanchez 1982).

Concluding discussion

The soils examined in the eastern region of Maracá Island are at least as nutrient-poor as acid and dystrophic rain forest and savanna soils elsewhere in the tropical Americas (Table 6.6 and 6.7). The characteristic acidity, low cation exchange capacity and low exchangeable base content of tropical soils are well illustrated for all the sites in both tables, including Maracá. Despite debates on edaphic controls on forest and savanna vegetation, these data also indicate the lack of any significant differences in soil chemistry in forest and savanna habitats throughout the region, and thus suggest that if there are edaphic controls, they are unlikely to be chemical ones. The very close relationship between rates of soil biochemical processes such as nitrogen mineralisation, and surface soil moisture content, or soil wetness, as controlled by the height of the groundwater table (Ross *et al.* 1992; Marrs *et al.* 1991) probably represents seasonal and more transient soil chemical conditions than those given in Table 6.6 and 6.7. The identification of waterlogging and high water table levels as a major control of the current location and form of the forest–savanna boundary on Maracá Island (Furley & Ratter 1990; Thompson *et al.* 1991) implicitly invokes chemical or, at least biochemical, edaphic controls.

In a compartment study of the distribution of nutrients in the *terra firme* forest system at San Carlos in Venezuela, Jordan (1989) reported that 56 per cent of the total ecosystem nitrogen, 83.2 per cent of the phosphorus, 23.6 per cent of the potassium, 13.1 per cent of the calcium and 24.3 per cent of the magnesium were present in the soil. Although these very high values for nitrogen and phosphorus are a little unusual for tropical rainforest systems, they draw attention to the potential importance of nutrient losses in eroded soil after deforestation.

Although not measured in any of the Maracá studies, phosphate fixation in many of the soils is probably responsible for excessively low phosphate availability. In acidic soils of pH 4.5–5.5, iron and aluminium sesquioxides and hydroxyoxides are primarily responsible for phosphorus fixation. Despite this, neither total soil phosphorus nor available phosphate are significantly correlated with soil iron and aluminium oxide content ($r = 0.514$ and $r = 0.033$ respectively) in the data presented by Nortcliff & Robison (1989) for a range of Maracá soils. Nor is there a significant correlation between total soil phosphorus and 'available' or Mehlich-extractable phosphate ($r = 0.374$). No experiments were carried out on Maracá to test specifically for phosphorus deficiency. Ross *et al.* (1992), however, suggest that the processes of nitrogen mineralisation and nitrification in forest and savanna soils on Maracá may be phosphorus-limited. Although Vitousek (1984) suggests that low mean annual litterfall in *terra firme* forest in Amazonia is most likely an indication of low phosphorus availability, Scott *et al.* (1992) found higher than average litterfall rates in *terra firme* forest on Maracá Island, and relatively high phosphorus content in the leaf litter. Both of these results contradict Vitousek's theory.

Since soils on Maracá Island are generally nutrient-poor, the relatively high soil erosion rates measured in experimentally cleared forest plots do

Table 6.6 Topsoil chemical characteristics for *terra firme* forest in the Amazon basin region of South America (top 10 cm depth).

(a) General characteristics

location	soil type	% clay	pH	% organic matter	% organic C	author
Surinam	ultic haplorthox	3.2	4.0		1.52	Poels (1987)
S. W. Venezuela (San Carlos)	tropaquod		4.52		3.41	Herrera (1979)
S. W. Venezuela		17	4.2		1.4	Eden (1974)
		22	4.1		0.7	
E. Peru (Yurimaguas)	typic paleudult	10	4.1		1.0	Alegre *et al.* (1988)
N. Bolivia (Rio Beni)	eutric cambisol	28	6.9		5.6	Haase (1992)
	ferric luvisol	23	6.5		2.2	
	plinthic luvisol	19	6.0		3.7	
E. Brazil (Para)	oxisol		4.91		3.99	Buschbacher *et al.* (1988)
	oxisol		4.41		3.21	
N. Brazil (Roraima)			5.4		1.21	Eden *et al.* (1990)
Maracá Island	grossarenic paleudult		4.4			Nortcliff & Robison (1989)
	grossarenic plinthic paleudult	9.1–39.7	4.6–5.1	1.1–6.8	0.5–2.25	Thompson *et al.* (1991) Furley (1989)

location	total N %	C/N ratio	available P (µg/g)	total P (µg/g)	exchangeable Ca	Mg	Na (meq/100g)	K	ECEC (meq/100g)	author
Surinam	0.11	14	2.1	54	0.46	0.10	0.06	0.07	3.48	Poels (1987)
S. W. Venezuela (San Carlos)	0.25	13.5		378	0.18	0.14	0.08	0.03		Herrera (1979)
S. W. Venezuela	0.09 / 0.06	15.5 / 11.7	1.2 / 0.75		0.2 / 0.1	0.06 / 0.02	0 / 0	0.03 / 0.03	7.39 / 6.65	Eden (1974)
E. Peru	0.11	9.09	8.0		0.2	0.13		0.08	3.4	Alegre et al. (1988)
N. Bolivia: eutric	0.43	13.02			23.6	1.67	0.52	0.20	26.0	Haase (1992)
ferric	0.20	11.0			4.6	1.67	0.54	0.19	7.0	
plinthite	0.28	13.21			8.2	1.92	0.20	0.31	10.7	
E. Brazil (Pará)	0.19 / 0.16	20.8 / 21.2	3.42 / 5.36	208 / 210	1.39 / 0.44	0.64 / 0.37		0.09 / 0.07		Buschbacher et al. (1988)
N. Brazil (Roraima)	0.16	7.6	3.8		2.63	1.57	0.03	0.13	5.0	Eden et al. (1990)
Maracá Island	0.022		0	33	0.111	0.14			1.26	Nortcliff and Robison (1989)
	0.4–2.4	0.01–0.3	1.0–14.0		0.21–0.84	0.15–0.7	0.0001–0.087	0.045–0.15	0.9–2.34	Thompson et al. (1991)
		0.002–0.04			0.02–3.52	0.14–0.63	0.13–0.43	0.06–0.35	0.32–4.49	Furley (1989)

Table 6.7 Topsoil chemical characteristics for savanna sites in South America (top 10 cm depth).

(a) General characteristics location	soil type	% clay	pH	% organic matter	% organic C	author
S. W. Venezuela		0	4.5		1.2	Eden (1974)
		22	4.1		3.8	
N. Bolivia	dystropept	29	4.1		1.07	Haase (1992)
	aquic haplorthox	32	4.8		1.8	
	aquic dystropept	28	4.9		1.94	
	oxic dystropept	27	4.6		3.4	
C. Brazil	typic acrustox	65	4.6		2.2	Smyth & Sanchez (1982)
	ustoxic-quartzpsamment	9	4.6		0.6	
C. Brazil	haplustox	45	4.9	3.1		Goedert (1983)
	acrustox	46	4.7	3.4		
N. Brazil		21	5.1		1.49	Eden et al. (1990)
Maracá Island	aquic haplorthox		4.3			Nortcliff & Robison (1989)
(Santa Rosa)	aquic haplorthox	4.4–30.3	4.3–5.3	0.6–4.0		Thompson et al. (1991)
	aquic haplorthox		4.7–5.6	0.1–2.1		Furley (1989)

(b) Soil nutrients.

location	total N %	C/N ratio	available P (µg/g)	total P (µg/g)	Ca	exchangeable (meq/100g) Mg	Na	K	ECEC (meq/100g)	author
S. W. Venezuela	0.08	15	0.05		0.1	0.02	0	0.06	5.18	Eden (1974)
	0.22	17.3			0.2	0.04	0	0.03	0.22	
N. Bolivia dystropept	0.27	3.92			0.14	0.15	0.33	0.15	5.18	Haase (1992)
a. haplor.	0.13	13.85			0.44	0.16	0.34	0.07	4.33	
a. dystro.	0.13	14.92			0.54	0.27	0.36	2.48	4.07	
o. dystro.	0.30	11.3			0.53	0.15	0.25	3.42	4.74	
C. Brazil t. acrustox			0.4		0.28	0.08		0.07	1.03	Smyth and Sánchez (1982)
u. quartzps.			1.0		0.31	0.03		0.02	0.89	
C. Brazil haplustox					0.25	0.15		0.10	2.4	Goedert (1983)
acrustox					0.60	0.40		0.08	2.58	
N. Brazil	0.08	18.63	2.6		0.47	0.2	0.06	0.13	2.36	Eden et al. (1990)
Maracá	0.22		1.96	384	0.33	0.69			3.116	Nortcliff and Robison (1989)
	0.27–1.39		0.02–0.15	1.5–12.1	0.04–0.43	0.013–0.42	0.0004–0.061	0.014–0.15	0.15–2.0	Thompson et al. (1991)
			0.014–0.059		0.02–1.19	0.16–0.9	0.15–0.26	0.14–0.52	0.54–2.87	Furley (1989)

not result in excessive nutrient loss, only rather high nitrogen, potassium and calcium losses in the wet season after total vegetation clearance. In the case of nitrogen, measurements of NH_4-N and NO_3-N in runoff waters indicated that around 5–10 times more nitrogen was eroded in sediment than was lost in runoff. In Table 6.5, these data are compared to the general nitrogen input–output budget presented by Herrera (1979) for San Carlos in Venezuela. The combined amounts of nitrogen in erosion and water runoff from totally cleared plots on Maracá is around twice that measured as leached and discharged into streams at San Carlos. In cleared plots, initial nutrient replenishment is through rainfall input. The losses of nitrogen in erosion and runoff from totally cleared plots on Maracá are nearly twice the rainfall input of nitrogen at San Carlos. Although Maracá soils are initially nutrient- (and nitrogen-) poor, it is clear that, over fairly short time periods, deforestation and subsequent soil erosion can deplete their small nutrient capital even further.

An awareness of high nutrient losses in eroded organic matter, particularly in tropical Africa, combined with much-reduced nutrient inputs due to curtailment of litter influx after deforestation, has led to the development of soil and crop management techniques, specifically designed to conserve soil organic matter (e.g. Sanchez *et al.* 1989). The Tropical Soil Biology and Fertility Programme (TSBF) of UNESCO is now pioneering these techniques in parts of tropical South America, including the Amazon basin. A series of experiments on agroforestry and legume cultivation practices at Yurimaguas in Peruvian Amazonia (Palm 1988) has yielded excellent results which indicate not only that such practices can prevent deterioration of soil fertility, but also that it may be possible to restore already degraded soils and to improve their fertility beyond that of adjacent forest and savanna soils.

Acknowledgements

The author is indebted to the Brazilian Environment Secretariat (SEMA) for the use of field sites on Maracá Island and to the Royal Geographical Society for both financial and logistical support. The administrative and practical help of Steve Bowles, Fiona Watson, Sarah Latham, Dr Jill Thompson and Duncan Scott was invaluable. Fieldwork support was provided by Professor John Thornes, Dr Stephen Nortcliff, Flávio Luizão, Dr João Ferraz, Bridget Gregory and Sulineide Ataide, and laboratory support by Regina Luizão, Katie Fawcet, Dawn Adams and Simon Wild. The use of laboratory facilities at the National Amazonian Research Institute (INPA) in Manaus is gratefully appreciated.

References

Alegre, J. C., Cassel, D. K. and Bandy, D. E. (1988), Effect of land-clearing methods on soil chemical properties of an Ultisol in the Amazon, *Soil Science Society of America, Journal*, 52, 1283–8.

Allen, S. E. (1989, second edition), *Chemical Analysis of Ecological Materials*, Oxford, Blackwell Scientific Publications.

Black, C. A. (1965), *Methods of Soil Analysis. Part 2. Chemical and Microbiological Properties*, Madison, Wisconsin, American Society of Agronomy.

Buschbacher, R., Uhl, C. and Serrão, E. A. S. (1988), Abandoned pastures in Eastern Amazonia. II. Nutrient stocks in the soil and vegetation, *Journal of Ecology*, 76, 682–99.

Crooke, W. M. and Simpson, W. E. (1972), Determination of ammonium in kjeldahl digests of crops by an automated procedure, *Journal of the Science of Food and Agriculture*, 22, 9–10.

Dias, A. C. P. and Nortcliff, S. (1985), Effects of two land clearing methods on the physical properties of an Oxisol in the Brazilian Amazon, *Tropical Agriculture* (Trinidad), 62, 207–12.

Dunne, T. (1977), Studying patterns of soil erosion in Kenya, *FAO Soils Bulletin*, 33, 109–32.

Eden, M. J. (1974), Palaeoclimatic influences and the development of savanna in southern Venezuela, *Journal of Biogeography*, 1, 95–109.

Eden, M. J., McGregor, D. F. M. and Vieira, N. A. Q. (1990), Pasture development on cleared forest land in northern Amazonia, *Geographical Journal*, 156, 283–96.

Furley, P. A. (1989), The soils and soil–plant relationships of the eastern sector of Maracá Island (Appendix 5), in Milliken, W. and Ratter, J. A. (eds.), *The Vegetation of the Ilha de Maracá*, Edinburgh, Royal Botanic Garden, 229–76.

Furley, P. A. and Ratter, J. A. (1990), Pedological and botanical variations across the forest–savanna transition on Maracá Island, *Geographical Journal*, 156, 251–66.

Goedert, W. J. H. (1983), Management of Cerrado soils of Brazil: a review, *Journal of Soil Science*, 34, 405–28.

Haase, R. (1992), Physical and chemical properties of savanna soils in Northern Bolivia, *Catena*, 19, 1119–34.

Haylett, D. G. (1960), Run-off and soil erosion studies at Pretoria, *South African Journal of Agricultural Science*, 3, 379–94.

Hecht, S. B. (1979), in Sanchez, P. A. and Tergas, L. E. (eds.), *Pasture Production in Acid Soils of the Tropics*, Cali, Colombia, CIAT, 65–80.

Henriksen, S. and Selmer-Olsen, A. R. (1970), Automatic methods for determining nitrite and nitrate in water and soil extracts, *Analyst*, 95, 514–18.

Herrera, R. (1979), *Nutrient Distribution and Cycling in an Amazon Caatinga Forest on Spodosols in Southern Venezuela*, unpublished Ph.D. thesis, University of Reading, England.

Herrera, R., Jordan, C. F., Klinge, H. and Medina, E. (1978), Amazon ecosystems: their structure and functioning with particular emphasis on nutrients, *Interciencia*, 3, 223–31.

Jordan, C. F. (1982), The nutrient balance of an Amazonian rain forest, *Ecology*, 63, 647–54.

Jordan, C. F. (1989), *An Amazonian Rain Forest. The Structure and Function of a Nutrient Stressed Ecosystem and the Impact of Slash and Burn Agriculture*, UNESCO: Man and the Biosphere Series, 2, New Jersey, USA, Parthenon Publishing Group.

Lal, R. (1981), Deforestation of tropical rainforest and hydrological problems, in Lal, R. and Russell, E. W. (eds.), *Tropical Agricultural Hydrology*, Chichester, John Wiley and Sons, Ltd, 131–40.

Lungren, L. (1980), Comparison of surface runoff and soil loss from runoff plots in forest and small-scale agriculture in the Usambara Mts., Tanzania, *Geografiska Annaler*, 62A, 113–48.

Maass, J. M., Jordan, C. F. and Sarukhan, J. (1988), Soil erosion and nutrient losses in seasonal tropical agroecosystems under various management techniques, *Journal of Applied Ecology*, 25, 595–607.

Marrs, R. H., Thompson, J., Scott, D. and Proctor, J. (1991), Nitrogen mineralisation and nitrification in terra firme forest and savanna soils on Ilha de Maracá, Roraima, Brazil, *Journal of Tropical Ecology*, 7, 123–37.

Milliken, W. and Ratter, J. A. (1989), *The Vegetation of the Ilha de Maracá*, Edinburgh, Royal Botanic Garden.

Murphy, J. and Riley, J. P. (1965), A modified single solution method for the determination of phosphate in natural waters, *Anal. Chim. Acta*, 27, 31–6.

Nortcliff, S. and Robison, D. (1989), *The Soils and Geomorphology of the Ilha de Maracá, Roraima. The Second Approximation*, Edinburgh, Royal Botanic Garden.

Nortcliff, S., Ross, S. M. and Thornes, J. B. (1990), Soil moisture, runoff and sediment yield from differentially cleared tropical rainforest plots, in Thornes, J. B. (ed.), *Vegetation and Erosion*, Chichester John Wiley and Sons, Ltd, 419–36.

De Oliveira Leite (1985), Interflow, overland flow and leaching of natural nutrients on an Alfisol slope of Southern Bahia, Brazil, *Journal of Hydrology*, 80, 77–92.

Palm, C. (1988), *Mulch Quality and Nitrogen Dynamics in an Alley Cropping System in the Peruvian Amazon*, unpublished Ph.D. thesis, North Carolina State University, USA.

Poels, R. L. H. (1987), *Soils, Water and Nutrients in a Forest Ecosystem in Surinam*, doctoral thesis, Agricultural University, Wageningen.

Roose, E. J. and Lelong, F. (1976), Les facteurs de l'érosion hydrique en Afrique tropicale. Études sur petites parcelles expérimentales de sol, *Rev. Geogr. Phys. Geol. Dyn*, 4, 365–74.

Ross, S. M. (1992), Soil and litter nutrient losses in forest clearings close to the forest–savanna boundary in Northern Brazil, in Proctor, J., Furley, P. A. and Ratter, J. A. (eds.), *Nature and Dynamics of Forest–Savanna Boundaries*, London, Chapman & Hall.

Ross, S. M., Luizão, F. J. and Luizão, R. M. M. (1992), Soil conditions and soil biology in different habitats across a forest–savanna boundary in Northern Brazil, in Proctor, J., Furley, P. A. and Ratter, J. A. (eds.), *Nature and Dynamics of Forest–Savanna Boundaries*, London, Chapman & Hall.

Ross, S. M., Thornes, J. B. and Nortcliff, S. (1990), Soil hydrology, nutrient and erosional response to the clearance of terra firme forest, Maracá Island, Roraima, northern Brazil, *Geographical Journal*, 156, 267–82.

Sanchez, A., Palm, C., Szott, T., Cuevas, E. and Lal, R. (1989), Organic input management in tropical soils, in Coleman, D. C., Oades, M. and Uehara, G. (eds.), *Dynamics of Soil Organic Matter in Tropical Ecosystems*, NifTAL Project, Honolulu, University of Hawaii Press, 125–52.

Sanchez, P. A. (1982), Nitrogen in shifting cultivation systems of Latin America, *Plant and Soil*, 67, 91–103.

Sanchez, P. A. and Salinas, J. G. (1981), Low-input technology for managing oxisols and ultisols in Tropical America, *Advances in Agronomy*, 34, 279–406.

Sarmiento, G. (1983), The Savannas of Tropical America, in Bourlière, F. (ed.), *Tropical Savannas*, Ecosystems of the World, 3, 245–87.

Scott, D. A., Proctor, J. and Thompson, J. (1992), Ecological studies on a lowland evergreeen rain forest on Maracá Island, Roraima, Brazil, II: Litter and nutrient cycling, *Journal of Ecology*, 80, 705–17.

Serrão, E. A. S., Falesi, I. C., Veiga, J. B. and Texeira, J. F. (1989), Productivity of cultivated pastures in low fertility soils of the Amazon of Brazil, in Sanchez, P. A. and Tergas, L. E. (eds.), *Pasture Production in Acid Soils of the Tropics*, Cali, Colombia, Centro Internacional de Agricultura Tropical (CIAT), 195–226.

Seubert, C. E., Sanchez, P. A. and Valverde, C. (1977), Effects of land clearing methods on soil properties of an Ultisol and crop performance in the Amazon jungle of Peru, *Tropical Agriculture* (Trinidad), 54, 307–21.

Smith, R. M. and Stamey, W. L. (1965), Determining the range of tolerable erosion, *Soil Science*, 100, 414–24.

Smyth, T. J. and Sanchez, P. A. (1982), Phosphate rock dissolution and availability in Cerrado soils as affected by phosphorus sorption capacity, *Soil Science Society of America, Journal*, 46, 339–45.

Thompson, J., Viana, V., Proctor, J., Ratter, J. A. and Scott, D. (1992), Contrasting forest–savanna boundaries on Maracá Island, Roraima, Brazil, in Proctor, J., Furley, P. A. and Ratter, J. A. (eds.), *Nature and Dynamics of Forest–Savanna Boundaries*, London, Chapman & Hall.

Vitousek, P. M. (1984), Litterfall, nutrient cycling and nutrient limitation in tropical forests, *Ecology*, 65, 285–98.

Weirsum, F. (1985), Effects of various vegetation layers of an *Acacia auriculiformis* forest plantation on surface erosion in Java, Indonesia, in El-Swaify, S. A., Moldenhauer, W. C. and Lo, A. (eds.), *Soil Erosion and Conservation*, Iowa Soil Conservation Society of America, 79–89.

Van Zon, H. J. M. (1980), The Transport of Leaves and Sediment over a Forest Floor. A Case Study in The Grand Duchy of Luxembourg, *Catena*, 7, 97–110.

7 *Peter A. Furley and James A. Ratter*

Soil and plant changes at the forest–savanna boundary on Maracá Island[1]

Introduction

Ecological and environmental boundaries are of particular interest in helping to explain the development and dispersal of plant communities. They represent tension zones where systems change, very often abruptly. They are rarely in stable equilibrium and, in ecology, they represent locations where one community is often advancing at the expense of another. Boundaries provide evidence for the dynamic nature of long-term evolutionary processes. Shifts in vegetation patterns also have practical significance in indicating forest advance, retreat or a potential for regeneration. In most cases, the precise nature of the boundary and the rates of change are unknown.

The aim of the present contribution is to illustrate the variety of forest–savanna transitions which exist on Maracá Island and to take a detailed model of one type of boundary to explain the dynamic processes which are currently shaping the forest edge. The botanical surveys, which form the basis of the work, together with some of the soil research are reported in Milliken & Ratter (1989).

Factors and processes affecting the boundary

A number of broad theories have been advanced to account for the sharp transitions between essentially woody plant communities and those dominated by shrubs and herbaceous plants. In more diffuse ecotones, with numerous possible transitional vegetation communities, it is likely that a combination of factors accounts for the change, whereas at abrupt boundaries it is probable that one or two local factors are responsible.

The principal factors may be grouped and summarised:

[1] This chapter is based on a paper which originally appeared in *The Geographical Journal*, 156:3, 251–66, under the title 'Pedological and botanical variations across the forest–savanna transition on Maracá Island.'

Climatic

The overall regional constraint upon forest advance is clearly climate and particularly the gradual increase in dry-season length and intensity. At the forest margins, it appears that short dry spells within the wet season, especially at the onset, can severely influence plant growth and make the forest edge vulnerable to other disturbing factors. It is not, therefore, the net amount of precipitation averaged over a period of years and available to plant growth, but distribution at critical times of the year plus storage over spells of water deficit, which are likely to be important. There are very few quantitative data to test these conjectures, although the overall climatic determinism is not in question.

Fire

It is generally agreed that expanding areas of savanna are most frequently associated with the incidence and severity of burning (White 1983). Fire has been shown to compress an ecotone and contribute to the abruptness of the boundary, and, furthermore, savanna trees and shrubs are clearly fire-adapted. The dispute lies in whether fire alone can cause savanna advance into established forest (for example into evergreen forest as suggested by Aubréville in 1966). In the opinion of Hopkins (1992), other factors are needed in addition to fire and cultivation, for savanna to develop from evergreen forest. The same change has been described following the opening of the forest by elephants in East Africa and the subsequent entry of fire (Buechner & Dawkins 1961; Belsky 1990).

Land use change

In addition to cultivation, which represents one of the extreme forms of human disturbance to forest, more subtle land-use pressures equally increase the vulnerability of the forest margins (Morgan & Moss 1965; Moss 1982). Since areas converted to agro-pastoralism following deforestation tend to be rapidly colonised and revert to at least a shrubby, secondary woody vegetation, it is considered that the direct action of humans alone would not generate savanna. However, prolonged disturbance and annual clearing, pesticide, herbicide and fertiliser attack, often combined with regular firing, will obviously keep any potential forest regeneration at bay (Hills & Randall 1968; Adejuwon & Adesina 1988; 1992). Furthermore, long-term settlement and cultivation may cause near-irreversible edaphic changes in the soils which may make them incapable of supporting forest growth (Schnell 1976; Frost *et al.* 1986).

Edaphic controls

Soil deterioration, which inevitably occurs after the nutrient-conserving mechanisms of established forest are removed (Jordan 1985), may inhibit the regrowth of woody plants at least for a protracted period. Oxidation and destruction of organic matter, removal of the protective litter acting as a mulch at the ground surface, dessication and accelerated exposure to weathering, leaching, runoff and erosion are likely both to reduce the ability of forest trees to recolonise and, conversely, to encourage savanna advance. In addition, however, there are many soils which naturally favour savanna vegetation. The white sands (*campinaranas*) of the Amazon basin forests, for example, are acidic, are excessively well drained, lack both organic and mineral nutrient ion reserves and are, therefore, always oligotrophic. Only specialised forest trees can adapt to such extreme conditions, often associated with ectomycorrhizae and other nutrient-conserving devices typical of exceptionally nutrient-poor localities. On sloping topography, the downslope colluvial accumulation of both nutrients and water may encourage the formation and development of a number of savanna and forest zones (Markham & Babbedge 1979; Furley 1992).

Water availability
The provision of virtually constant supplies of water, whether from precipitation, continuously high atmospheric humidity, groundwater or soil, is an obligatory requirement of humid tropical forests. A combination of marginal climate, poor soil–water conservation and a lack of groundwater within reach of roots, or a combination of these, will militate against forest advance or regeneration. The unreliability of water sources is likely to shift the boundary in favour of savanna.

Palaeoenvironmental factors
In addition to contemporary dynamic processes affecting the forest–savanna boundary, the distribution of savannas must also reflect past climatic and environmental changes at any given locality. There are, for example, savanna patches within forest which are believed to represent relics of past arid climates and are correlated with glacial maxima during the Pleistocene (Adjanohoun & Assis 1968; Bellier *et al.* 1969 in Africa; Whitmore & Prance 1987 in the New World tropics). However, it is difficult to account for these solely as a result of past climate, since forest has managed to engulf surrounding areas. They are probably maintained by edaphic factors and they in turn may reflect geomorphological changes during dry phases in recent geological time (Ab 'Sáber 1982).

    Even a brief examination of these theories indicates the variety of causal factors which may operate at the forest margin. It reinforces the notion that it is a combination of constraints that accounts for the absence of forest along the tortuous mosaic of vegetation which frequently characterises the boundary.

Savanna and forest distributions and their junctions on Maracá Island

Maracá Island lies at the climatic boundary for eastward forest advance in Roraima and also, coincidentally, at the westward margins of the present

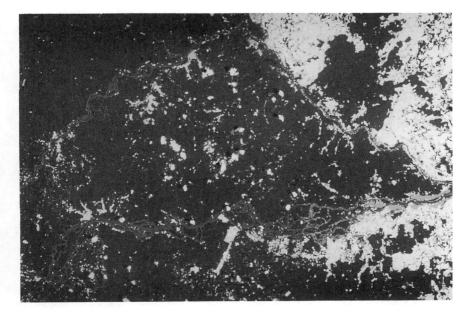

Figure 7.1 LANDSAT TM (Thematic Mapper) image of Maracá Island, 1985. The photograph shows the transition between forest (dark) to the west and savanna (pale) to the east. The island itself is circumscribed by two branches of the Uraricoera River, the southern one being extremely braided. The island vegetation is predominantly forest, but is 'mottled' by pale colours representing non-forested patches. These consist of savanna but also linear tracts showing the tangled shrub and low tree vegetation typical of *vazantes* (periodic stormlines). The geometric outline of the fazenda at the agricultural frontier can be seen in the mid-bottom of the photograph.

agricultural frontier (Eden & McGregor 1989; Furley & Mougeot 1993). For these reasons, the savanna laps around the eastern side of the island, although the two branches of the Uraricoera River form the current barriers to movement (Figure 7.1).

Within the confines of the island, which has a maximum east–west spread of 70 km and a north–south width of 30 km and a total area of some 101,000 ha, the satellite imagery shows up a number of non-forested areas. These comprise aquatic sites, rocky outcrops and some previously disturbed areas (*capoeiras*) now being actively recolonised by forest species, as well as tracts of savanna. The savanna sites have been classified by Milliken & Ratter (1989) as: (1) campo (grassland) with scattered trees, predominantly *Curatella americana* L. and *Byrsonima crassifolia* (L.) Kunth; (2) seasonally wet campo, sometimes referred to as hyperseasonal savanna (Sarmiento 1988, 1992); and (3) *vazante*, which is a mostly treeless form

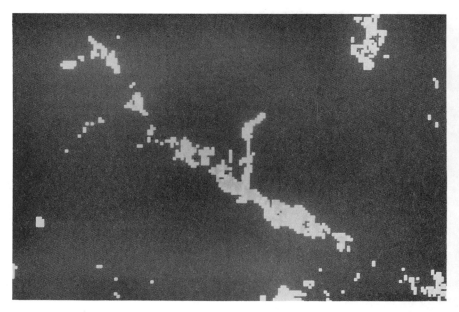

Figure 7.2 Details of the vegetation on Maracá Island (LANDSAT TM 1985). By
enlarging the scale on the image processor, the details of savanna patches and the
linear *vazante* can be clearly identified. Note that the smallest pale patches represent individual pixels of c. 30×30 m.

of vegetation running through the forest in elongated strips up to 100 m
or more in width. The seasonally wet campos form the predominant
savanna type behind the riverine levées and on the seasonally wet interior
depressions, whereas the drier campos often form scattered pacthes well
inside the forest, frequently as totally isolated islands (Figure 7.2). The
vazantes can be seen to follow gently inclined drainage courses which must
serve to evacuate storm floods and contain water for much of the wet
season but which are otherwise dry with characteristic flora and soil
properties.

Methodology

Representative transects were taken across the forest–savanna boundaries
over the course of two field seasons at each of the following savanna sites:

A. Forest–hyperseasonal savanna
  i.   Santa Rosa: a slight depressional basin, some 3 km long by 1 km
       wide, linked to the northern branch (Santa Rosa Channel) of the
       Uraricoera River, and forming a discrete island within forest.

ii. 'Angico': situated at the eastern extremity of the *terra firme* forest on the island, overlooking seasonally wet campo.

B. Island savannas of mostly dry campo or campo cerrado
(open arboreal savanna)
   i. Savannas of this type surround the wet hyperseasonal savannas at Santa Rosa and elsewhere; in these locations they form narrow bands at slightly higher and better drained sites and abut on to the forest.
  ii. Isolated, discrete islands within the forest; there appear to be a number of patches smaller than the 20 × 20 m pixels identified on the LANDSAT TM imagery.

C. Vazante
Several sub-types are apparent from field surveys and satellite image interpretation but observations reported here are restricted to
   i. major linear forms: Preguiça Trail
  ii. minor drainage lines, sufficiently small to be relatively unaffected by floods and sometimes marked by lines of buriti palms (*Mauritia flexuosa* L.f.), as at Santa Rosa.

At each site, detailed botanical observations have been made both of the general character of the vegetation (using point-centred-quarter techniques) and of individual species distribution along transect lines. Sequences of soil profiles were sited to reflect the changes in plant communities and soil samples were taken, by horizon, for subsequent analysis. Details of field and laboratory methods are given in Milliken & Ratter (1989).

Soil and plant community variations across the boundaries

In this report, the general model of forest–hyperseasonal savanna will be examined in greater detail and with particular reference to the 'Angico' transect. The analysis of this site is prefaced by a brief account of the other boundaries found on the island to give a context to the research project.

1. Forest–savanna transitions at the island savannas and
vazante *locations*
Several sites were examined along the Preguiça Trail (Figure 7.3). For the purposes of the present discussion, a simplified grouping will be presented. The southern part of the Preguiça Trail leads into the Maracá channel, the southern branch of the Uraricoera River. A succession of different vegetation communities extends from the river inland and the Trail crosses the large *vazante* shown earlier in Figure 7.2. Of particular interest are the two discrete *Curatella americana/Byrsonima crassifolia* island campos (units 8 in Figure 7.4), separated by low thicket or *carrasco* (unit 7). Attention

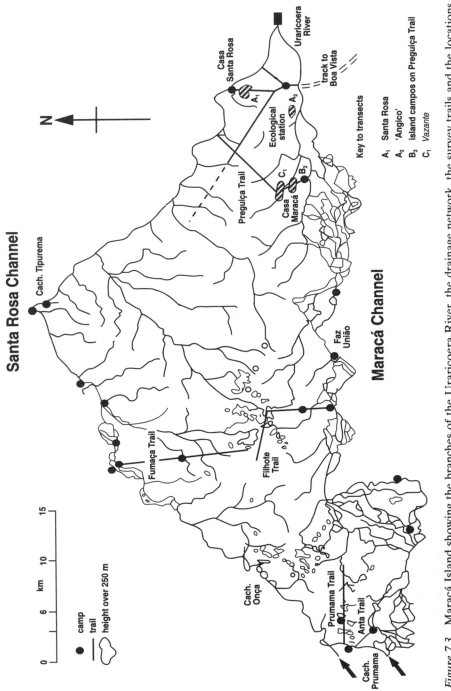

Figure 7.3 Maracá Island showing the branches of the Uraricoera River, the drainage network, the survey trails and the locations of the forest–savanna transitions examined.

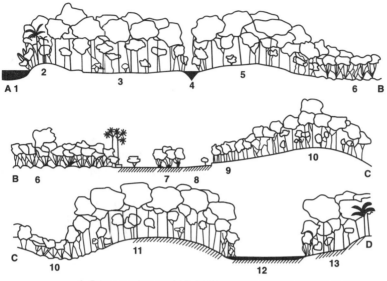

A–D is a continuous SSE–NNW transect approx. 3 km in length

Key: hatched areas represent the transitions examined:
1   Maracá Channel.
2   levee with mixed riverine forest.
3   tall forest dominated by *Peltogyne gracilipes* and *Pradosia surinamensis* on damp ground.
4   the Igarapé stream.
5   Forest similar to 3, but slightly taller and on drier ground.
6   dense thicket on hummocked ground.
7   thicket similar to 6.
8   *Curatella americana / Byrsonima crassifolia* campo.
9   marginal thicket (carrasco) vegetation.
10   low forest with campina influence.
11   tall forest with extreme dominance of *Peltogyne gracilipes*.
12   *vazante* vegetation.
13   tall forest dominated by *Pradosia surinamensis*.

Figure 7.4   Schematic profile of the vegetation at the southern end of the Preguiça Trail.

will then be drawn to the *vazante* area (unit 12) dividing two tall stretches of forest (units 11 and 13).

The low thicket consists of an extremely dense cover of small, multi-trunked, deliquescent trees and shrubs reaching up to *c*.5 m, made up of species characteristic of the forest edge. The results of the survey worked out at 4882 trees (at least 3 cm dbh) per hectare, but even this does not give a true reflection of the density because the spaces between trees were packed with more slender individuals which did not fall within the survey (Milliken & Ratter 1989:114 & Table 39). The campo sites were grassland covered with a scattering of shrubs and low trees of *Curatella* and *Byrsonima*.

The *vazante* zone is virtually treeless, although the physiognomy and species composition of different *vazantes*, which have a wide distribution on the island, have been observed to vary considerably. At the present site, the vegetation reaches 60–200 cm and consists of tall herbs and low shrubs such as *Mimosa pigra* L., *Senna alata* (L.) Roxb., *Melochia simplex* St. Hil., *Canna glauca* L., *Costus scaber* R. & P., *Thalia geniculata* L., *Heliconia psittacorum* L.f., *Scleria sprucei* C. B. Cl. and numerous grasses, covered by a tangle of herbaceous vines (Milliken & Ratter 1989: Table 52). The two main components of the vegetation seem to be semi-aquatic species which flourish in the flood conditions of the wet season and die back to underground perennating organs during the dry season, and land plants which flourish in dry periods, notably tall gasses and herbaceous leguminous and convolvulaceous vines.

The forest margins to either side of the *vazante* are abrupt, forming steep, sharp walls. The southern forest (unit 11) is dominated by the widespread tree *Peltogyne gracilipes* Ducke, whereas the northern forest (unit 13) has *Pradosia surinamensis* (Eyma) Penn. as the most abundant tree. The *Peltogyne gracilipes* forest is remarkable for the small number of tree species present and is readily identified during the dry season because of the distinctive, deciduous crowns. *Pradosia surinamensis* is the most common of the eastern *terra firme* forest species and, with the Peltogynes, comprises over half of the trees (at least 30 cm dbh) on the Preguiça Trail.

Soil variations complement the plant communities and provide evidence for both edaphic control and dynamic changes in the vegetation. Taking first of all the distribution of key surface soil properties, it can be seen (Figure 7.5.a) that the distribution of the sum of the exchangeable cations highlights the high *vazante* values, the intermediate forest levels, the consistently low campo figures and the slight increase within the low thicket community. The total cation graph reflects the major contribution of calcium and magnesium. A similar pattern is observed for the distribution of soil organic properties with carbon and nitrogen trends highly correlated and matching the trends displayed for the cations (Figure 7.5.b).

Turning to the acidity and pH distributions (Figure 7.5.c), it can be seen that pH changes relatively little, most values lying between 4 and 5.5 and within half a pH unit for either solute. On the other hand, total exchangeable acidity (particularly the exchangeable aluminium component) reaches a peak at the *vazante* site with lower values in the forest to either side, the *Peltogyne* forest having very low exchangeable aluminium levels. The campo and low thicket sites have levels lower than the *vazante* or the northern *Pradosia* forest.

One further field observation, for which quantitative analysis is not yet available, is the striking difference in soil texture. *Vazante* soils are

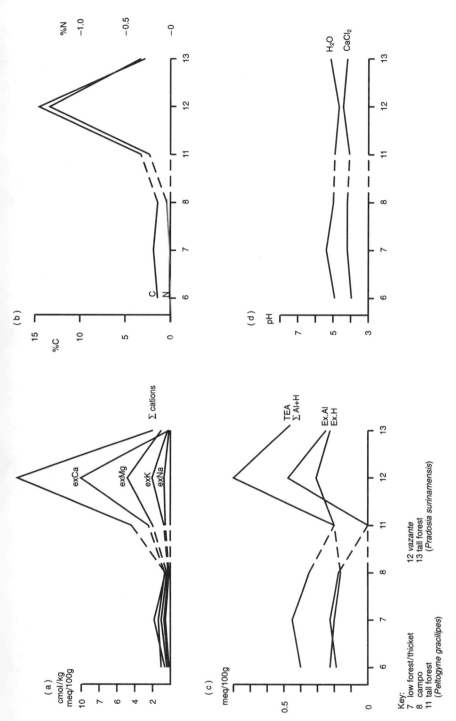

Figure 7.5 Variations in surface soil properties across the forest transitions along the southern Preguiça Trail:
(a) Exchangeable cations
(b) Organic matter
(c) Exchangeable acidity
(d) pH

massive clays, dark, organic and clearly good reservoirs of moisture and nutrients despite the high exchangeable acidity. Forest soils are acidic, of sandy loam texture with intermediate levels of organic matter and nutrients. However, the campos are characterised by acidic, nutrient-poor, low-organic soils and are also typified by extremely sandy textures with high porosity and drainage potentials. They are, in other words, typical of the dystrophic white sands found in many areas of the Amazon, with soil properties which would inhibit forest advance.

Despite their isolation, these island campos contain characteristic arboreal cerrado species. Further, the low thicket comprises species associated with forest margins and, within the thicket, there are numerous specimens of *Curatella americana* and *Byrsonima crassifolia* – which suggest that thicket has replaced savanna and thereby slightly ameliorated the surface soils.

The conclusions from these observations are that:

(a) The soils very clearly match contemporary vegetation patterns.
(b) The isolated savannas are found over oligotrophic soils and may represent the last obstacles to the closing of the forest.
(c) The low thicket forms a link in the succession from campo to a forest cover and, in the process of establishment, has perhaps modified its surface soil properties.
(d) The low forest/thicket is advancing substantially into previously grassy areas, as evidenced by typical cerrado trees found well within the contemporary woody vegetation.
(e) The sharpest boundaries, at the sides of the *vazante*, coincide with an embryonic valley form discharging storm flow.

2. The Santa Rosa and 'Angico' transects

Santa Rosa   The *Curatella americana–Byrsonima crassifolia* campo is a very widespread vegetation type in the New World tropics, stretching from Mexico to Paraguay (Milliken & Ratter 1989). It occurs to the south and east of Maracá Island and extends into Venezuela in the north and to the Rupununi Highlands of Guyana further east. At Santa Rosa, it forms the drier margins (Bi on page 97). The vegetation consists of a scattering of shrubs and small trees, rarely more than 6 m tall, within grassland. The trees have the typical fire-resistant, contorted form and leathery leaves characteristic of the cerrados in central Brazil. Leaves of *C. americana* are impregnated with silica to such an extent that they have been used as sandpaper. The tree is so predominant that its cover value index on a representative 50 × 50 m plot is 145 compared with the other principal species – 27 for *B. crassifolia*, 9 for *Swartzia grandifolia* Bong. ex. Benth., 7 for *Vitex schomburgkiana* Schauer, with no other species reaching 6 (Milliken & Ratter 1989: 153, Table 48). The low campina forest at the south–west end of the transect is dense and varied with trees about 8–12 m tall (Milliken & Ratter 1989: Table 36) and with a sharp forest edge (Figure 7.6). To the north–east, the forest transition from campo passes several minor vegetation zones, eventually passing into thicket and a more diffuse ecotone into forest. This forest appears to be a depauperate version of typical *terra firme* type with a high proportion of colonising and marginal species.

The most striking surface soil changes over the boundary include high acidity levels in the non-forested areas, matching peaks of organic matter and base cations (Figure 7.7). It is rapidly apparent that the forest–savanna boundaries differ at either end of the transect.

Since the savanna is seasonally very wet with the lowest parts of the basin flooded, it was felt necessary to monitor groundwater and surface-water changes. Observations were made over the course of a year (by D. Scott and J. Thompson, working with J. Proctor), and showed that the central campo was severely affected by saturation. The groundwater rose to within a postulated 20 cm rooting depth for some three months, whereas areas within the forest, at least at the southern end, were unaffected by groundwater even at the wettest times of the year (Figure 7.8).

'Angico'   This short transect runs orthogonally to the slope from the low plateau on which the ecological station is situated, down to the extensive wet campo covering much of the eastern end of the island (Figure 7.9). The transect runs from a mesotrophic variant of the *terra firme* forest, through an abrupt transition with *Curatella americana*-dominated arboreal cerrado to a low shrubby and predominantly wet herbaceous and near treeless campo.

The transect is considered in more detail in this paper because it represents the clearest model of a seasonally water-dominated forest margin. The low forest, which reaches 10–15 m, is also of interest because it is characterised by the deciduous tree *Anadenanthera peregrina* (L.) Speg. var. *peregrina* (the 'angico'), which was found on the island only on this slope and is related, in central Brazil, to higher levels of calcium and magnesium (Ratter *et al.* 1973, 1978). Conspicuous trees associated with the angico are *Cochlospermum orinocense* (Kunth) Steud. and *Didymopanax morototoni* Decne. & Planch. and the palm *Maximiliana maripa* (Correa) Drude. (Milliken & Ratter 1989: Table 14). See Figure 7.10.

The first phase of the pedological work attempted to characterise the changes in nutrient status by means of a trench cut across the boundary with three major profile sites. It is readily apparent that significantly higher exchangeable cation levels are found in the forest, principally made up of calcium and magnesium and to a lesser extent potassium. The increased values upslope of the forest margin are marked by slightly higher pH levels, organic carbon percentages and (although the significance, if any, is

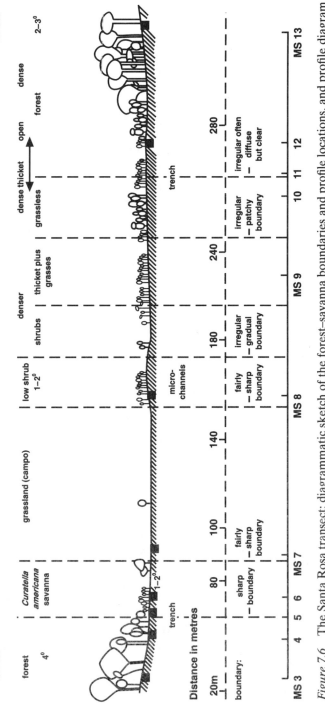

Figure 7.6 The Santa Rosa transect: diagrammatic sketch of the forest–savanna boundaries and profile locations, and profile diagram of the tree species distribution.

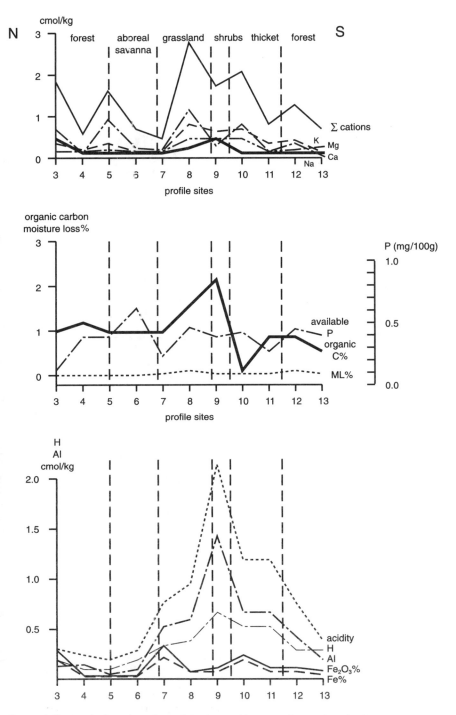

Figure 7.7 Variations in selected surface soil properties across the forest–savanna boundaries at Santa Rosa.

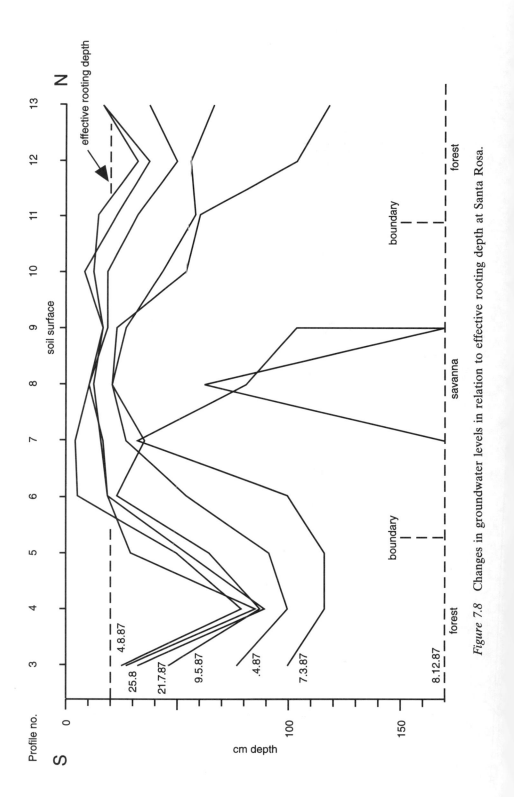

Figure 7.8 Changes in groundwater levels in relation to effective rooting depth at Santa Rosa.

Figure 7.9 Site of the 'Angico' transect and the nature of the forest–savanna boundary to the east of Maracá Island. The photograph shows the pattern of riverine forest (or gallery forest – *mata ciliar*), the wetlands and swamps (where the track to the ecological station is marked) and the general forest–savanna boundary. The photograph is taken looking west along the southern branch into Maracá Island on the right.

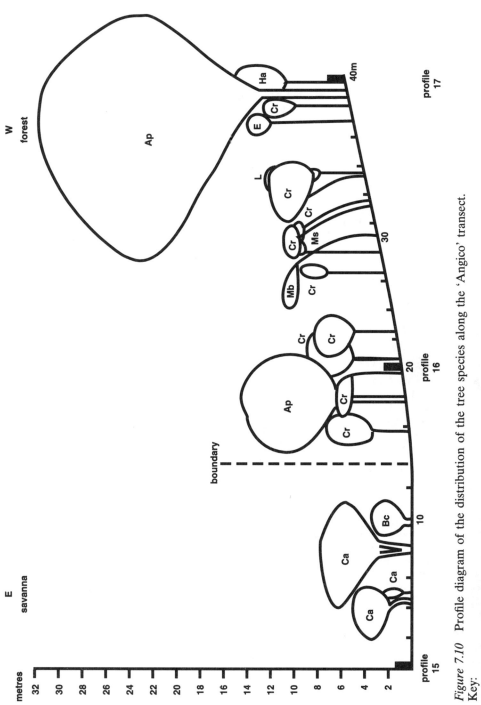

Figure 7.10 Profile diagram of the distribution of the tree species along the 'Angico' transect.

Key:

Ap *Anadenanthera peregrina* (L.) Speg. var.
      peregrina ('angico')
Bc *Byrsonima crassifolia* (L.) Kunth
Ca *Curatella americana* L.
Cr *Casearia rubicunea* (Poir.) Badlk.

E   *Erythroxylum* sp.
Ha *Himatanthus articulatus* (Vahl) Woods.
L   *Licania* sp.
Mb *Machaerium birovulatum* Micheli
Ms *Myrcia* cf. *splendens* (Sw.) DC.

not clear) higher iron oxide levels with a drop in soil acidity. Profile 16, which is sited exactly on the boundary, takes an intermediate position between campo and forest (Figure 7.11).

Although these surface-soil parameters neatly reflect the change in plant communities, they are unlikely, by themselves, to have determined the boundary. There are many other instances on the island of soil properties similar to the campo levels, where low forest or thicket has successfully invaded and colonised. the shape of the slope and the hyperseasonal character of the campo suggested that seasonal flooding was also important and its significance at the Santa Rosa site had already been appreciated.

Consequently, the trench was monitored over a cycle of wet and dry seasons (by D. Scott and J. Thompson). From March until April 1987, groundwater levels dropped consistently. From May until August, with the onset of the wet season, the levels rose until the savanna site had groundwater to within 10 cm of the surface (and periodically to the surface). After September, the groundwater levels declined with a further drying phase. Figure 7.12 shows the distribution of the saturated zone over these wetting and drying phases and the heights within the profiles to which the water rose. The interesting point is at the boundary where, at the height of the wet season, the groundwater rose to around tree-rooting depth, saturating the soil downslope but leaving the forest upslope still dry. Furthermore, detailed examination of the soil profiles indicated that mottling (indicating at least periodic gleying) exactly coincided with the rooting depth at about the forest margin. The conclusion, therefore, is that seasonal flooding over a long period has reached to about the contemporary forest margin and that the downslope saturation and flooding would inhibit further forest advance into the *campo cerrado* and campo zones. Consequently, it can be argued that the forest–savanna boundary has reached a temporary halt at this point and that further forest advance, which has been identified in a number of other areas, would require a widespread change in the groundwater regime. On the other hand, savanna could migrate upslope if a combination of climatic drying and fire reduced the potential for forest regeneration. At present there is no evidence for such forest retreat.

Indications of migration rates for the forest edge

As indicated earlier, there are a number of sites where evidence can be adduced for forest advance, thereby substantiating ideas put forward for other areas of Brazil (see Furley 1992, Ratter *et al.* 1973, 1978, Ratter 1986, 1992).

Typical of this evidence is the discovery of well-established trees, characteristic of the savanna, currently lying well within the forest boundary. Of these, *Curatella americana* is the most common species encountered on

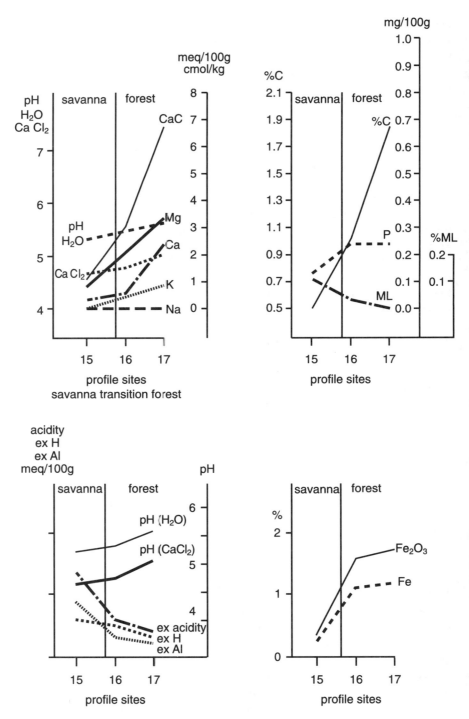

Figure 7.11 Variations in selected surface soil properties across the forest–savanna boundary on the 'Angico' transect.

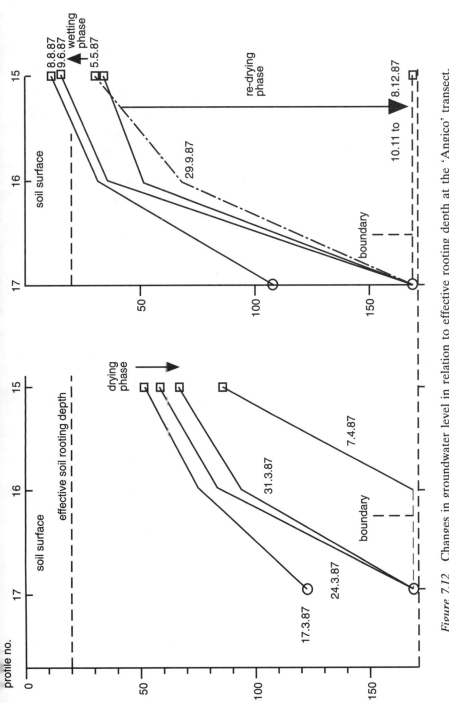

Figure 7.12 Changes in groundwater level in relation to effective rooting depth at the 'Angico' transect.

Maracá. This suggests that the thicket or forest has advanced at least by the distance such trees are found within the forest, and within the lifetime of the individual tree. Some trees are found over 10 m into the forest and appear to be no more than ten years old, which would therefore represent a rapid rate of advance. (Milliken & Ratter 1989:157)

There is also a thriving community of forest-margin plants. Many species are typical of edge sites and trees may overhang the campo, such as the wide-crowned *Andira surinamensis* (Bondt.) Splitg. ex Pulle, small palms (e.g. *Bactris maraja* Mart.), small shrubs (for example *Casearia spinescens* (Sw.) Benth. and a marginal thicket of vines including *Davilla aspera* (Aubl.) Benoist. It is not difficult to envisage a gradual increase in shade (nursery effect) and augmented organic litter levels which, with decomposition and nutrient recycling, could encourage forest encroachment. Thus surface soils at the margin may reflect an ameliorating trend whilst the subsoils may remain oligotrophic.

Conclusions

Research into the nature and mobility of the forest–savanna boundaries on Maracá Island has revealed a variety of ecotones and diverse explanations for their current distribution and migration.

At least three major types of transition are apparent. The most frequent form, predominantly in the eastern sector, is the forest–hyperseasonal savanna boundary. This is exemplified clearly at the 'Angico' site and in a more complicated set of transitions at Santa Rosa. The principal causal factor seems to be the upper limit of seasonal flooding and, since this level appears to have been constant for some time, the boundary is itself relatively stable at the 'Angico' site but possibly more mobile over the gentler gradients of the Santa Rosa depression.

A second clear-cut boundary occurs at *vazante* sites. At these locations, which are common throughout the island, a sharp wall of forest abuts on to the typically low, shrubby and herbaceous storm-drains which form the valley savannas. The embryonic valleys are characterised, at the sites examined, by spectacularly different soils presumably brought down by periodic floods from considerable distances, possibly allogenic to the island and therefore of greater age than the alluvial and proto-alluvial deposits found over most of the lower elevations.

The third variety of forest–savanna boundary which was encountered consists of discrete island-like *campo cerrados* scattered well into the forest. Those sites which could be reached and examined were characterised by white sand soils. The oligotrophic nature of the soils neatly mirrors the cerrado type of vegetation. The islands do, however, appear to be contracting, as low thicket (carrasco) and low open forest (campina) and presumably ultimately tall forest, succeed in colonising the patches. They may represent the last relict outposts of the supposed Pleistocene savannas.

Acknowledgements

The forest–savanna boundary research formed a part of the Royal Geographical Society Maracá Rainforest Project and the support of the Royal Geographical Society, INPA (Instituto Nacional de Pesquisas da Amazônia) and SEMA (Secretaria Especial do Meio Ambiente) is gratefully acknowledged. In the field, the help of William Milliken (botanical survey), Jill Thompson, Duncan Scott and John Proctor (forest regeneration) was particularly appreciated.

References

Ab 'Sáber, A. N. (1982), The paleoclimate and paleocology of Brazilian Amazonia, in Prance, G. T. (ed.), *Biological Diversification in the Tropics*, New York, Columbia University Press, 41–59.

Adejuwon, J. O. and Adesina, F. A. (1988), Vegetation patterns along the forest–savanna boundary in Nigeria, *Singapore Journal of Tropical Geography*, 9: 1, 18–32.

Adejuwon, J. O. and Adesina, F. A. (1992), The nature and dynamics of the forest–savanna boundary in south-western Nigeria, in Furley, P. A., Proctor, J. and Ratter, J. A. (eds.), *Nature and Dynamics of Forest–Savanna Boundaries*, London, Chapman & Hall.

Adjanohoun, E. and Assis, A. L. (1968), Essai de création de savanes incluses en Côte d'Ivoire forestière, *Université d'Abidjan, Annales de la Faculté des Sciences*, 4: 237–56.

Aubréville, A. (1966), Les lisières forêt-savanes des régions tropicales, *Adansonia*, 6, 175–87.

Bellier, L., Gillon, D., Gillon, Y., Guillaumet, J-L. and Perraud, A. (1969), Recherches sur l'origine d'une savane incluse dans le bloc forestier du Bas-Cavally (Côte d'Ivoire) par l'étude des sols et de la biocenose, *Cahiers Mémoires. Office de la Recherche Scientifique et Technique Outre-mer (ORSTOM), Série Biologique*, 10, 65–94.

Belsky, J. (1990), Tree/grass ratios in East African savannas: a comparison of existing models, *Journal of Biogeography*, 17, 265–70.

Buechner, H. K. and Dawkins, H. C. (1961), Vegetation change induced by elephants and fire in Murchison Falls National Park, Uganda, *Ecology*, 42, 752–66.

Eden, M. J. and McGregor, D. F. M. (1989), Ilha de Maracá and the Roraima region, in *Maracá Rainforest Project, First Report: Geography*, London, Royal Geographical Society.

Frost, P., Medina, E., Menaut, J. C., Solbrig, O., Swift, M. and Walker, B. (eds.) (1986), Responses of savanna to stress and disturbance, *Biology International*, Special Issue 10.

Furley, P. A. (1989), The soils and soil–plant relationships of the eastern sector of Maracá Island (Appendix 5), in Milliken, W. and Ratter, J. A. *The Vegetation of the Ilha de Maracá*, Edinburgh, Royal Botanic Garden.

Furley, P. A. (1992), Edaphic controls at the forest–savanna boundary, in Furley, P. A., Proctor, J. and Ratter, J. A. (eds.), *Nature and Dynamics of Forest–Savanna Boundaries*, London, Chapman & Hall.

Furley, P. A. and Mougeot, L. J. A. (1993), Introduction and chapter 1 in Furley, P. A. (ed.), *The Rainforest Frontier: Settlement and Change in Brazilian Roraima*, London, Routledge.

Hills, T. L. and Randall, R. E. (eds.) (1968), The ecology of the forest–savanna boundary, in *Proceedings of the IGU Humid Tropics Symposium, Venezuela 1964*, Department of Geography, McGill University, Montreal, Quebec.

Hopkins, B. (1993), Ecological processes at the forest–savanna boundary, in Furley, P. A., Proctor, J. and Ratter, J. A. (eds.), *Nature and Dynamics of Forest–Savanna Boundaries*, London, Chapman & Hall.

Jordan, C. (1985), *Nutrient Cycling in Tropical Forests*, Chichester, John Wiley & Sons Ltd.

Markham, R. H. and Babbedge, A. J. (1979), Soil and vegetation catenas on the forest–savanna boundary in Ghana, *Biotropica*, 1:3, 224–34.

Milliken, W. and Ratter, J. A. (1989), *The Vegetation of the Ilha de Maracá*, Edinburgh, Royal Botanic Garden.

Morgan, W. M. and Moss, R. P. (1965), Savanna and forest boundary in western Nigeria, *Africa*, 35, 206–95.

Moss, R. P. (1982), *Reflections on the Relationships between Forest and Savanna in Tropical West Africa*, Discussion Papers in Geography, 23, University of Salford.

Ratter, J. A. (1986), *Notas sobre a vegetação da Fazenda Agua Limpa (Brasília, D. F., Brasil)*, Texto Universitário, 3, Brasília, Universidade de Brasília.

Ratter, J. A. (1992), Transitions between *cerrado* and forest vegetation in Brazil, in Furley, P. A., Proctor, J. and Ratter, J. A. (eds.), *Nature and Dynamics of Forest–Savanna Boundaries*, London, Chapman & Hall.

Ratter, J. A., Richards, P. W., Argent, G., Gifford, D. R. (1973), Observations on the vegetation of northeastern Mato Grosso 1. The woody vegetation types of the Xavantina–Cachimbo Expedition area, *Philosophical Transactions of the Royal Society*, B: 266, 449–92.

Ratter, J. A., Askew, G. P., Montgomery, R. F. and Gifford, D. R. (1978), Observations on the vegetation of northeastern Mato Grosso 2. Forest and soils of the Rio Suiá-Missu area, *Proceedings of the Royal Society of London*, B: 203, 191–208.

Sarmiento, G. (1988), *The Ecology of Neotropical Savannas*, Harvard University Press.

Sarmiento, G. (1992), A conceptual model relating environmental factors and vegetation formations in the lowlands of tropical South America, in Furley, P. A., Proctor, J. and Ratter, J. A. (eds.), *Nature and Dynamics of Forest–Savanna Boundaries*, London, Chapman & Hall.

Schnell, R. (1976), *La Flora et la Végétation de l'Afrique Tropicale*, Paris, Gauthier-Villars. Introduction à la Phylogéographie des pays tropicaux, 3.

White, F. (1983), *The Vegetation of Africa*, Paris, UNESCO.

Whitmore, T. C. and Prance, G. T. (1987), *Biogeography and Quaternary history in Tropical America*, Oxford Monographs in Biogeography No. 3, Oxford, Clarendon Press.

8 *Peter A. Furley, T. C. D. Dargie and C. J. Place*

Remote sensing and the establishment of a geographic information system for resource management on and around Maracá Island

Introduction

The management of natural resources in north-west Roraima is particularly conducive to the use of remote sensing (RS) techniques and geographical information systems (GIS). The clear-cut patterns of savanna and forest, the approximate coincidence of land-use and vegetation zones, the pattern of flooding during the wet season and the importance of topographic and drainage features, together with their close relationship to soil, are well suited to interpretation and analysis using a combination of these methods.

Prior to the SLAR (Side-Looking Airborne Radar) surveys in the early 1970s, there was little or no accurate information for much of the state, an area larger than the UK (230, 104 sq km). Projeto Radam, the radar survey of Amazonia, later extended to the whole country, generated volumes of data (Brasil 1975), mapped at the reconnaissance scale of 1 : 250,000, reduced for publication to 1 : 1,000,000 (Furley 1986). Information under the headings of geology, geomorphology, soils and land evaluation, vegetation and land use potential, provided the first comprehensive data available for natural resource assessment or development planning.

Subsequent to Projeto Radam, there was little work within Roraima until recently, either in resource surveys at a more detailed scale or utilising remote sensing. There has, however, been a regional analysis of the incidence of burning and deforestation from NOAA-AVHRR satellite images, which give a capability for frequent monitoring at a small scale – 1 sq km (Cross 1990; Fearnside *et al.* 1990). The US earth resources satellites, LANDSAT MSS (Multi-Spectral Scanner) and TM (Thematic Mapper) and the French system SPOT have also been used either singly or comparatively (Nelson *et al.* 1987; Table 8.1). The Brazilian environmental agency (previously IBDF and currently IBAMA) has monitored deforestation at a more detailed scale, by manually overlaying images to give a time sequence (Brasil 1983).

As part of the Maracá Rainforest Project, RS and GIS techniques were used to obtain data for areas too difficult to reach by ground survey and to provide a spatial database for interpretation and analysis. There were three principal objectives:

1. To provide a detailed vegetation map of the island from satellite images.
2. To provide a regional land cover assessment of the area around the island, particularly encompassing the agricultural frontier between Maracá and Boa Vista to the east.
3. To compare the MSS data for 1978, representing one of the earliest clear images available, with TM data for 1985, being one of the latest available prior to fieldwork in 1987/88.

Background: analysis of Projeto Radam data

This extremely ambitious project was never aimed at more than a reconnaissance level of data collection and interpretation. It provided a rapid, broad scale of information in order to shape the path of development planning. Its tremendous achievement was to give the first comprehensive picture of natural resources in the Brazilian Amazon. Projeto Radam was inevitably generalised and demanded more detailed follow-up surveys which, as it turned out, could not be afforded. These were carried out until recently only in limited areas outside Roraima. For example, the soil work on Maracá Island was restricted to one soil survey and one soil fertility site in an area of 70 km from east to west by 30 km from north to south.

The survey does, however, provide a very useful baseline and context for resource evaluation. Consequently, a GIS for Roraima as a whole has been constructed and 100-sq-km grids have been digitised into the database for analysis. Examples of the single attribute maps or coverages are given in Figures 8.1 to 8.4. A number of features are outstanding, such as the approximately north–south trend of the forest–savanna boundary, the density of the drainage pattern, and the spectacular relief associated with the residual mountains or *tepuis*, notably the Tepequém area to the north of the island (Figure 8.5). The GIS analysis also permits overlay interpretation of one attribute upon another. Figure 8.6 illustrates the relationship of selected aspects of vegetation against soil type using the query facility of a relational database language.

The scale of Projeto Radam does not permit this type of analysis to be extended in any depth and the errors resulting from the limited data quality are considerable. The exercise was of value mostly to set up a working GIS which can be utilised and upgraded as more detailed and accurate data are made available in the future.

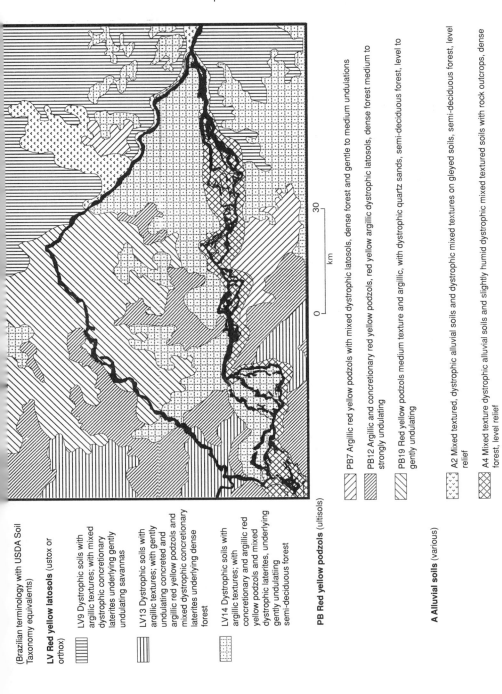

LV Red yellow latosols (ustox or orthox)

LV9 Dystrophic soils with argillic textures; with mixed dystrophic concretionary laterites underlying gently undulating savannas

LV13 Dystrophic soils with argillic textures; with gently undulating concreted and argillic red yellow podzols and mixed dystrophic concretionary laterites underlying dense forest

LV14 Dystrophic soils with argillic textures; with concretionary and argillic red yellow podzols and mixed dystrophic laterites, underlying gently undulating semi-deciduous forest

PB Red yellow podzols (ultisols)

PB7 Argillic red yellow podzols with mixed dystrophic latosols, dense forest and gentle to medium undulations

PB12 Argillic and concretionary red yellow podzols, red yellow argillic dystrophic latosols, dense forest medium to strongly undulating

PB19 Red yellow podzols medium texture and argillic, with dystrophic quartz sands, semi-deciduous forest, level to gently undulating

A Alluvial soils (various)

A2 Mixed textured, dystrophic alluvial soils and dystrophic mixed textures on gleyed soils, semi-deciduous forest, level relief

A4 Mixed texture dystrophic alluvial soils and slightly humid dystrophic mixed textured soils with rock outcrops, dense forest, level relief

Figure 8.1 Soil attribute data for Maracá Island.

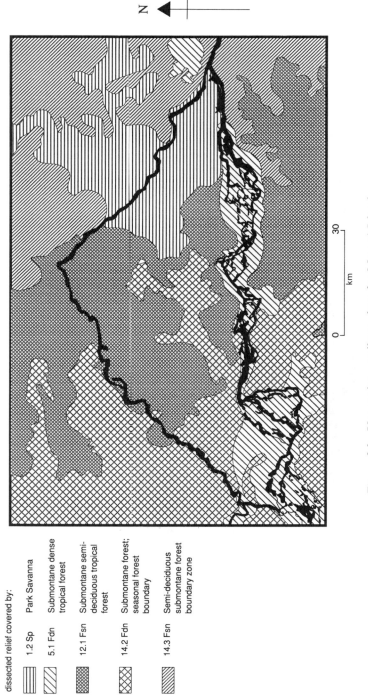

Figure 8.2 Vegetation attribute data for Maracá Island.

dissected relief covered by:

1.2 Sp   Park Savanna

5.1 Fdn   Submontane dense
tropical forest

12.1 Fsn   Submontane semi-
deciduous tropical
forest

14.2 Fdn   Submontane forest;
seasonal forest
boundary

14.3 Fsn   Semi-deciduous
submontane forest
boundary zone

0   30
km

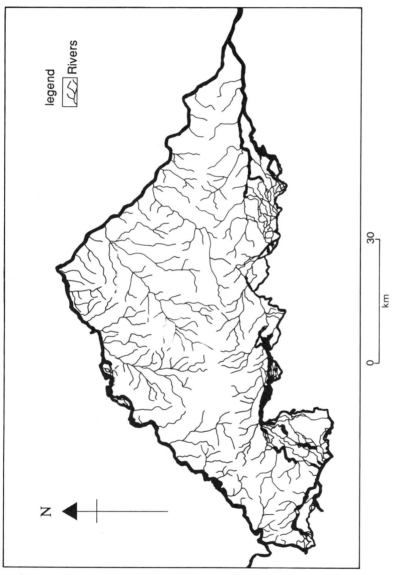

Figure 8.3 Drainage attribute data for Maracá Island.

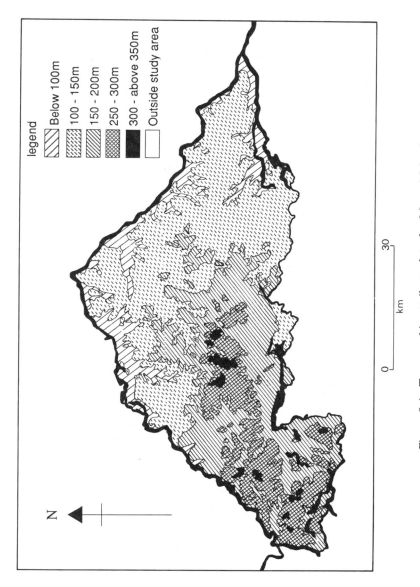

Figure 8.4 Topographic attribute data for Maracá Island.

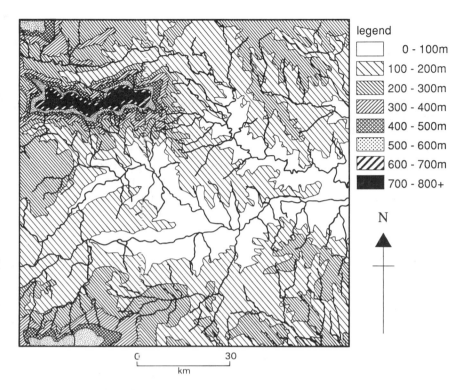

legend

	0 - 100m
	100 - 200m
	200 - 300m
	300 - 400m
	400 - 500m
	500 - 600m
	600 - 700m
	700 - 800+

N

0   30
    km

Figure 8.5 Outstanding relief to the north of Maracá Island: the residual formations (*tepuis*) at Tepequém.

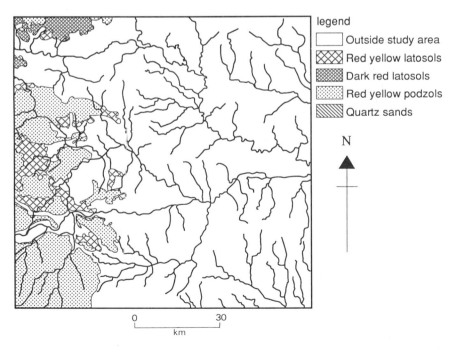

legend

	Outside study area
	Red yellow latosols
	Dark red latosols
	Red yellow podzols
	Quartz sands

N

0   30
    km

Figure 8.6 Example of GIS overlay facility: the soils underlying dense forest in and around Maracá Island.

Assessment of land cover and vegetation from LANDSAT data

1 Maracá Island
The principal objective of the RS analysis was the compilation of a map
showing the spatial distribution of vegetation on Maracá Island. There
were considerable problems of survey for an area of 101,000 ha, even with
a large team of scientists working in the field for over a year. Much of the
area could not be visited, although the overall density of observations and
the quality of the 'ground-truthing' was very high for the Amazon region.
The detailed results for the botanical and other surveys have been published elsewhere (e.g. Milliken & Ratter 1989; Milliken & Ratter, in press).
A black-and-white air photo mosaic (1 : 70,000) enabled a preliminary
geomorphological and drainage interpretation to be made (Eden, 1989
unpublished), but it was evident that satellite imagery would be necessary
to provide biological data for the larger part of the island.

Numerous problems became apparent in utilising the available
LANDSAT MSS and TM images. Despite some ten years of satellite passes,
the availability of images with little or no cloud cover was extremely limited. The MSS image of 1978 and the TM image of 1985 were amongst the
best available and provided a seven-year period for comparison. For the
purposes of producing a vegetation classification, the TM data set of 1985
was utilised, as it was more up to date and the spectral and spatial properties
of TM imagery are superior to MSS (Table 8.1). However, the 1985 data
were not ideal, as the island itself was bisected by the orbit paths of the
satellite, the eastern third being on PATH/ROW 232/58 and the western
two-thirds being on PATH/ROW 233/58. This bisection caused problems
of geometric fidelity between the images and, owing to the time interval
between the images (thirty-nine days), the spectral properties were different,
primarily because of differing atmospheric conditions.

The geometric correction required in order to stitch the two sections
together was limited by the quality of the ground control points (GCPs)
which were taken from the largest scale topographic maps available (1 :
100,000). A final correction was produced which gave a very favourable
root mean square error of 27 m for the western section and 29 m for the
eastern section. These figures are probably over-optimistic for the whole
image, but the resulting fit of the two sections, and the quality of correspondence with the available map data, were very good under the circumstances.

Despite these difficulties, a vegetation zoning has been completed which
can be used as a base map for future ecological research (Figure 8.7). The
scale of the map can be adjusted according to the data input and a GIS
database ensures that future information can be geo-referenced and thereby directly compared. The map output is currently produced and the data
are stored using the ARC INFO software package. These data can be
downloaded to a PC if funds become available for basic computer facilities
at the research station.

Table 8.1 Satellite flight characteristics of Earth Resources Satellites.

	NOAA-AVHRR	LANDSAT MSS	LANDSAT TM	SPOT 1 & 2
launch date	12 Dec 84 (9) 17 Sep 86 (10) Sep 88 (11)	23 Jul 72 (1) 22 Jan 75 (2) 05 Mar 78 (3) 16 Jul 82 (4) 01 Mar 84 (5)	16 Jul 82 (4) 01 Mar 84 (5)	22 Feb 86 (1) 22 Jan 90 (2)
orbit	NPSS	NPSS	NPSS	NPSS
altitude (kms)	833–870	919	705	830
inclination	98.7–98.9°	99.09°	98.2°	98.7°
coverage	82° N–82° S	82° N–82° S	81° N–81° S	81° N–81° S
repeat cycle	12 hours	18 days	16 days	26 days
equator crossing time	02.30 (9, 11) 14.30 (9, 11) 07.30 (10) 19.30 (10)	09.30 (1, 2, 3) 09.45 (4, 5)	09.45	10.30
spatial resolution	1.1 km [LAC] 4.0 km [GAC]	80 m	30 m 120 m [6]	20 m [XS] 10 m [PAN]
swath width	3000 km	185 km	185 km	60 km

continued

Table 8.1 (cont.)

	NOAA-AVHRR	LANDSAT MSS	LANDSAT TM	SPOT 1 & 2
		[a b]		
spectral	0.58– 0.68[1]	0.50– 0.60[1, 4]	0.45– 0.52[1]	0.51–0.73[PAN]
resolution	0.73– 1.10[2]	0.60– 0.70[2, 5]	0.52– 0.60[2]	0.50–0.59[1]
(wavelength)	3.55– 3.93[3]	0.70– 0.80[3, 6]	0.63– 0.69[3]	0.61–0.68[2]
(µm)	10.30–11.30[4]	0.80– 1.10[4, 7]	0.76– 0.90[4]	0.79–0.89[3]
	11.30–12.50[5]		1.55– 1.75[5]	
			10.40–12.50[6]	
			2.08– 2.35[7]	

( )   – Satellite number
NPSS – Near polar sun-synchronous
LAC – Local area coverage
GAC – Global area coverage
[1]   – Spectral band number
[a]   – Landsat 1, 2, or 3
[b]   – Landsat 4 or 5, band numbers renamed
[PAN] – SPOT panchromatic
[XS] – SPOT multispectral

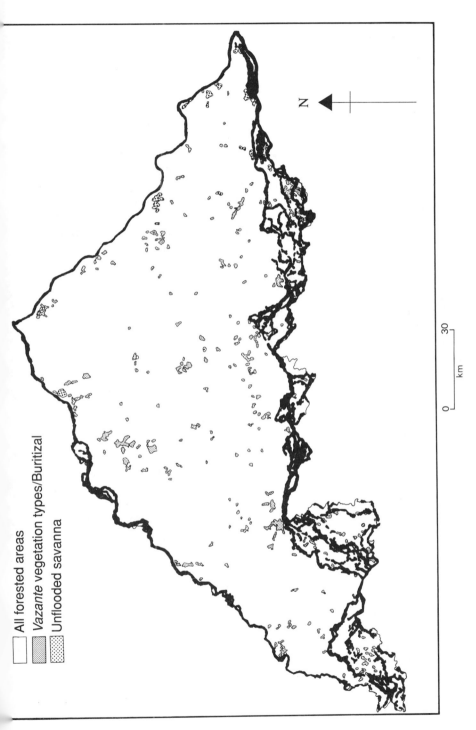

All forested areas

Vazante vegetation types/Buritizal

Unflooded savanna

N

0   30

km

Figure 8.7 Simplified vegetation classes of Maracá Island. Most of the island is covered by forest but, as shown, there are numerous non-forested tracts scattered over the island, only identified by satellite imagery and downloaded to a GIS using ARC INFO.

The spectral differences between the western and eastern sections were overcome by using a small section of the island which was in the overlap region of the two orbit paths. The assumption was made that, for the area of overlap for the period between the two images (thirty-nine days), no significant change had occurred in the spectral properties of the vegetation at canopy level. Therefore, any spectral difference was primarily due to atmospheric differences between the two dates. In order to correct the differences, a histogram-matching procedure was used, where the eastern section of overlap produced a reference histogram for each band, to which the respective histogram of the western section was matched. The functions calculated from this procedure were then used to alter all the values for the western two-thirds of the island. A number of intermediate procedures, including filtering, ratioing and principal components analysis were then used in order to maximise the differentiation of the vegetation communities.

The classification procedure was essentially unsupervised, on account of the very limited ground-truth available across the whole of the area. The unsupervised clustering procedure generated twenty-five spectral clusters, which were then used as spectral signatures in a minimum-distance classification. The resulting classes were then interpreted with the assistance of the field botanists. Interpretations were improved with the help of oblique aerial photography taken during the field work on Maracá Island during 1987/88. However, the interpretation was limited by the timing of the field-work and the extent of the ground-truth available.

For the final classification, the twenty-five classes were simplified to twelve, two of these being associated with cloud cover (Dargie & Furley 1993). Figure 8.7 shows a fourfold grouping, which is the maximum level of detail possible in black and white. The classification attempts a comprehensive coverage of the island and there will inevitably be errors in extrapolations from limited sites known in detail on the ground. The final distributions should be seen as a first attempt to produce a vegetation zoning for the island rather than the definitive map. Copies of the three A3 colour prints of the vegetation classes can be obtained from the Department of Geography, University of Edinburgh. A by-product of the image processing was the generation of a set of areal statistics for the various classes (Table 8.2).

Determination of the spatial distribution and quantification of the vegetation classes provided the basis for a GIS analysis of the data. The map output can be generated in a variety of forms and at a number of different scales. As it is geo-referenced, the vegetation distribution can be compared with other data sets to determine relationships between vegetation and environmental variables such as soil or drainage. The analysis and map composition can be performed in a number of GIS software systems, for instance ARC/INFO or ERDAS, which can be mounted on IBM PC-compatible computers. Such a system could readily be installed at the research station on the island at modest cost.

Table 8.2 Vegetation zones on Maracá Island.

Class	Area (ha)	%
Semi-deciduous closed canopy forest	34,136.102	33.56
Intermediate forest types	14,709.961	14.46
Evergreen closed canopy forest	36,215.961	35.60
Open canopy forest types	2,979.090	2.93
Buritizal	1,855.260	1.82
Vazante vegetation types	1,318.050	1.30
Unflooded savanna	478.890	0.47
Shallow water/emergent vegetation	4,108.590	4.04
Trees overhanging water	1,899.810	1.87
Deep water	2,380.410	2.34
Cloud cover	1,020.420	1.00
Cloud shadow	621.630	0.61
	101,723.852	100.00

2 Land cover assessment

A second objective was to identify and classify land cover types over the broad area approximately 200 km square from Boa Vista to Maracá. Figure 8.8 illustrates the classes identified on one quarter scene LANDSAT TM. The black-and-white reproduction does not do justice to the ability of the technique to differentiate vegetation zones. Nevertheless, clear patterns are evident and comparison of successive satellite passes could provide an effective monitoring capability of land-use change. This can also be quantified using a relational database and GIS.

3 Monitoring land cover change using multidate imagery

The capability of measuring change is one of the principal assets of remote sensing. Of particular interest, in the region around Maracá, is the level of deforestation following the westward migration of the agricultural frontier and the related change in land use of both forest and savanna ecosystems. The full details of the methodology, error assessment and results are given in Dargie & Furley (1993).

LANDSAT 2 (MSS) data for 1978 and LANDSAT 5 (TM) data for 1985 were compared over a total area of nearly 10,500 sq km. (Figure 8.9, Table 8.3 and 8.4). The methodology included the creation of subscenes, replacement of missing scan lines in the 1978 data set, destriping the 1978 data to reduce the effect of six-line banding caused by miscalibration of the sensor and, finally, geometric correction of the images. The establishment of training areas involved training on cover types from ground data and from inference, and gave an idea of the probability of accurate classification:

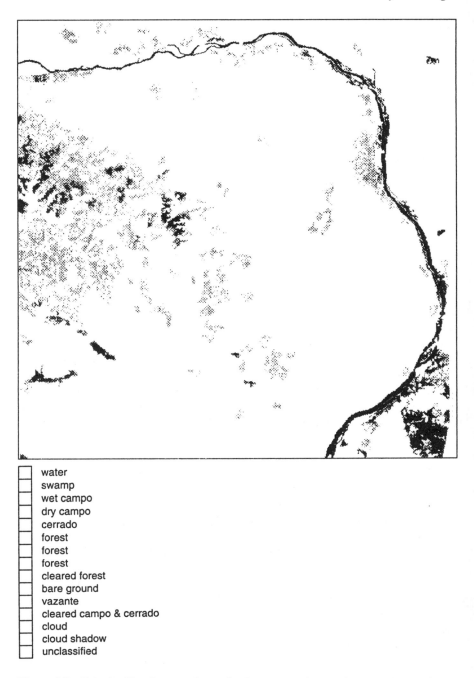

water
swamp
wet campo
dry campo
cerrado
forest
forest
forest
cleared forest
bare ground
vazante
cleared campo & cerrado
cloud
cloud shadow
unclassified

Figure 8.8 Principal land cover classes in the area to the north-west of Boa Vista.
(Black & white print from colour monitor of LANDSAT TM image; Boa Vista
marked on Uraricoera River.)

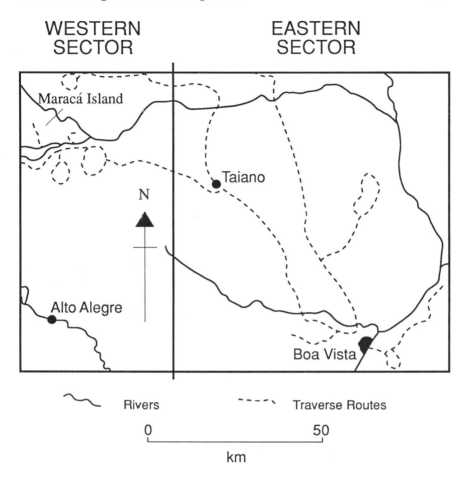

Figure 8.9 Image boundaries and field traverses in the study area.

Table 8.3 Image details.

Landsat 2 Multispectral Scanner (MSS)
15 February 1978   249.58   Bands 4–7
16 February 1978   250.58   Bands 4–7
    Pixel size c. 80m

Landsat 5 Thematic Mapper (TM)
15 September 1985   232.58   Bands 3–5
    Pixel size c. 30m

Table 8.4 Study area statistics.

TM pixel total   11,608,000
Total area (based on 30 m pixel size)   10,447.2 km²

Western sector
TM pixel total   3,981,544
Total area   3,583.4 km²

Eastern sector
TM pixel total   7,625,456
Total area   6,863.8 km²

(a) Geometrical correction
    1. image-to-map (UTM) 1985 TM data fitted to co-ordinates from IBGE 1:100,000 map sheets; cubic convolution, 30 m pixel size; accuracy ± 50 m
    2. image-to-image 1978 MSS images converted to corrected 1985 TM image with resampled 30 m pixels
      a. western 1978 sector ± 4 pixels accuracy
      b. eastern 1978 sector ± 1 pixel accuracy

(b) Training methods
    1. cover types trained on ground data
    2. cover types trained on inference:
    cloud, cloud shadow
    burnt campo and cerrado
    cleared campo and cerrado
    cleared forest
    forest types (single-band density slicing)
    1978 swamp, wet campo and dry campo mosaic

    Training areas per cover type
    1. several, scattered throughout the image
    2. minimum total of 1000 pixels to calculate mean variance and inter-band co-variance

(c) Classification: maximum likelihood – 95 per cent probability of pixel belonging to one cover type class, accepting that there will be unclassified pixels (unlike island vegetation map). At least two cycles of training-area definition, purification and classification were needed to produce acceptable classified images.

Image comparison: Pixel counts of changes (transition patterns) were derived by comparing the class of each 1978 pixel with its 1985 equivalent, and then by assembling results into transition matrices for eastern and western sectors.

Results and conclusions

The land-use survey is summarised in Figure 8.8, with twelve land-cover units identified plus cloud, cloud shadow and unclassified units. These have been reduced to four in the black-and-white reproduction. Transition matrices and cover totals were calculated and a number of observations can be made:

1   Open cover types, which include water, swamp, wet and dry campo (grassland), bare ground and cerrado (shrubby savanna), make up almost 60 per cent of the study area. They reveal a complex pattern of inter-type change between the two image dates. This pattern probably represents a seasonal flux between types within an overall balance for all classes.

2   There is a very strongly marked seasonal change. Much of the dry season cerrado changes to wet season swamp and wet campo, and confirms the field observations that much of the cerrado area is seasonally water-logged or very wet.

3   There are large unexpected reversals within the pattern of seasonal fluxes in land cover. These reversals suggest that improved training is still required to clarify seasonal change, probably by redefining the transition boundaries for swamp, wet and dry campo areas.

4   Forest losses are significant despite the relative remoteness of the area. The raw statistics are given in Table 8.5.

Table 8.5 shows that there has been a significant loss even in the remote western margins of the forest edge (over 4 per cent) and a very large loss has occurred in the more developed eastern sector (nearly 30 per cent) between 1978 and 1985. This gives an overall 10 per cent loss from the total 1978 baseline forest cover. Losses in the west appear to be mainly in upland and valley forests and seem to be mostly associated with colonisation, usually with a nucleated settlement core and rectalinear feeder road system joined linearly to other parts of the region. This is well demonstrated by Alto Alegre and other sites studied during the land development programme (Dargie & Furley 1993; Mougeot & Léna 1993). In the east, the very high rates of forest depletion relate to valley and floodplain locations and this is most likely to be the valuable riverine or *várzea* forest. The forest losses appear to be associated with the growth of commercial agriculture such as rice or horticultural developments (Barrow & Paterson 1993).

These figures are immensely significant, given the perceived isolation of

Table 8.5 Loss of forest.

	western sector	Forest area (km^2) eastern sector	total area	% total area
1978 MSS	1848.6	525.5	2374.1	22.72
1985 TM	1773.5	375.7	2149.2	20.57
Change	−75.1	−149.8	−224.9	
% change	−4.06	−28.51	−9.47	
	western sector	Cleared forest area (km^2) eastern sector	total area	% total area
1978 MSS	137.2	46.6	183.8	1.76
1985 TM	160.0	189.6	349.6	3.34
Change	+22.8	+143.0	+165.8	
% change	+16.62	+306.87	+90.21	

the area. However, they also need to be treated with caution, because the calculations for forest loss and cleared land do not always balance (especially in the western sector), and some of the losses can be attributed to misinterpretation of the original forest area (as wetland swamp, *vazantes* or non-forested storm-flow lines, or wet savanna). A further possible source of error is that the 1978 MSS data may have overestimated the forest area, because of the difficulties in interpreting linear forest features such as strings of buriti palm (*veredas*) and storm-flow wetlands (*vazantes*) at the 80 m pixel scale. This also applies to the eastern sector, where much of the cleared forest – as defined in 1985 – may actually be swampy areas of *varzea* converted to rice production.

Interestingly, large areas of the cleared forest identified in 1978 are recorded as forest in 1985. This may indicate abandonment of cleared areas and would be consistent with the high levels of pasture abandonment noted over eastern Amazonia (Serrão *et al.* 1988). Furthermore, and only evident in the 1985 image because of its recent nature, there is considerable conversion of cerrado (whether wet or dry campo, cerrado in the strict sense or open cerrado interspersed with patches of bare ground) into dry rice and improved pasture. This represented only 0.35 per cent of the area examined but, from field observations, appeared to be expanding rapidly.

The use of remote sensing has enabled a map of the island vegetation to be produced. Despite the fact that most of the island distributions are extrapolated from known ground sites, and that the coverage for the west was markedly less comprehensive than in the east, the map is nevertheless an invaluable baseline for future biological research. Remote sensing also generated the first detailed land cover assessment for the north-western region of Roraima. Further, comparison of land cover changes over time has given a graphic view of the pace of disturbance in an area normally perceived as relatively unaffected by development. The establishment of a geographical information system for Maracá Island also permits manipulation of the existing database together with future additions.

References

Barrow, C. & Paterson, A. (1993), Agricultural diversification: the contribution of rice & horticultural producers, in Furley, P. A. (ed.), *The Rain Forest Frontier: Settlement and Change in Brazilian Roraima*, London, Routledge.

Brasil (1975), *Projeto Radambrasil, Levantamentos de recursos naturais*, Rio de Janeiro, Ministério da Agricultura, 8, Folha NA.20 Boa Vista, Folha NB.20 Roraima, Folha NB.21; 9, Folha NA.21 Tumucumaque; 18, Folha SA.20 Manaus.

Brasil (1983), Alteração da cobertura vegetal natural do Território de Roraima Anexo Relatório Técnico, Brasília, Ministério da Agricultura.

Cross, A. (1990), *Tropical Deforestation and Remote Sensing: The Use of NOAA/ AVHRR Data over Amazonia*, Report to the EEC, Geneva, UNEP/GRID.

Dargie, T. C. D. & Furley, P. A. (1993), Monitoring environmental change, in Furley, P. A. (ed.), *The Rain Forest Frontier: Settlement and Change in Brazilian Roraima*, London, Routledge.

Fearnside, P. M., Tardin, A. T. & Meira Filho, L. G. (1990), *Deforestation Rate in Brazilian Amazonia*, Brasilia, INPE/INPA, National Secretariat of Science and Technology.

Furley, P. A. (1986), Radar surveys for resource evaluation in Brazil: an illustration from Rondônia, in Eden, M. J. & Parry, J. T. (eds.), *Remote Sensing and Tropical Land Management*, Chichester, John Wiley & Sons Ltd, 70–99.

Milliken, W. & Ratter, J. A. (1989), *The Vegetation of the Ilha de Maracá*, Edinburgh, Royal Botanic Garden.

Milliken, W. & Ratter, J. A. (in press), *Maracá: Ecology of an Amazonian Rain Forest*, Manchester, Manchester University Press.

Mougeot, L. J. A. & Léna, P. (1993), Forest clearance and production strategies in northern Roraima, in Furley, P. A. (ed.), *The Rain Forest Frontier: Settlement and Change in Brazilian Roraima*, London, Routledge.

Nelson, R., Horning, N. and Stone, T. A. (1987), Determining the rate of forest conversion in Mato Grosso, Brasil using LANDSAT MSS and AVHRR data, *International Journal of Remote Sensing*, 8, 1767–84.

Serrão, E. A. S. & Toledo, J. M. (1988), *Sustaining Pasture-based Production Systems for the Humid Tropics*, paper presented to the MAB Conference on Conversion of Tropical Forest to Pasture in Latin America, Oaxaca, Mexico.

9 *Michael J. Eden, Duncan F. M. McGregor and Nelson A. Q. Vieira*

Pasture development on cleared forest land near Maracá Island[1]

In recent decades, pasture development for cattle ranching has been a prime cause of deforestation in Amazonia. Such clearance has mostly occurred since the 1960s, and has principally focused on Pará and Mato Grosso States in Brazil and the eastern lowlands, or *oriente*, of Colombia and Peru. Accurate data on the forest area involved are not available, but it probably totals at least 20 million hectares in Brazilian Amazonia and some 6–7 million hectares in the Colombian and Peruvian *oriente* (Bunyard 1989; Domínguez 1987; Margolis 1988a, b; Serrão & Toledo 1988). Unfortunately, the derived pastures, which are established with introduced grasses like colonião (*Panicum maximum* Jacq.), jaraguá (*Hyparrhenia rufa* (Nees) (Stapf) and kikuyu (*Brachiaria humidicola* (Rendle) (Schweik.), are not readily sustained in a productive condition, and, after a few years of use, support only very low cattle densities (less than 0.5 animals per hectare) or are abandoned. However, by continuing to establish fresh pastures in the forest, cattle ranchers are able to maintain beef production, albeit at the expense of the forest resource.

As the shortcomings of pioneer ranching of this kind have become apparent, studies have been initiated into the ecological dynamics of derived pasture systems and on the prospects for establishing more sustainable ranching on the cleared forest land (Santhirasegaram 1975; Falesi 1976; Hecht 1981; Fearnside 1979, 1980; Serrão *et al.* 1979; Buschbacher *et al.* 1988; Serrão & Toledo 1988). Although important progress is being made in these studies, they have only been undertaken in a limited number of areas, mainly in eastern Brazilian Amazonia and in parts of the Peruvian and Colombian *oriente*, and there is as yet only partial understanding of the complex soil–plant–animal interactions involved. Against this background, the present study examines ecological aspects of forest clearance

[1] This paper originally appeared in *The Geographical Journal*, 156: 3, 283–96, under the title 'Pasture development on cleared forest land in northern Amazonia.'

for pasture in the vicinity of Maracá Island in northern Roraima, Brazil. In this region of semi-evergreen seasonal forest, located on the western margin of the Rio Branco–Rupununi savanna, forest clearance has as yet only occurred on a small scale, but it has extended over a period of decades and, with increasing migration into the region, may well accelerate in the future. In these circumstances, it is appropriate to investigate the nature and impact of local pasture development as a basis for considering longer-term management strategies.

The study formed part of the Royal Geographical Society's Maracá Rainforest Project (1987–88) and was undertaken from the Maracá ecological station under the auspices of the then Secretaria Especial do Meio Ambiente (SEMA). The study examined changing pasture status over time through investigation of (a) a spatial sequence of adjacent pastures of different ages; (b) changing soil physical and chemical conditions over the sequence; and (c) associated management variables in the area. The findings show many similarities to conditions reported elsewhere in Amazonia, although in the present area grazing levels appear to be relatively low and pasture use generally sustained, albeit at low levels of productivity.

Forest clearance for pasture development has been investigated in other parts of Amazonia. It has been previously asserted that soil nutrient levels in derived pastures of this kind generally improve with time and that pastures, when well-managed, will maintain themselves for many years (Falesi 1976). This view has in the past led to official encouragement of large-scale pasture development, particularly in Brazilian Amazonia (Fearnside 1980). However, much of the land that has been cleared only achieves good pasture productivity for three to five years, after which pasture performance declines and weed invasion increasingly becomes a problem (Serrão *et al.* 1979; Serrão & Toledo 1988). Often such pastures are later abandoned, at least on a temporary basis. Pasture deterioration of this kind reflects various factors, including adverse soil conditions, the reduced vigour of introduced grasses over time, and the vulnerability of the grasses to pests and diseases. The process of pasture deterioration and associated weed invasion is accelerated in areas of heavier and more continuous grazing (Serrão *et al.* 1979; Serrão & Toledo 1988).

Adverse soil conditions are a serious constraint on pasture productivity. Initial forest clearance and burning enhance the supply of available soil nutrients, although losses occur as a result of leaching and erosion immediately following clearance. Even so, in eastern Amazonia, available calcium and magnesium levels reportedly remain relatively high in pasture soils, pH values stay in the range 5.5–6.5, and exchangeable aluminium generally remains low (Serrão *et al.* 1979). Available phosphorus levels, however, are exceedingly low in most older pastures, and, particularly on clayey soils, are considered to be the most serious constraint on the maintenance of pasture productivity; over time, soil nitrogen supplies may also become limiting (Hecht 1981; Serrão *et al.* 1979; Serrão & Toledo 1988). In addition, soil physical changes, particularly topsoil compaction, are reported and may also have adverse effects on the growth and maintenance of pasture grasses; such compaction results in reduced infiltration and may increase sheetwash erosion (Hecht 1981).

Various pest and disease problems are encountered in Amazonian pastures. The vulnerability of *Brachiaria* spp., especially *B. decumbens*, to attacks of spittle bug (*Deois* spp., *Zulia* spp.) has been widely reported, and similar damage is inflicted on grasses like *Digitaria* spp. and *Cynodon* spp. Under the prevailing humidity, fungal diseases are likewise reported to affect seed production seriously in the widely-used *Panicum maximum* (Silva & Magalhães 1980; Hecht 1981; Serrão & Toledo 1988).

Weed invasion is also a critical problem in derived pastures, and is particularly acute in areas of lower soil fertility (Fearnside 1979). Under such conditions, woody weeds rapidly invade pasture land, especially where forage grasses have lost their initial vigour and are subject to grazing pressure, and they make time-consuming and expensive weed control necessary (Dantas & Rodrigues 1980; Hecht 1981). Burning of weedy pastures is often practised, but, although disposing of existing weed material, it does little to arrest general decline in pasture quality. The condition of pastures is further aggravated by overgrazing, which in turn accelerates soil deterioration and weed invasion. In spite of its damaging impact, overgrazing is often an attractive economic option, since cleared, albeit degraded, land can be readily sold at a profit and the proceeds re-invested in further profitable, but damaging, clearance of forest land (Fearnside 1980; Hecht 1981).

In spite of the ecological problems outlined above, substantial forest clearance for pasture is occurring in parts of Amazonia, and ranching is likely to remain an attractive pioneer exploitation system as long as new forest land can be readily acquired for clearance. In Brazil, the process has been encouraged in recent decades by provision of fiscal incentives for the development of commercial ranching. However, the short-sighted nature of such exploitation, which results in extensive and rapid degradation of forest land, is increasingly acknowledged and official attempts are periodically made to curtail its expansion. In Brazil, this has lately been pursued through an environmental protection programme, *Nossa Natureza*, which was established in 1989 in response to growing local and international criticism of the extent of forest clearance (Neto 1989a, b). It remains to be seen how effective this initiative will be under new government direction, but, given the persisting attraction of land investment as an inflationary hedge and the absence of acceptable alternative modes of livestock rearing for forest areas, current pioneer ranching is not easily going to be arrested. In several areas, particularly in Brazilian Pará and in parts of the Peruvian and Colombian *oriente*, experimental work has been initiated into the development of grass–legume pastures based on low inputs of phosphates and other fertilisers, but investigations remain at a relatively early stage and such pastures have yet to be established on any commercial scale (Serrão & Toledo 1988; Eden 1990).

Study area

The study area is located to the south of Maracá Island in northern Roraima, Brazil. The area is approximately 130 km north-west of Boa Vista, the capital of Roraima, and lies in an area of semi-evergreen seasonal forest adjacent to the western margin of the Rio Branco – Rupununi savanna. The regional climate is of seasonal tropical type, with mean monthly temperatures in the range 26–29 °C. Annual rainfall is estimated at 2300 mm, of which some 75–80 per cent falls during the months April to August.

The study area lies on the southern flank of the Guiana Shield. The local landscape is gently to moderately dissected in character, and is located on the higher margin of an end-Tertiary planation surface, with local elevation of 120–140 m above sea level. Slope angles are commonly 6–10°, with local amplitude of relief at 25–35 m. Soils in the area are developed over weathered Shield rocks, mainly micaceous schists with some granitic and gneissic materials. Both residual and colluvial parent materials are encountered. These are relatively fine-textured, giving rise to soils with sandy loam to sandy clay loam topsoils, grading to sandy clay to clay at depth. In places, plinthite or ironstone gravel may be present. Most soils are acid, with low cation exchange capacity and low to moderate base saturation; they are mainly ultisols or inceptisols (Brasil 1975; Nortcliff & Robison 1988). In places, soils of higher base saturation, provisionally classified as alfisols, are also developed over specific parent materials. In general, the soils of adjacent forest and savanna sites share similar parent materials, although the savanna soils are commonly degraded as a function of plant cover. Analytical data for representative forest soils are given in Table 9.1.

The forest in the area is semi-evergreen seasonal forest of hylaean type. The taller trees are 30–35 m in height, with occasional emergents reaching 40 m or so; the largest trees attain approximately 100 cm dbh. Characteristic large emergent species include *Jacaranda copaia* (Aubl.) D. Don, *Anacardium giganteum* Hancock ex Engl., and *Micropholis melinoniana* Pierre. The majority of the trees are evergreen, but some species like *Tabebuia uleana* (Kranzl.) A. Gentry and *Lueheopsis duckeana* Bussett lose their leaves during the dry season (Milliken & Ratter 1989; Eden *et al.* 1991).

Adjacent to the study area lies the extensive Rio Branco–Rupununi savanna, which locally supports an open bunch-grass community, attaining 1 m or so in height and consisting mainly of *Trachypogon spicatum* (L.f.) Kuntze, various panicoid grasses and *Bulbostylis paradoxa* Nees. Dispersed trees and shrubs are present, including *Curatella americana* L.,

Table 9.1 Analytical data for representative forest soils at Fazenda Patchuli and Fazenda Pau Roxo, near Maracá.

	texture sand	silt (%)	clay	organic carbon (%)	pH	exchangeable Ca	Mg	Na (meq/100 g)	K	Al	H	ECEC (meq/100 g)	total N (%)	available P (ppm)
(a) Fazenda Patchuli[1]														
0–25 cm	55	12	33	0.40	4.3	0.10	0.08	0.06	0.06	0.03	0.93	1.26	0.08	2.2
25–50 cm	50	12	38	0.35	4.3	0.06	0.08	0.06	0.04	0.03	0.70	0.97	0.06	2.1
50–75 cm	45	14	41	0.43	4.2	0.06	0.08	0.07	0.05	0.04	0.58	0.88	0.06	1.5
75–100 cm	36	16	48	0.35	4.3	0.10	0.10	0.08	0.05	0.04	0.58	0.95	0.07	0
(b) Fazenda Pau Roxo[2]														
0–25 cm	67	11	22	0.47	5.6	0.90	0.30	0.06	0.10	tr	0.27	1.63	0.09	1.6
25–50 cm	59	10	31	0.68	5.3	0.64	0.32	0.06	0.10	tr	0.25	1.37	0.04	2.2
50–75 cm	55	11	34	0.51	5.2	0.10	0.60	0.07	0.29	tr	0.34	1.40	0.04	1.9
75–100 cm	47	9	44	0.40	5.4	0.04	0.84	0.10	0.53	0.02	0.39	1.92	0.03	2.3

[1] Free-draining midslope profile, developed over *in situ* schistose parent material.
[2] Free-draining local summit profile, developed over fine-grained metamorphic parent material.

Byrsonima crassifolia (L.) Kunth, and *Bowdichia virgilioides* Kunth. Cattle were first introduced to the region in the late eighteenth century (Kelsey 1972), whereupon they spread rapidly across the savanna, but it has only been in recent decades that there have been any significant efforts to extend ranching on to adjacent forest land. One area where this has occurred is immediately to the south of Maracá Island, where a few small ranches, 1000–2000 ha in extent, have been established. The area first became accessible in the early 1950s when a dirt road was constructed from Boa Vista and local clearance began on a small scale. However, most of the derived pasture is more recent, dating from the late 1970s and 1980s, and has largely been a response to the construction of the Manaus – Boa Vista road and the enhanced marketing opportunities that this provides for local cattle producers. Where derived pastures, based on introduced grasses like colonião (*Panicum maximum*) and kikuyu (*Brachiaria humidicola*), have been established on ranches near Maracá, zebu cattle have also been brought in.

Methods

The present investigation is based on four adjacent ranches located to the south of Maracá. They are Fazenda Nova Olinda, Fazenda Canada and Fazenda Pau Roxo, whose land lies along the Uraricoera River, and Fazenda Patchuli, which is some 9 km to the south (Figure 9.1). Fazenda Patchuli and Fazenda Nova Olinda are under common ownership, as are Fazenda Canada and Fazenda Pau Roxo. All the ranches contain tracts of semi-evergreen seasonal forest, derived pasture and natural savanna, wherein field investigation and sampling were undertaken.

Soil profiles were widely examined within the study area and soil samples collected in adjacent forest, derived pasture and savanna. Such synchronic sampling was intended broadly to simulate a time-sequence from mature forest, through clearance and early cultivation, to younger and then older derived pastures. Soils of adjacent savanna areas were sampled for comparative purposes. The general intention was to sample sites of similar inherent soil characteristics as a basis for isolating changes attributable to land cover and usage. It was recognised that some inherent variability would exist between sites, but assumed that this would not generally mask changes of interest.

At Fazenda Patchuli, for example, sampled sites were located over a distance of some 2 km along an access track that extended from undisturbed forest, through cleared forest land, into natural savanna; relatively uniform conditions of parent material and of undulating convexo-concave relief characterised the area. A similar local sampling pattern was adopted in respect of Fazenda Nova Olinda/Canada and of Fazenda Pau Roxo. In addition to representative profile sampling, topsoil samples (0–10 cm) were

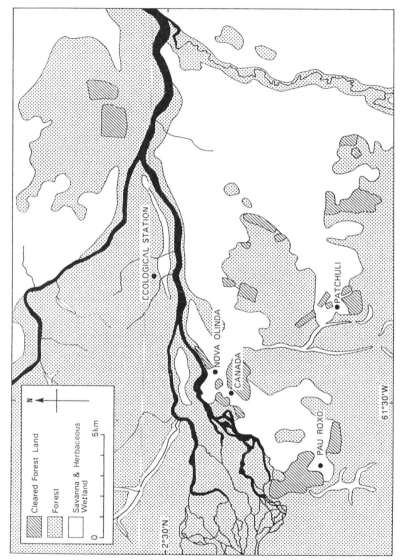

Figure 9.1 Study area to the south of Maracá Island. Cleared forest areas are derived from aerial photographs, LANDSAT TM images and field observation.

collected in each area. In total, topsoil samples were obtained for seven sites in forest, nineteen sites in forest land cleared for pasture, and six sites in savanna. At each site, four replicate topsoil samples were obtained for laboratory analysis, together with three core samples ($c.$ 115 cm^3) from which bulk density determinations were made. The samples were individually collected at randomly-selected points within an area of approximately 30 × 30 m in the central part of each site. All samples were obtained at the end of the rainy season (August–September 1987), some six months or so after the annual cutting and burning period in the area.

Laboratory analyses have been undertaken as follows: organic carbon was determined by the Walkley-Black method; exchangeable calcium, magnesium, sodium, hydrogen and aluminium were extracted with 1 M potassium chloride and exchangeable potassium with 0.02 M hydrochloric acid and were measured by atomic absorption spectrophotometer or flame photometer; available phosphorus was determined using the Bray 1 method; total nitrogen was determined using a micro-kjeldahl procedure; pH was measured in a 1 : 2.5 suspension in water. Effective cation exchange capacity (ECEC) is expressed as the sum of exchangeable bases, aluminium and hydrogen. Bulk density determinations were made after oven-drying to constant weight at 105 °C; particle size analysis was undertaken using the pipette method (Black *et al.* 1965).

No attempt was made to obtain quantitative data on pasture composition or plant biomass, but general information on plant conditions was collected at all sites. Dominant plant species were recorded in pasture and savanna sites, with specimens collected for identification as necessary. On one cleared forest site at Fazenda Nova Olinda, quantitative data were obtained on residual timber and other forest debris remaining after cutting and burning. Surface forest debris (twigs, bark, charcoal, etc.) was collected in twenty 0.5 × 0.5 m quadrats at the site, and weighed after drying to constant weight. Volumetric sampling of large timber debris was undertaken along four 30 × 1 m transects, and total dry weight estimated on the basis of representative bulk density wood samples. Total calcium, magnesium, sodium, potassium and phosphorus content of representative ashed samples of the above were determined by atomic absorption spectrophotometer (calcium, magnesium), flame photometer (sodium, potassium) and UV spectrophotometer (phosphorus) after digestion in 1 M HNO$_3$, and total nitrogen was obtained by micro-kjeldahl procedure (Black *et al.* 1965).

Data on stock levels, areas of clearance, general ranch management and the like were obtained by informal questioning of local ranchers and their managers and other assistants.

Forest clearance for pasture

Pasture establishment in the study area follows a relatively uniform pattern. Forest trees are generally cut by axe or chainsaw during the dry season from September to March, and, after partially drying out, the resultant debris is fired. Foliage and small branches are mostly consumed, but larger branches and trunks generally survive the initial burn with only superficial charring. Ash and fine charcoal debris are unevenly distributed over the newly-exposed topsoil.

Initially, the cleared land is devoted to subsistence crops, which take advantage of the enhanced soil nutrient supply provided by burning of plant debris. The main crops, which are normally planted to coincide with initial rains in April or May, are maize and dry rice, with a range of subsidiary crops like beans, bananas, manioc and water melons. Grass cuttings are usually planted amidst the food crops. In earlier times, colonião (*Panicum maximum*) was the commonest pasture grass in use, together with jaraguá (*Hyparrhenia rufa*), but since about 1980 kikuyu grass (*Brachiaria humidicola*) has been widely adopted.

During the initial cropping period, hand weeding is often undertaken, but as time passes increasing shrubby invasion occurs. In the subsequent dry season, the accumulated woody weeds are generally cut by hand and the site re-burnt. This disposes of the weed debris and depletes remaining timber debris. After the burn, the grass cuttings re-establish themselves and an initial pasture is created. This is normally achieved in the second rainy season after clearance, although in places food cropping may be continued for a second, or even third, year and pasture establishment delayed accordingly.

Once established, the introduced forage grasses like colonião (*Panicum maximum*) and kikuyu (*Brachiaria humidicola*) develop a more or less continuous ground cover. New kikuyu growth provides a well-developed ground layer, commonly 30–50 cm in thickness, which is relatively effective in suppressing early weed growth. Erect colonião likewise displays vigorous initial growth, readily attaining 2 m or more in height, although the pasture often becomes more weedy at an early stage. In all cases, however, woody weeds soon establish themselves in pastures, and, given time, would readily dominate the community as the initial stage of forest regeneration.

Among the commoner regenerating woody plants are the palms *Maximiliana maripa* (Correa) Drude and *Astrocaryum aculeatum* G. F. W. Meyer, which are common understorey species in local forest stands, various leguminous shrubs such as *Mimosa* spp., and sundry forest and other trees (Table 9.2). In the face of persisting woody regrowth, periodic hand cutting of weeds necessarily continues in pastures, while ranchers also make local use of the biocide Tordon for removing more persistent weeds such as jurubeba (*Solanum* sp.). In most cases, pastures are burned each dry season in order to dispose of weed material and renew the grass cover. Recurrent burning also serves to dispose of residual, decomposing timber debris in pastures. Such debris is substantially reduced within four to six

Table 9.2 Common woody weeds in derived pastures in the vicinity of Maracá (preliminary list).

Aegiphila sp.	Verbenaceae	tree
Astrocaryum aculeatum G. F. W. Meyer	Palmae	tree
Bauhinia sp.	Leguminosae	tree
Chamaecrista nictitans (L.) Moench ssp. *disadena* (Steud.) I. & B. var. *disadena*	Leguminosae	shrub to 1.5 m
Cochlospermum orinocense (Kunth) Steud.	Cochlospermaceae	tree
Curatella americana L.	Dilleniaceae	tree
Dalbergia sp.	Leguminosae	tree
Desmodium incanum (Sw.) DC.	Leguminosae	herb to 75 cm
Eupatorium sp.	Compositae	tree
Maximiliana maripa (Correa) Drude	Palmae	tree
Mimosa debilis Humb. & Bonpl. ex Willd.	Leguminosae	shrub to 1.5 m
M. pudica L. var. *tetrandra* (Willd.) DC.	Leguminosae	shrub to 1.5 m
M. schrankioides Benth.	Leguminosae	climber to 2.5 m
Psidium sp.	Myrtaceae	shrub to 2.0 m
Senna obtusifolia (L.) Irwin & Barneby	Leguminosae	shrub to 1.0 m
Solanum sp.	Solanaceae	shrub to 2.5 m
Tabebuia sp.	Bignoniaceae	tree
Vitex schomburgkiana Schauer	Verbenaceae	tree

years of clearance and mostly absent in older pastures, although dead standing trunks may persist for many years.

Although this initial pasture sequence after forest clearance recurs throughout the area, there is considerable variation apparent in the condition of older pastures. In places, pastures originally planted to colonião were still well-established on land that had been cleared ten years or more ago. Elsewhere colonião pastures of similar age were substantially invaded with woody weeds, or, in a few cases, seemingly so degraded that they were only able to support a low cover of native grasses and herbaceous and shrubby weeds. Most older pastures, however, contained a substantial cover of grasses and/or woody weeds, and no evidence was apparent of any general, early deflection of cleared forest land to open bunch-grass savanna. In places, a few isolated examples of *Curatella americana* occurred in older weedy derived pastures, but the characteristic *Trachypogon–Curatella* association of the savanna was not generally extending on to cleared forest land. Since the present derived pastures were all examined at the end of the rainy season (August–September 1987) and in no cases had been burnt since the previous dry season, it was assumed that their variable condition was mainly a response to differential soil degradation and/or recent stock levels.

Precise data on stock levels in the area are not easily acquired, with levels having in any case been rather variable in recent times. The ranches investigated contain both derived pastures and savanna, both of which are variously used for grazing. The main operation in the area is fattening stock on derived pastures, for which purpose animals are bought in from adjacent savanna ranches. Stock turnover is relatively high, and considerable fluctuations occur in cattle numbers and grazing pressure. At Fazenda Patchuli, which reportedly contained 340 zebu cattle at the time of investigation, between one and two animals per hectare were being maintained on some 250 ha of derived pasture. Similar cattle densities existed at Fazenda Canada, with 500 head distributed over some 300 ha of derived pasture, and at Fazenda Nova Olinda with 350 head spread over 50 ha of derived pasture and on adjacent natural savanna. Fazenda Pau Roxo likewise supported an estimated 400 animals, but, with a greater area of derived pasture available (500 ha), had lately experienced lesser overall cattle density (less than one animal per hectare). Even by Amazonian standards, carrying capacities in the area were rather low.

Soil and pasture conditions

Adverse soil conditions, particularly in respect of available phosphorus, are generally considered to limit pasture productivity on cleared forest land in Amazonia (Fearnside 1979, 1980; Serrão *et al.* 1979). As a basis for investigating this hypothesis in the vicinity of Maracá, soils were examined in adjacent forest, derived pasture and savanna.

In respect of soil physical conditions, some clear sequential changes are apparent. This is mainly so in respect of topsoil bulk density (0–10 cm), which, as elsewhere in Amazonia (Hecht 1981), increases relatively rapidly following conversion of forest to pasture. On the basis of three adjacent determinations at each site, bulk density values under forest were found to average 1.20 g/cm^3. Values increase in the years after clearance and, in older pastures, attain a mean of 1.52 g/cm^3. The latter values match those recorded in adjacent savanna sites (Table 9.3).

Topsoil exposure and compaction by trampling contribute significantly to the pattern of bulk density change after forest clearance. How far such change affects pasture growth is currently unclear, both in terms of the persistence of introduced forage species and their competitiveness with native woody weeds. The bulk density values recorded in pasture sites, even older ones, do not appear to be sufficiently high to impede root penetration significantly, but some malaeration effects may be apparent

Table 9.3 Topsoil bulk density of land cover types near Maracá. Values in bold type are significantly different from those immediately above at the 95 per cent level (Mann-Whitney U test – one-tailed probabilities).

	n =	bulk density (g/cm³)	standard error
forest	21	1.20	0.03
first-year clearance	12	1.21	0.05
young pastures (2–4 years)	24	**1.36**	0.01
old pastures (> 4 years)	24	**1.52**	0.02
savanna	9	1.52	0.03

(Landon 1984). Equally, reduced infiltration rates and consequent accelerated surface runoff and sheetwash erosion may adversely affect soil moisture supply and topsoil nutrient levels. At the same time, it is evident that some older pasture sites in the study area, with higher bulk density values (1.45–1.57 g/cm³) in sandy loam to sandy clay loam topsoils, support a well-developed colonião cover, indicating that soil compaction is not a general constraint on growth of pasture species.

In respect of soil chemical conditions, some broad patterns are apparent in the study area. Under forest, acid soil conditions generally prevail, and cation exchange capacity is low. Available phosphorus values are also low (Tables 9.4–9.7). Significant variation exists within the area in respect of forest soils, primarily as a function of parent materials. The main contrast is between Fazenda Patchuli, Fazenda Nova Olinda and Fazenda Canada in the east (Tables 9.4 and 9.5) and Fazenda Pau Roxo to the west (Table 9.6). In the former area, more acid topsoils are encountered, with relatively low levels of exchangeable bases. They contrast with the latter area, where topsoils are less acid and have significantly higher levels of exchangeable calcium and magnesium; nitrogen levels are also higher. Available phosphorus levels, however, do not differ significantly between the two areas.

General soil chemical data (Table 9.7) show some expected effects of forest clearance and burning in the study area. This is apparent in first-year clearance sites where increased values for topsoil pH, exchangeable bases (calcium, magnesium, potassium) and available phosphorus are most evident. However, there is considerable inter-site variability in the data and no consistent pattern of change emerges. In this respect, it is noted that sampling of first-year clearance sites occurred some six to eight months

Table 9.4 Topsoil (0–10 cm) analytical data for forest and cleared forest sites at Fazenda Patchuli. (Each value is the mean of four analyses at each site.)

	organic carbon %	pH	exchangeable (meq/100g)						ECEC (meq/100g)	total N (%)	available P (ppm)
			Ca	Mg	Na	K	Al	H			
forest	1.03	4.6	1.53	1.24	0.01	0.14	0.42	1.12	4.46	0.12	3.7
	2.13	4.6	0.10	0.49	0	0.09	0.31	0.82	1.81	0.14	3.6
first-year clearance	0.99	6.4	3.17	3.19	0.02	0.17	0.61	0.25	7.41	0.11	4.6
	1.44	6.3	4.39	1.37	0	0.16	0	0.15	6.07	0.13	7.6
young pastures (2–4 years)	1.73	5.6	2.96	0.87	0	0.21	0.05	0.22	4.31	0.11	6.7
	2.13	5.5	1.37	0.53	0	0.22	0.07	0.37	2.56	0.13	3.4
	1.88	5.2	0.19	0.45	tr	0.20	0.17	0.49	1.50	0.12	3.3
old pastures (6–25 years)	2.41	5.7	3.40	0.50	0	0.21	0.03	0.24	4.38	0.14	4.9
	1.36	5.4	1.08	0.33	0	0.09	0.08	0.29	1.87	0.10	3.5

Table 9.5 Topsoil (0–10 cm) analytical data for forest and cleared forest sites at Fazenda Nova Olinda and Fazenda Canada. (Each value is the mean of four analyses at each site.)

	organic carbon	pH	exchangeable (meq/100g)						ECEC (meq/100g)	total N (%)	available P (ppm)
			Ca	Mg	Na	K	Al	H			
forest	2.33	5.2	1.29	0.60	0.05	0.11	0.27	0.56	2.88	0.12	5.9
	0.78	5.0	0.09	0.06	0.15	0.07	0.10	0.28	0.75	0.08	3.3
first-year clearance	4.78	5.1	3.24	0.96	0	0.32	1.11	1.50	7.13	0.24	15.1
young pastures	3.25	5.5	2.31	0.86	0	0.18	0.39	1.01	4.75	0.16	5.5
	2.46	5.6	2.80	0.78	0	0.32	0.28	0.62	4.80	0.13	8.4
old pastures	2.42	5.9	4.14	0.55	0.16	0.10	0.01	0.12	5.08	0.12	1.9
	1.71	5.9	2.66	0.37	0.19	0.20	0	0.14	3.56	0.11	24.3
	2.53	6.9	7.68	0.29	0.14	0.20	0	0.10	8.41	0.13	4.5
	1.64	5.4	1.69	0.23	0.13	0.08	0.02	0.17	2.32	0.09	4.3

Table 9.6 Topsoil (0–10 cm) analytical data for forest and cleared forest sites at Fazenda Pau Roxo. (Each value is the mean of four analyses at each site.)

Fazenda Pau Roxo samples for forest are significantly different (95 per cent level, Mann-Whitney U test: two-tailed probabilities) from Fazenda Patchuli/Nova Olinda/Canada samples for forest taken together for all measured characteristics, with the exception of exchangeable sodium and available phosphorus.

| | organic carbon | pH | exchangeable (meq/100g) | | | | | | ECEC (meq/100g) | total N (%) | available P (ppm) |
			Ca	Mg	Na	K	Al	H			
forest	0.64	5.9	2.62	3.60	0.01	0.12	0	0.15	6.50	0.15	2.7
	0.74	6.3	5.65	1.31	0.01	0.25	0	0.15	7.37	0.18	3.3
	0.84	5.9	7.12	3.71	0.01	0.13	0	0.21	11.18	0.25	3.9
first-year clearance	0.72	6.9	5.01	2.81	0.01	0.10	0	0.10	8.03	0.16	2.8
young pastures	0.53	6.7	4.13	0.64	0.01	0.18	0	0.18	5.14	0.14	2.8
	0.63	5.7	3.67	0.87	tr	0.27	0	0.14	4.95	0.19	1.7
old pastures	0.69	6.1	2.45	0.50	0.02	0.09	0	0.19	3.25	0.10	0.8
	0.43	5.6	5.98	1.98	tr	0.32	0	0.13	8.41	0.22	2.2

Table: 9.7 Topsoil (0–10 cm) analytical data for forest and cleared forest sites at all four fazendas. SE is specified in brackets.

		forest (n = 28)	first-year clearance (n = 16)	young pastures (n = 28)	old pastures (n = 32)
	organic C %	1.21 (0.15)	1.98 (0.46)	1.80 (0.20)	1.65 (0.18)
	pH	5.4 (0.14)	6.2 (0.27)	5.7 (0.13)	5.9 (0.10)
exchangeable	Ca	2.63 (0.57)	3.95 (0.73)	2.49 (0.39)	3.64 (0.55)
	Mg	1.57 (0.38)	2.09 (0.64)	0.71 (0.07)	0.59 (0.10)
	Na	0.03 (0.01)	0.01 (0)	tr (0)	0.08 (0.01)
	K	0.13 (0.01)	0.19 (0.03)	0.23 (0.02)	0.16 (0.02)
	Al	0.16 (0.065)	0.43 (0.22)	0.14 (0.05)	0.03 (0.02)
	H	0.47 (0.08)	0.50 (0.20)	0.43 (0.10)	0.17 (0.02)
	(meq/100 g)				
	ECEC (meq/100 g)	5.00 (0.77)	7.17 (0.93)	4.01 (0.38)	4.67 (0.59)
	total N %	0.16 (0.01)	0.16 (0.01)	0.14 (0.01)	0.13 (0.01)
	available P (ppm)	3.8 (0.28)	7.6 (1.62)	4.6 (0.55)	5.8 (2.21)

after initial cutting and burning of the forest and that, in the interim, the land was variously cropped with nutrient-demanding maize and/or dry rice. It is thus assumed that much of the initial soil nutrient boost from burning was already depleted at the time of sampling.

Subsequently, in derived pastures, there is some indication of nutrient levels declining in relation to areas of first-year clearance. However, on account of the delayed sampling mentioned above, differences between areas of first-year clearance and young pastures are presumably less than would otherwise be the case. In overall terms, nutrient levels in pasture

Table 9.8 Topsoil (0–10 cm) analytical data for old pasture (6–25 years) and savanna sites in the vicinity of Maracá. Values in bold type in column 2 are significantly different from those in column 1 at the 95 per cent level (Mann-Whitney U test – two-tailed probabilities).

	old pastures (6–25 years) (n = 32)	savanna (n = 24)
clay (%)	17	21
organic carbon (%)	1.65	1.49
pH	5.9	**5.1**
exchangeable Ca (meq/100g)	3.64	**0.47**
exchangeable Mg (meq/100g)	0.59	**0.20**
exchangeable Na (meq/100g)	0.08	0.06
exchangeable K (meq/100g)	0.16	0.13
exchangeable Al (meq/100g)	0.03	**0.53**
exchangeable H (meq/100g)	0.17	**0.97**
ECEC (meq/100g)	4.67	**2.36**
total N (%)	0.13	**0.08**
available P (ppm)	5.8	2.6

sites are not exceptionally low; again there is considerable inter-site variability, but it is notable that no consistent nutrient differences exist between younger and older pastures.

The same is the case in respect of soil organic matter. Derived pastures in the area show rather variable values, but there is no significant difference between younger and older pastures. Conversely, pasture values commonly exceed those under forest (Tables 9.4–9.7). This is the case in spite of the regular burning of litter and other organic debris in derived pastures, and is contrary to expectation (Detwiler & Hall 1988). It may reflect the contribution of decomposing herbaceous root material to soil organic matter (Weaver *et al.* 1987), but probably also results from additions of fine charcoal at the soil surface (Hecht 1981; Ernst & Tolsma 1989).

Finally, a general distinction exists between older derived pastures and adjacent savanna sites (Table 9.8). The latter have more acid topsoils and contain significantly lower levels of exchangeable calcium and magnesium, with correspondingly higher levels of exchangeable hydrogen and aluminium. Nitrogen levels in the savanna are also lower, although neither organic carbon nor available phosphorus shows a significant decline.

Discussion

Soil fertility

In general, the above soil chemical data show similarities to those reported elsewhere in Amazonia (Falesi 1976; Serrão *et al.* 1979; Hecht 1981). This is particularly so in respect of pH values and associated exchangeable calcium and magnesium which remain relatively high in derived pastures over time, and of exchangeable aluminium which remains correspondingly very low or absent. There is also some similarity in respect of available phosphorus. In the vicinity of Maracá, initial increase in available phosphorus is evident in most first-year clearance sites as a consequence of burning forest debris, although no consistent decline is apparent as pastures themselves age (Tables 9.4–9.7). As elsewhere, however, available phosphorus levels in derived pastures at Maracá are, with occasional exceptions, very low and certainly below those regarded as adequate for most crops (Landon 1984). In eastern Amazonia, no great importance was attached by Falesi (1976) to low phosphorus levels in derived pastures, but, as subsequently demonstrated (Serrão *et al.* 1979; Fearnside 1979, 1980), phosphorus is usually the most limiting nutrient to pasture productivity, causing poor-quality growth irrespective of other fertility indicators. This is assumedly also the case in the present area. In this respect, Cochrane *et al.* (1985) indicate that the low available phosphorus in many forest topsoils in Roraima is due to fixation as iron or aluminium phosphate under very acid soil conditions. However, the present derived pasture soils are often no more than moderately acid and unlikely to induce such fixation, which implies that other factors regulate supply. Further laboratory investigation of this is currently being undertaken.

Evaluating the absence of a clear temporal decline in the topsoil chemical fertility of established pastures at Maracá is difficult given the relatively limited number of samples and the intra-site variability. In interpreting the data available, it can be seen that as well as the initial boost to soil fertility from cutting and burning the forest, medium-term nutrient inputs are provided by gradual decomposition of residual timber debris (Hecht 1981; Uhl 1987). Under the seasonal climate at Maracá, such decomposition usually extends over a period of five to six years. Thereafter, occasional dead standing trunks are found in derived pastures, but little else of the original forest phytomass remains. Few data are available on this continuing nutrient flux to the pasture system, but its importance is confirmed by preliminary information obtained in the present study. Thus, in one first-year cultivation site at Fazenda Nova Olinda, it is estimated that the residual timber and other forest debris remaining after initial burning totalled

Table 9.9 Total nutrient supply in forest debris in recently cleared field area at Fazenda Nova Olinda, near Maracá. The area was burnt in January/February 1987, and sampled in September 1987.

	timber	surface organic debris (twigs, bark, charcoal, etc.)	total
total volume (m³/ha)	140.5	n/a	n/a
total dry weight (t/ha)	110.1	7.2	117.3
total Ca (kg/ha)	171.4	121.1	292.5
total Mg (kg/ha)	55.0	18.7	73.7
total Na (kg/ha)	2.2	0.3	2.5
total K (kg/ha)	129.1	4.9	134.0
total P (kg/ha)	45.9	3.2	49.1
total N (kg/ha)	509.4	52.3	561.7

some 117 tonnes per hectare (dry weight). The material, sampled some seven months after the original forest burn, contained a substantial nutrient capital, which is presumably being gradually released to the pasture system (Table 9.9).

In respect of long-term nutrient supply, the situation is less clear. There is considerable nutrient variability among older pastures, but no overall nutrient decline is apparent in comparison to younger pastures. It is assumed that this largely reflects relatively efficient nutrient cycling in the pasture system, and consequent low net nutrient loss under conditions of recurrent dry-season burning and wet-season regeneration of forage and woody weed plants. This might, at first sight, be expected to produce a positive correlation between topsoil nutrient content and total above-ground biomass in older pastures, but of this there is no indication in the present data. Instead, it appears that soil nutrient levels, at least at the end of the growing season, are more a function of differential sequestration by the plant biomass (Buschbacher *et al.* 1988) than an indicator of the overall nutrient status of the soil–plant system. In this respect, the influence of woody weeds is no doubt important in view of their assumed relative efficiency in utilising soil nutrients, particularly phosphorus (Jordan 1985); nitrogen fixation presumably also occurs among the leguminous shrubs that commonly exist in derived pastures. Admittedly, the presence of woody weeds does nothing to improve pasture quality directly, but, as with any incipient forest regeneration, woody regrowth serves to increase overall nutrient retention in the soil–plant system. The difference in the present case, however, is that nutrient accumulation in the biomass is regularly reversed by dry-season burning, which presumably leads to some slow net nutrient loss from the system.

In general, considerable inter-site variability is apparent in topsoil conditions in established pastures. This is no doubt partly a function of soil parent materials, but, as suggested above, nutrient flux within the soil–plant system itself is also a critical variable. This in turn reflects the status and usage of the pasture itself. In these circumstances, there is clearly much benefit to be gained from an integrated analysis of the soil–plant nutrient dynamics of derived pastures.

By comparison with derived pastures, topsoil nutrient conditions in the savanna near Maracá are significantly less favourable in most respects. In general, soil parent materials in the savanna are not fundamentally different from those of adjacent forest or cleared forest sites, but the soils have apparently been degraded by sheetwash erosion and nutrient leaching during an extended period of savanna cover. In consequence, the savanna has a low soil–plant nutrient capital and low above-ground biomass.

Grazing intensity and land management
In general, derived pastures in the vicinity of Maracá have not as yet been grossly degraded in respect of nutrient supply, and, even when cleared for a decade or two, are periodically used for grazing purposes. Compositionally, derived pastures are distinct from adjacent savanna and show little indication of deflection to the status of the latter. However, there is considerable variation in the condition of older pastures, which contain different amounts of forage grass and invading woody and herbaceous weeds. No clear correlation is evident between topsoil nutrients and pasture status, and it is assumed that other factors, notably stock levels and associated variables such as frequency of weeding, amount of fencing, and incidence of rotational grazing, influence the condition of older pastures. Unfortunately, at the individual pasture level, there is little precise information on such management variables and, particularly in respect of stock levels, conditions have fluctuated considerably over time. However, there are qualitative data available at the ranch level which allow some general observations to be made.

In this respect, it is evident that Fazenda Patchuli has of late experienced more 'progressive' pasture management. This is reflected in its somewhat higher stock densities (between one and two animals per hectare), more regular clearance of woody weeds, and increased attention to stock rotation. In recent years, the ranch has introduced kikuyu grass (*Brachiaria humidicola*) on all its new pastures. Against this background, the ranch contains some of the most degraded older pastures in the area, which, even with recent ploughing and replanting, support only a low cover of native grasses and herbaceous and shrubby weeds.

At Fazenda Nova Olinda and Fazenda Canada, whose derived pastures are adjacently located near the Uraricoera River, stock levels of between one and two animals per hectare recur. At Fazenda Nova Olinda, which is jointly owned with Fazenda Patchuli, fenced pastures exist and rotational grazing is practised. This contrasts with Fazenda Canada which has experienced limited management in recent years. However, both ranches, and particularly Fazenda Canada, contain older pastures which, although still in use for grazing, are mostly degraded and contain common to abundant woody weeds.

In contrast, derived pastures at Fazenda Pau Roxo are in better condition, apparently as a result of lower stock densities (less than one animal per hectare). New pastures, which continue to be planted with colonião, are very weedy as a function of the more open nature of the grass layer, but older pastures, although containing many woody weeds, support a dense colonião layer, 2.0–2.5 m in height. As indicated, forest soils at Fazenda Pau Roxo have higher levels of exchangeable bases and are less acid than elsewhere, but low available phosphorus levels persist, and the main variable affecting the condition of older pastures is taken to be lower stock levels.

Conclusion

As yet, only preliminary conclusions can be drawn about the pasture system in the vicinity of Maracá Island. Some soil physical degradation is apparent as pastures age, although it is unclear to what extent this influences pasture growth. In respect of soil nutrient supply, no progressive deterioration is apparent as established pastures age; older pastures vary in soil nutrient content, but are not measurably less fertile than younger pastures. In absolute terms, nutrient levels in derived pastures are not particularly low, with the exception of available phosphorus which is assumed to be as limiting to pasture productivity as elsewhere in Amazonia (Serrão *et al.* 1979; Fearnside 1979). In general, the variable condition of older pastures appears to be related to grazing levels, with more degraded and/or weedy pastures being associated with increased stock densities (between one and two animals per hectare), and more favourable older pastures with lower stock densities (less than one animal per hectare). In both cases, grazing is sustainable in so far as all derived pastures remain in use, with no indication of older ones yet being abandoned. However, the economic return on using older pastures is obviously very low, and it is the occupance or ownership of the land, rather than its yield, that is valued.

The present ranching system in the vicinity of Maracá Island thus relies on continuing forest clearance to maintain and/or increase overall beef production, and no indication exists of the local emergence of more intensive and sustainable methods of livestock rearing. It is true that clearing, temporarily exploiting, and then selling forest land in Amazonia has long been a profitable strategy for the individual rancher (Fearnside 1980; Hecht 1981), but it is increasingly recognised that this approach, with its implicit continuance of forest clearance, is by no means in the longer-term national interest. It may be that, in the future, possibilities will emerge for more intensive fertiliser-based pasture systems or for grass–legume systems with supplementary fertiliser inputs, but of this there is no immediate prospect in the present area or indeed any guarantee of future viability. At present, what exists in the area is another example of low-grade pioneer land colonisation, founded on the exploitation of the nutrient capital of the forest system. Even though the pasture system is currently maintained at a low level of productivity, its long-term prospects are poor and its reliance on continuing forest clearance inappropriate.

Even so, the soil–plant dynamics of pioneer ranching systems of this kind are still poorly understood, and need further investigation in respect of the present function of such systems and their prospects for improved productivity on a sustainable basis. Relevant work of this kind is being undertaken elsewhere in Amazonia (Buschbacher *et al.* 1988; Serrão & Toledo 1988), but in northern Roraima, where only limited forest clearance for pasture has yet occurred, minimal pasture research has been started. The present study aims to provide a baseline for the area, but it exposes as many problems as it solves. In this respect, further specific information is required on (a) the influence of soil physical constraints on pasture conditions, particularly topsoil compaction and surface runoff and erosion, (b) the nature of soil phosphorus supply and its relationship to pasture productivity, (c) nutrient supplies in the pasture biomass and their relationship to soil nutrients, and (d) changes in pasture status and management over time. Given increased understanding of the dynamics and potential of existing ranching systems, it is arguable that more realistic planning decisions can be made in respect of the future use of Amazonian forest land, whether for livestock rearing, alternative productive activities, or conservation.

Acknowledgements

Grant assistance was received by all three authors from the Ford Foundation/ Royal Geographical Society, by Duncan McGregor from the Carnegie Trust for the Universities of Scotland, and by Michael Eden from the Central Research Fund of the University of London. Grateful acknowledgement is made of logistical and other assistance provided by the Royal Geographical Society Maracá Rainforest Project, and by Brazilian government agencies, notably the *Secretaria Especial do Meio Ambiente*, the *Instituto Nacional de Pesquisas da Amazônia*, and the *Empresa Brasileira de Pesquisa Agropecuária*. Laboratory analyses were undertaken by Margaret Onwu and cartographic work by Ron Halfhide and Justin Jacyno. Plant identifications were made at the Royal Botanic Gardens, Kew and Edinburgh.

References

Black, C. A., Evans, D. D., White, J. L., Ensminger, L. E. and Clark, F. E. (1965), *Methods of Soil Analysis*, Madison, American Society of Agronomy.

Brasil (1975), Projeto Radambrasil, *Levantamento de recursos naturais*, Rio de Janeiro, Ministério da Agricultura, 8. Folha NA.20 Boa Vista, Folha NB.20 Roraima, Folha NB.21; 9, Folha NA.21 Tumucumaque.

Bunyard, P. (1989), Brazil and the Amazonian pact, *The Ecologist*, 19, 86–7.

Buschbacher, R., Uhl, C. and Serrão, E. A. S. (1988), Abandoned pastures in eastern Amazonia. II. Nutrient stocks in the soil and vegetation, *Journal of Ecology*, 76, 682–99.

Cochrane, T. T., Sánchez, L. G., de Azevedo, L. G., Porras, J. A. and Garver, C. L. (1985), *Land in Tropical America*, Cali, Centro Internacional de Agricultura Tropical.

Dantas, M. and Rodrigues, I. A. (1980), Plantas invasoras de pastagens cultivadas na Amazônia, *Boletim de Pesquisa, EMBRAPA/CPATU*, Belém, 1, 1–23.

Detwiler, R. P. and Hall, C. A. S. (1988), Tropical forests and the global carbon cycle, *Science*, 239, 42–7.

Domínguez, C. A. (1987), La colonización como ampliación del espacio de dominación. In Kohlhepp, G. and Schrader, A. (eds.), *Homem e natureza na Amazônia*, 271–8, Tübingen, Geographisches Institut der Universität Tübingen.

Eden, M. J. (1990), *Ecology and Land Management in Amazonia*, London, Belhaven.

Eden, M. J., Furley, P. A., McGregor, D. F. M., Milliken, W. and Ratter, J. A. (1991), The impact of forest clearance and burning on soil properties in northern Roraima, Brazil, *Forest Ecology and Management*, 38, 283–90.

Ernst, W. H. O. and Tolsma, D. J. (1989), Mineral nutrients in some Botswana savanna types, in Proctor, J. (ed.), *Mineral Nutrients in Tropical Forest and Savanna Ecosystems*, 97–120, Oxford, Blackwell Scientific Publications.

Falesi, I. C. (1976), Ecossistema de pastagem cultivada na Amazônia brasileira, *Boletim Técnico, EMBRAPA/CPATU*, Belém, 1, 1–193.

Fearnside, P. M. (1979), Cattle yield prediction for the Transamazon highway of Brazil, *Interciencia*, 4, 220–5.

Fearnside, P. M. (1980), The effects of cattle pasture on soil fertility in the Brazilian Amazon: consequences for beef production sustainability, *Tropical Ecology*, 21, 125–37.

Hecht, S. B. (1981), Deforestation in the Amazon basin: magnitude, dynamics and soil resource effects, *Studies in Third World Societies*, 13, 663–84.

Jordan, C. F. (1985), *Nutrient Cycling in Tropical Forest Ecosystems*, Chichester, John Wiley & Sons Ltd.

Kelsey, T. F. (1972), *The Beef Industry in the Roraima Savannas: a Potential Supply for Brazil's North*. Ph.D. dissertation, Gainesville, University of Florida.

Landon, J. R. (ed.) (1984), *Booker Tropical Soil Manual*, Harlow, Longman.

Margolis, M. (1988a), Threat from Amazon burn-off, *The Times*, London, 6 September.

Margolis, M. (1988b), Brazil moves to save rain forests, *The Times*, London, 13 October.

Milliken, W. and Ratter, J. A. (1989), *The Vegetation of the Ilha de Maracá*, Edinburgh, Royal Botanic Garden.

Neto, R. B. (1989a), Outside influences resented, *Nature*, 338, 286.

Neto, R. B. (1989b), Disputes about destruction, *Nature*, 338, 531.

Nortcliff, S. and Robison, D. (1988), *The Soils and Geomorphology of the Ilha de Maracá, Roraima. The Second Approximation*, Department of Soil Science, University of Reading.

Santhirasegaram, K. (1975), Management of legume pastures in a tropical rainforest ecosystem of Peru, in Bornemisza, E. and Alvarado, A. (eds.), *Soil Management in Tropical America*, 434–52, Raleigh, Soil Science Department, North Carolina State University.

Serrão, E. A. S., Falesi, I. C., de Veiga, J. B. and Neto, J. F. T. (1979), Productivity of cultivated pastures on low fertility soils in the Amazon of Brazil, in Sanchez, P. A. and Tergas, L. E. (eds.), *Pasture Production in Acid Soils in the Tropics*, 195–225, Cali, Centro Internacional de Agricultura Tropical.

Serrão, E. A. S. and Toledo, J. M. (1988), *Sustaining Pasture-based Production Systems for the Humid Tropics*, paper presented at MAB Conference on Conversion of Tropical Forests to Pasture in Latin America, Oaxaca, Mexico, October 1988.

Silva, A. de B. and Magalhães, B. P. (1980), Insetos nocivos às pastagens no Estado do Pará, *Boletim de Pesquisa, EMBRAPA/CPATU*, Belém, 8, 1–20.

Uhl, C. (1987), Factors controlling succession following slash-and-burn agriculture in Amazonia, *Journal of Ecology*, 75, 377–407.

Weaver, P. L., Birdsey, R. A. and Lugo, A. E. (1987), Soil organic matter in secondary forests of Puerto Rico, *Biotropica*, 19, 17–23.

A tentative interpretation of the Quaternary geomorphology of Maracá Island, based on an analysis of soils developed on residua and drift deposits

Introduction

Recently there has been increasing interest in tropical forested areas and their incalculable and irreplaceable biodiversity. Much has been written about the rate at which the forests are disappearing and the need to protect and study the biodiversity before it disappears. Considerably less has been written about how one would systematically study the millions of hectares that remain, given the diversity that exists in a single hectare. An obvious step is to characterise well those areas that are already protected, such as Maracá. There is also interest in developing rapid methods of identifying and characterising other key areas of potentially high biodiversity (Wolf 1991). Similarly, people have attempted to identify useful indicators of biodiversity. One approach is to map units of soils and geomorphology and use this to help stratify the study of vegetation.

While many people regard tropical soils as uniformly nutrient-poor, there is increasing awareness that soils under tropical forest are quite diverse and that this influences the nature of the ecosystem. Furthermore, the degree of biodiversity is related not only to current soil characteristics, but also to the geomorphological and paleoclimatic history of the area (Brown & Prance 1987). These authors hypothesised that the degree of diversity could be related to former areas of forest refugia, which in turn were related in part to soil conditions. Unfortunately, much of what is known about the history of the Amazon basin has been extrapolated from studies in central, southern and eastern Amazonia (Bigarella & Ferreira 1985). The Ecological Survey of Maracá provides several advantages for increasing our understanding. The island lies in the northern, less studied part of the basin. The area is, in effect, the boundary between two of the three morphostructural regions in Amazonia: the pre-orogenic shields and the sub-Andean depression (Projeto RADAMBRASIL 1975). This means that within close proximity on the island there are examples of ecosystems on soils developing on residual rock as well as several different kinds of Quaternary drift such as one finds farther to the south near Manaus.

Preliminary indications from the interior of the island pointed to polycyclical developments. In other words, there appeared to be remains of surfaces representing different stages in the history of the island. We can only hypothesise at this point the implications of this for the distribution of the vegetation.

The analysis below stemmed from the fieldwork conducted for the soil survey (Robison & Nortcliff 1991). Therefore the point of view has a pedological bias and is more simple than if we had set out to study the geomorphology for its own sake. However, we believe that it is useful to collate the available evidence and interpret it in terms of a likely geomorphological progression and the implication it might have for simplifying or stratifying future ecological studies.

Method

Prior to the fieldwork, aerial photographs (1 : 70,000) and radar images (1 : 250,000) were analysed. Based on the remotely sensed images, the island was divided into physiographic regions which were likely to represent geomorphological homogeneity (Figure 10.1.a). Given that a trail system did not exist on the island before the expedition, a hypothetical trail system was devised that would allow for ground-truthing each of the ten physiographic units. Thus, much of the time was consumed adding trails to the existing system which would allow us to visit each of the ten units.

The units were as follows:

Unit 1
This is essentially a dissected plinthite landscape, with the ferralitic duricrust overlain by a thin deposit of quartzitic sand. The abundance of rounded gravel and sand cemented in the duricrust suggests that this area was the destination of unsorted, eroded material from farther north. During the period devoted by the surface labelled N3, it was a low point on the landscape, where over a long stable period iron was deposited, cementing the colluvial material.

Unit 2
The Preguiça Trail. Sorted sediments overlying weathered granite. Alternating bands of sandy and clayey material higher and better drained than unit 4.

Unit 3
Quartzite hills. Based on the aerial photographs, we estimate that there are three pockets of hills that are composed of metamorphic rocks. The

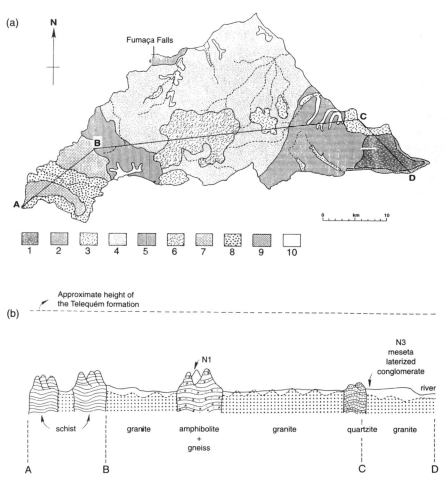

Figure 10.1.a   Physiographic regions (Robison & Nortcliff 1991).
 1 plinthite with quartzite overlay
 2 sediments over weathered granite
 3 metamorphic rock
 4 low hills
 5 flat and well drained
 6 central uplands
 7 schist intrusion hills
 8 low ridges
 9 flood plain
10 *vazante*
Figure 10.1.b   Schematic and geological profile and relic land surfaces.

rocks are resistant to weathering and the tops of the hills are covered in stone mulch.

Unit 4
The Fumaça Trail. This largest unit is composed of low gradient hills with granite ridges and infilled valleys. The drift is mainly quartz sand. The unit is more poorly drained than 2. Evidence suggests that the Santa Rosa Channel crossed this unit west to east, before cutting through the Fumaça falls.

Unit 5
This flat, well-drained unit was formed by sorted, high base, fine sediments. The deposition could have occurred during N3, at the same time as the laterization of unit 1.

Unit 6
Central uplands. At the island's centre, the tall hills are capped with fine sediments that underwent a significant period of soil formation. These are surrounded by hills composed of high-base igneous intrusions sometimes partially metamorphosed.

Unit 7
Purumame Hills. Two sets of steep hill composed of schist intrusions.

Unit 8
Sorted sediments forming low ridges. Generally poorly drained with surface sediment.

Unit 9
Contemporary flood plain, with low base sediments.

Unit 10
Vazantes. Elevated swamps with nearly closed drainage, possibly relics of the surface labelled N3. Filled with fine organic sediments.

Within each unit, the trails served as transects, along which we dug soil pits in representative sites and collected rock samples. Where possible, these transect pits were associated with the vegetation surveys. In addition, river outcroppings provided valuable evidence about the geomorphology of the island, but these are reported elsewhere (Martini 1988). Unfortunately, due to the difficult accessibility of the central highlands, there was only visual appraisal of the vegetation with which to compare our geomorphological information. The central highlands could, in the future, provide some of the more unusual ecological information.

The mineralogical analysis reported below used X-ray diffraction (XRD) on unoriented powder mounts following methods according to Brown and Brindley (1980). The total element analysis was performed by X-ray fluorescence spectroscopy (XRFS) according to Norrish and Chappel (1976).

Results

Based on analysis of the soil profiles, we found it useful to divide the surface of the island into two broad groups: those related to residual rock formations and those related to drift. In an area where Pre-Cambrian rocks and Quaternary alluvium exist in close proximity, this proved a useful division in the field and in the laboratory. Residual soils, by definition, have undergone relatively little turbation and retain or reflect the primary minerals in the parent rock. By contrast, the drift has undergone at least one cycle of erosion, sorting and deposition and this helps account for many of the differences found in the field. It should be stated that the residual soils or those directly influenced by parent rock may not account for more than 10 per cent of the surface of the island. However, these areas could be considerably more important in terms of the biological diversity of the island.

Even taking into account the fundamental difference between residua and drift, Table 10.1 shows that there were considerable differences within as well as between these broad groups in terms of chemical composition. While the amphibolite had the highest amounts of total calcium and magnesium, the highest levels of aluminium and silicon were found in drifts. However, another drift had the highest levels of phosphorus, mainly from the organic fraction. Thus it is useful to distinguish between the different types of residua and drift and to consider their implications.

Residua
We identified the outcroppings of four major rock formations in our transects; granite, mica-schist, quartzite and amphibolite/gneiss (Figure 10.1.b). The most widespread are the granite ridges in units 2, 4 and possibly 8. Because the relief associated with this formation is not steep, the soils are not undergoing radical rejuvenation as are the residual soils in units 3, 6 and 7. Table 10.1 shows that the parent material on these granite ridges is high in silicon and, relative to other residual soils, low in total iron, aluminium and the bases. The vegetation was low forest with frequently uprooted trees. The shallow rooting appeared to be related to dense subsoils with high aluminium saturation (Nortcliff & Robison 1989). The mixed *terra firme* forest resembles the forest on the eastern side of the island (F1 in Milliken & Ratter 1989) but has occurrences of *Peltogyne gracilipes* and is described in transect 10 of the vegetation survey (Milliken & Ratter 1989). The soils here have acidic pH values and low levels of

Table 10.1 Total element analysis of subsoil samples forming on four rock types and four drift types.

	sample no.	SiO_2	Fe_2O_3	Al_2O_3	CaO	K_2O	P_2O_5	MgO
Rock type								
granite	435	85.2	1.07	16.53	< 0.01	1.02	0.01	0.00
schist	134	56.89	6.08	24.33	< 0.01	4.21	0.01	0.16
amphibolite	585	45.80	14.58	20.99	4.19	0.20	0.02	3.69
quartzite	383	68.30	9.95	6.13	< 0.01	0.05	0.13	< 0.01
Drift type								
low base status Quaternary N1	352	92.90	0.53	4.17	0.01	0.21	0.01	< 0.01
high base status Quaternary N3	415	60.28	7.12	22.00	0.03	1.45	0.06	0.09
fine sediments N1	545	46.50	7.16	27.93	< 0.01	0.84	0.01	< 0.01
fine sediments very recent	471	41.93	8.854	22.93	0.41	0.87	0.32	0.54

exchangeable calcium and potassium and an unusually low calcium–magnesium ratio.

The second residual formation is the schist-based Purumame Hills at the western edge of the island (unit 7). This parent material is high in total amounts of potassium, moderate in iron and silicon, and low in aluminium, calcium and magnesium. The topography is steep, and consequently the soils are undergoing constant turbation. Even so, the soils are poor, with an acidic pH, low cation exchange capacity and low levels of all exchangeable cations. The calcium–magnesium ratio is greater than one (Table 10.2). The vegetation is F2, open, mixed *terra firme* forest much more similar in species composition to central Amazonia than is the eastern part of the island. It has the highest number of plant species per unit area of the transects, and does not contain *Peltogyne gracilipes*. It is described in detail on transects 12 and 13 of the vegetation survey (Milliken & Ratter 1989). These hills appear from satellite images to be a fragment of an important geomorphological unit of the Roraima area, the Planalto Dissecado Norte de Amazonia (Projeto RADAMBRASIL 1975).

The third residual formation is found on the quartzite hills (unit 3). The quartzite appears more resistant to weathering than the other rocks on the island, and almost unweathered boulders form a coarse mulch on the summit surfaces. The vegetation is sparse *terra firme* forest with much *Maximiliana maripa* at the summit and tall forest with *Peltogyne* and *Bombacopsis quinita* at the base. The area affected by these rocks appears limited to a few hills, but leads to the formation of unusual, very red soils of moderate fertility (Nortcliff & Robison 1989). Table 10.2 presents the information for the subsoil at the crest of a quartzite hill with low cation exchange capacity resulting from the coarse texture of the material, but a moderately high percentage base saturation and calcium–magnesium ratio. The soils on the flank, by comparison, were found to have calcium–magnesium ratios of less than one.

The final residual formation was that of the high base metamorphic intrusions in the central highlands (unit 6). Table 10.1 shows that the rocks are very high in calcium and magnesium with soils forming that have among the highest levels of exchangeable calcium and magnesium reported for lowland tropical forests. However, the potassium and phosphorus are low, again illustrating nutrient imbalances inherited from the parent rock. The vegetation is dominated by *Ecclinusa guianensis* on the summits and again, *Peltogyne* forests on the lower flanks (Milliken, personal communication, 1989).

Drift

In addition to different rock types, the island possesses considerable evidence of the polycyclical history of the area and perhaps of northern Amazonia. It is likely that the entire region, including the island, was

Table 10.2 Selected chemical analyses of soil materials overlying four rock deposits and four drift deposits.

Rock/drift type	sample no.	pH	CEC	exch. Ca	exch. Mg cmol$_c$/kg	exch. K	total N mg/g	Mehlich P ppm
granite	435	4.92	3.93	0.09	0.47	0.02	0.005	0.11
schist	134	4.71	2.93	0.03	0.01	0.01	0.020	0.11
amphibolite	585	6.03	21.57	19.81	5.75	0.05	0.024	0.06
quartzite	383	5.22	2.93	0.80	0.20	0.01	0.026	0.56
low base status	352	5.02	2.01	0.00	0.05	0.02	0.000	0.28
Quaternary N1 high base status	415	5.46	10.14	0.16	0.55	0.12	0.026	0.11
Quaternary N3 fine sediments N1	545	5.21	2.64	0.07	0.01	0.00	0.009	0.06
fine sediments very recent	475	6.06	21.29	3.98	5.69	0.03	0.045	0.84

covered in Pre-Cambrian times by the Tepequém (Roraima) formation (Projeto RADAMBRASIL 1975). None of this formation is left on the island, the closest example being the Serra de Tepequém to the north. Since then there would have been repeated cycles of denudation and deposition to arrive at the contemporary land surface on the island.

In our transects we identified four surfaces (landmarks of possible important points in the Quaternary history of the island) and suggest a diagrammatic interpretation in Figure 10.2. A significant period of environmental stability may be shown by the surface labelled N1, of which we found remnants over 100 m above stream level in the central highlands. The soils on these remnants have a chemical composition and high kaolinite quantities which suggest long weathering. On the other hand, Figure 10.3 shows that the kaolinite is highly crystalline compared to another kaolinitic soil (sample 230). This could be explained by a long period of stability allowing for the recrystallisation of kaolinite. Hughes (1980) presents a tentative scheme for tropical soils suggesting that the crystallinity of kaolinite initially increases with age and then decreases. Hughes found kaolinite in soils near Manaus to have a relatively high crystallinity, and the soils considered, both coarse and fine textured, are similarly low in exchangeable cations.

These hills are surrounded by intrusions of amphibolite and gneiss which we hypothesise protected these vestiges of N1 from erosion (Figure 10.2). Though a vegetation transect was not possible on this surface, visual comparison suggests that the vegetation resembles the western end of the island, which in turn is more like the vegetation near Manaus than the forest on the eastern part of the island and *Peltogyne* was not in evidence (Milliken, personal communication, 1989). While the soils differ from the western side in appearance, they are similar in terms of acidity, low base saturation and a calcium–magnesium ratio greater than one.

N2 appears to have been associated with the lowest base level, with stream levels slightly below those at present. There are indications that the igneous and metamorphic outcroppings in the two river courses were scoured to below present stream levels, then subsequently covered with alluvium. In places this sediment is fine, such as outcroppings up the Maracá Channel, while in others it is coarse, mixed with rounded gravel. In both instances, however, the sediments were laterised during a period that we call N3. We did not recognise any paleosols from N2, partly, we assume, because there has been infill since then, and partly because the stream level may have differed only a little from current stream levels and therefore would be easily confused with the contemporary land surface.

N3 appears to have been formed during a period of long-term stable soil formation with a base level a few metres higher than at present. This higher sea level appears to have been accompanied by extensive impeded drainage in the area and a long period of isostatic stability which allowed

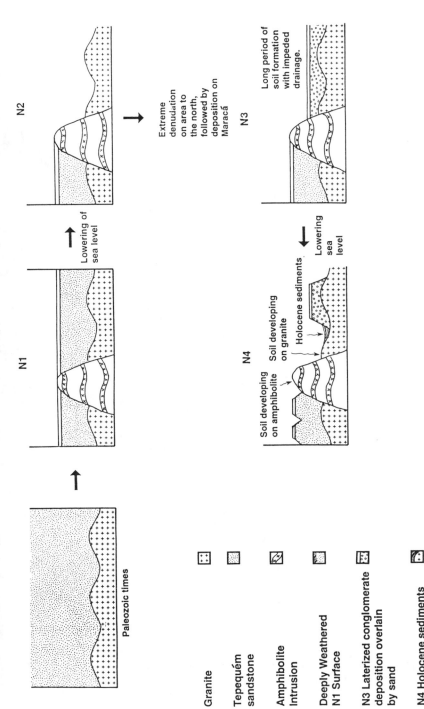

Figure 10.2 A diagrammatic interpretation of the Quaternary history of Maracá.

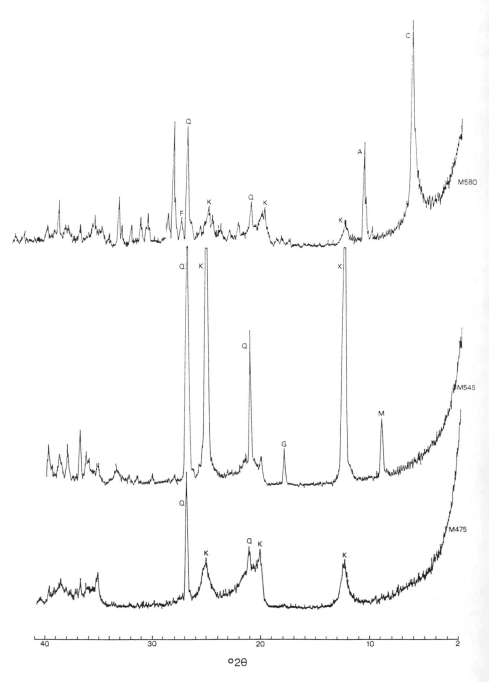

Figure 10.3 Comparison of X-ray diffraction traces of 'whole soil' mounts. All taken at same instrument settings. M580 is a soil developing on an amphibolite intrusion. M545 is a soil developing on N1 in the central highlands. M475 is from N4 alluvial soil. (Q = quartz, K = kaolinite, M = mica, C = chlorite, A = anorthite, and G = goethite.)

Note on M545 that not only the kaolinite but also the mica is 'recrystallizing' at the top of N1. Further evidence of the weathering is given by the goethite peak. No igneous rock will have that kind of kaolinite peak; it is therefore a deposit. M475 is a Quaternary deposit with a normal kaolinite peak.

for large amounts of iron to be deposited. A characteristic of this surface is the ironstone layer, whether in fine or coarse sediments. The ecological station is located on N3, which locally is composed of cemented conglomerate sediments overlain by a thick layer of sand. Based on our transects and remote sensing analysis, this formation is mainly limited to the eastern end of the island, and is much more common in the savanna areas to the east of the island. This unit has a mixed *terra firme* vegetation (F1) but is generally devoid of *Peltogyne*. The soils have very low cation exchange capacities and very low calcium–magnesium ratios.

It appears that between N3 and N4 there was another period of isostatic adjustment associated with a lowering of the base level to the present level (Figure 10.1.b). The effect has not been uniform on the island. Units 1 and 5 (supposedly under water during N3) have been dissected, leaving adequate internal drainage and leaving the laterite layers under unit 1 as outcroppings. By contrast, units 2, 4 and 8 were not dissected and have poor internal drainage. The microtopography on these units is unusual. With very dense subsoils (and possibly impermeable material underneath), it appears that most of the drainage occurs along the surface, even on coarse sediments, where one would expect rapid percolation. From a geomorphological point of view, these units appear unstable. That is, they appear to be actively in a process of denudation. The vegetation on these poorly drained units has comparatively low species diversity and was characterised by the predominance of *Peltogyne gracilipes* (transects 14–16 in the vegetation survey, Milliken & Ratter 1989). The soils generally have low cation exchange capacities and very low calcium–magnesium ratios. They also show signs of being seasonally saturated with water.

A related observation is that relatively recently, perhaps between N3 and N4, the Santa Rosa Channel flowed eastwards across the island from above the Fumaça falls (unit 4). Many of the features such as water-rounded boulders, deposits of rounded stones and the orientation of fluvial deposits lead to this conclusion. At some point fairly recently, the river broke through at the Fumaça falls to join the Uraricaá before turning south–east. Site 470 probably represents a deposit of this period, being a fine sediment with relative low contents of SiO_2 and intermediate contents of Fe_2O_3, CaO and MgO. At depth the soils are of relatively high fertility (Table 10.2).

Discussion

The surfaces that we identified in general are congruent with those found in the literature, though these refer to observations taken over a great distance. For example, a similar pattern of erosion and deposition has been illustrated for the northern, or Venezuelan, side of the Guiana Shield (Haffer 1987). Klammer (1978) identified five surfaces up to 100 m above stream level, but close to the mouth of the Amazon. Trying to establish the relative age of the different surfaces is more difficult. Bigarella and Ferreira (1985) emphasise the major pediplanations during the Tertiary. They consider that, at the lower elevations in the Amazon basin, there are no surfaces older than the Tertiary, and their youngest pediplanation surface, which they name Pd1, is considered to be Plio-Pleistocene. It is possible that the hills on the western and central parts of the island are remnants of Pd1, and of the Planalto Dessecado Norte da Amazônia (Projeto RADAMBRASIL, 1975). It follows that N1, at the same elevation as the summits of these hills, could be as old as the Plio-Pleistocene (approximately 1.5 million years).

Since then there appears to have been considerable activity. It is thought that there have been regular glacial periods, occurring every 100,000 years, with shorter interglacial periods in between (Dickinson & Vinji 1987). Clearly N2 through N4 represent the latter part of the Quaternary, and perhaps only the last two or three glacial periods. Further study is needed to determine the ages better and to search for other surface remnants. Various swamps and closed lagoons on the island (*vazante*) may provide an excellent opportunity for palynological study.

Whatever the exact age and sequence of the surfaces, there appears to be a vegetational pattern related to these geomorphological features that has relevance to future studies both on and off the island. There are two extreme *terra firme* forest types at opposite ends of the island and most of the species in one type are not found at the other (Milliken & Ratter 1989). They are both forests on nutrient-poor, well drained soils, so these differences cannot be explained edaphically by a difference in fertility. In between these forests there is a third type with an unusual predominance of *Peltogyne gracilipes* which is rare elsewhere in Amazonia (Milliken & Ratter 1989). This type of forest covers much of the surface of the island in our units 2 and 4.

We have preliminarily found three variables that appear correlated with this distribution of the vegetation. In all the situations where *Peltogyne* is dominant there is a low calcium–magnesium ratio. That is, there is more exchangeable magnesium than calcium. With one exception in our sample, the reverse is true. With the exception of unit 1, everywhere we found the low calcium–magnesium ratio we also found *Peltogyne*. Except for unit 1, this nutrient imbalance was associated with evidence of seasonal surface flooding and subsoil saturation. Finally, all of the areas that have a predominance of *Peltogyne* are what we regard as N4: the current erosional surface on Quaternary sediments. *Peltogyne* was generally not dominant in the areas that we identified as residual or the remnants of older surfaces.

Conclusion

Though we cannot be certain from our as yet limited number of samples, it appears clear that geomorphological analysis is useful for understanding the distribution of vegetation, at least in this part of Amazonia. From a geomorphological point of view, Maracá represents a dynamic situation. Currently Maracá lies at the transition between rain forest and savanna. In addition, it is an example of the transition between dissected high plain and the lower areas of the Amazon basin. Being at this boundary, the island reveals evidence for a complex series of erosional and depositional events, particularly in the Quaternary. These events have probably been superimposed upon parts of the island in the last two million years and result in a mosaic of drift material and residual material directly derived from underlying Pre-Cambrian rock. These residual materials by remaining *in situ* reflect the nature of the parent rock. In contrast, the remaining parts of the island have been subject to a series of erosional and depositional events. This results in a much more diverse set of soil-forming materials. Both have implications for ecological composition, and preliminary comparisons suggest there could be a direct relationship with major differences in vegetation on the island.

It is generally accepted that these different surfaces are explained by the repeated cycles of glaciation, with the related changes in temperature and rainfall. There is however, considerable discrepancy in the age that is associated with the different surfaces.

Acknowledgements

Stephen Nortcliff acknowledges support from the Royal Society Grant-in-Aid Scheme which enabled him to participate in the Maracá Project.

References

Bigarella, J. J. and Ferreira, A. M. M. (1985), Amazonian geology and the Pleistocene and the Cenozoic Environments and Paleoclimates, in Prance, G. T. and Lovejoy, T. E. (eds.), *Key Environments: Amazonia*, Oxford, IUCN and Pergamon Press, 49–71.

Brown, J. and Brindley, G. W. (eds.), (1980), *Crystal Structures of Clay Minerals and their X-Ray Identification*. London, Mineralogical Society.

Brown, K. S. Jr and Prance, G. T. (1987), Soils and Vegetation, in Whitmore, T. C. and Prance, G. T. (eds.), *Biogeography and Quaternary History in Tropical America*, Oxford, Oxford Scientific Publications, 19–45.

Dickinson, R. E. and Virji, H. (1987), Climate change in the humid tropics, especially Amazonia, over the last twenty thousand years, in Dickinson, R. E. (ed.), *The Geophysiology of Amazonia*, Chichester, John Wiley & Sons Ltd, 91–101.

Haffer, I. (1987), Quaternary history of tropical America, in Whitmore, T. C. and Prance, G. T., *Biogeography and Quaternary History in Tropical America*, New York, Oxford University Press, 1–18.

Hughes, J. C. (1980), Crystallinity of kaolin minerals and their weathering sequence in some soils from Nigeria, Brazil and Colombia, *Geoderma*, 24, 317–25.

Klammer, G. (1978), Reliefentwicklung im Amazonasbecken und plio-pleistozane Bewegungen des Meeresspiegels, *Zeitschrift für Geomorphologie N.F.*, 22, 390–416.

Martini, J. M. (1988), *Projeto Geologia – Ilha de Maracá: Relatório Final*, Manaus, Departamento Nacional de Produção Mineral.

Milliken, W. and Ratter, J. A. (1989), *The Vegetation of the Ilha de Maracá*, Edinburgh, Royal Botanic Garden.

Norrish, K. and Chappel, B. W. (1976, 2nd edition), X-ray fluorescence spectrometry, in Zussmann, J. (ed.), *Physical Methods of Determinative Mineralogy*, London, Academic Press, 201–72.

Nortcliff, S. and Robison, D. M. (1989), The soils and geomorphology of the Ilha de Maracá, Roraima: the second approximation, *Report of the Ecological Survey of Projeto Maracá*, RGS/SEMA.

Projeto RADAMBRASIL (1975), *Geomorfologia*, 8.

Robison, D. M. and Nortcliff, S. (1991), Os solos da Reserva Ecologica de Maracá, Roraima: Segunda Approximaçã, *Acta Amazónica*, 21, 409–24.

Wolf, E. C. (1991), Survival of the rarest, *Worldwatch Magazine*, 4: 2, 12–20.

Appendix: Membership of the Maracá Rainforest Project

1. Ecological Survey

INPA = Instituto Nacional de Pesquisas da Amazônia (National Amazon Research Institute in Manaus)

Botany

Dr James Ratter (botanist/ecologist)	Royal Botanic Garden, Edinburgh
Dr Ângelo Augusto dos Santos (ecologist)	INPA–Ecologia
Dra Maria Lúcia Absy (palynologist)	INPA–Botânica
Dra Maria das Graças Medina Arrais (bromeliads)	University of Piauí
Peter Edwards (ferns)	Royal Botanic Gardens, Kew
Carlos Alberto Alves Freitas (ferns)	INPA–Botânica
Dr Raymond Harley (Labiatae herbs)	Royal Botanic Gardens, Kew
Dr Mike Hopkins (ecologist)	University of Papua New Guinea
Dra Isonete de Jesus (fungi)	INPA–Botânica
Gwilym Lewis (legumes)	Royal Botanic Gardens, Kew
Pedro Augusto Suárez Mera (algologist/limnologist)	INPA–Limnologia
William Milliken (ecologist)	Royal Geographical Society
Dr Marçal Queiroz Paulo (lichens)	University of Paraíba
Dra Marlene Freitas da Silva (angiosperms)	INPA–Botânica
Edileuza Sette Silva (lichens)	Museu Integrado, Roraima
Cynthia Sothers (ecologist)	Worldwide Fund for Nature – Manaus
Luis Augusto Gomes de Souza (legumes)	INPA–Agronomia
Brian Stannard (parasitic Loranthaceae)	Royal Botanic Gardens, Kew
Prof. Lauro Xavier Filho (lichens)	University of Paraíba

Entomology

Nair Otaviano Aguiar (Coleoptera)	INPA/University of Amazonas
Luis Fernando Reys Aguiar (dragonflies)	Museu Nacional, Rio de Janeiro
Adelmar Gomes Bandeira (termites)	INPA
Dr Forbes Benton (ants, Phoridae)	CEPLAC (Cocoa Research Centre), Itabuna, Bahia
Erica Helena Buckup (spiders)	Fundação Zoobotânica do Rio Grande do Sul
José Ramiro Botelho (ectoparasites)	University of Minas Gerais, Belo Horizonte
Carlos Roberto Brandão (ants)	University of São Paulo
Lúcio Antônio de Oliveira Campos (bees)	University of Viçosa, Minas Gerais
Eliana Maria Cancello (termites)	University of São Paulo, Zoologia
Cláudio José Barros de Carvalho (Diptera)	University of Paraná, Curitiba
Dra Mirna Martins Casagrande (butterflies)	University of Paraná, Curitiba
Márcia Souto Couri	Museu Nacional, Rio de Janeiro
Ana Celeste Ferreira (Plecoptera)	INPA –Entomologia
Maria Helena Galileo (Coleoptera)	Fundação Zoobotânica do Rio Grande do Sul
Marcos Vinicius Bastos Garcia (bees)	WWF, Manaus
Sandra Harrison	Museu Nacional, Rio de Janeiro
Dr Pierre Jolivet (beetles, ant plants)	University of Viçosa, Minas Gerais
Dr Pedro Marcos Linardi (ectoparasites)	University of Minas Gerais, Belo Horizonte
Prof. Arno Antônio Lise (spiders)	Museu de Ciências Naturais, Porto Alegre, Rio Grande do Sul
Paulo Machado (ectoparasites)	University of Minas Gerais, Belo Horizonte
Maria Aparecida de Leão Marques (spiders)	Fundação Zoobotânica do Rio Grande do Sul
Hugo Mesquita (Odonata)	INPA–Entomologia
Dr Olaf Hermann Hendrik Mielke (butterflies)	University of Paraná, Curitiba
Padre Jesús Moure (bees)	University of Paraná, Curitiba
Francisco Peralta (bees)	INPA–Entomologia
Dr José Albertino Rafael (horseflies)	INPA–Entomologia
Dr Anthony Raw (wasps)	University of Brasília
Prof. Gilberto Righi (annelids)	University of São Paulo
Raquel Telles M. Sampaio (aquatic insects)	INPA–Entomologia
Jaime Maia dos Santos (nematodes)	University of Viçosa, Minas Gerais
Rosa Maria do Socorro dos Santos	INPA–Entomologia
Manoel do Nascimento Silva	Department of Education, Roraima

Og Francisco Fonseca de Souza (termites) — University of Viçosa, Minas Gerais

Maria Elizabeth L. de Souza (Hemiptera) — Fundação Zoobotânica do Rio Grande do Sul

Dr Ivaldo Ferreira Vilela (ants) — University of Viçosa, Minas Gerais

Zoology

Dr José Márcio Ayres (primates) — Museu Paraense Emílio Goeldi, Belém

Adrian Barnett (small mammals) — Independent

Prof. Roberto Cavalcante (birds) — University of Brasília, Ecologia

Mário Cohn-Haft (birds) — INPA/WWF Minimum Critical Size of Ecosystems

Elton Pinto Colares (giant otters) — INPA–Biologia de Água Doce

Aléxia Celeste da Cunha (small mammals) — INPA

Efrem Jorge Ferreira (fish) — INPA–Biologia de Água Doce

José Manuel Fragoso (peccaries) — University of Florida

Natália Inagaki (primates) — Museu Paraense Emílio Goeldi, Belém

Michelle Jegu (fish) — INPA

Olavo Lira (fish) — INPA

Dra Maria Cristina Dreher Mansur (molluscs) — Fundação Zoobotânica do Rio Grande do Sul

Márcio Martins (frogs) — INPA–Ecologia

Rogério Gribel Soares Neto (bats) — INPA–Ecologia

Andrea Portela Nunes (primates) — University of Rio de Janeiro/INPA

Mark O'Shea (reptiles) — Independent

Sharon Pollard (bats) — WWF/INPA–Ecologia

Paulo Petry (fish) — INPA–Biologia de Água Doce

Aldenora Lima de Queiroz (mammals) — INPA–Ecologia

George Rebelo (caimans) — INPA–Ecologia

Profa. Cecília Volkmer Ribeiro (sponges) — Fundação Zoobotânica do Rio Grande do Sul

Barbara Ann Robertson (zooplankton) — INPA–Limnologia

Fif Robinson (bats) — University of Oxford

José Maria Cardosa da Silva (birds) — Museu Paraense Emílio Goeldi, Belém

Maria Nazareth Ferreira da Silva (bats) — INPA–Ecologia

Douglas Stolz (birds) — INPA

Aylton Saturnino Teixeira (fish) — INPA–Biologia/Limnologia

Prof. Célio Murilo Carvalho Valle (mammals) — University of Minas Gerais, Belo Horizonte

Andy Whittaker (birds) — INPA/WWF Minimum Critical Size of Ecosystems

Jansen A. S. Zuamon (fish) — INPA–Biologia/Limnologia

2. Land Development

Dr Peter Furley	University of Edinburgh
Dr Christopher Barrow	University College, Swansea
Dr Thomas Dargie	University of Sheffield
Michael Eden	University of London
Dr John Hemming	Royal Geographical Society
Dr Philippe Léna	Museu Paraense Emílio Goeldi, Belém
Dr Duncan McGregor	University of London
Dr Luc Mougeot	Núcleo de Altos Estudos Amazónicos, University of Pará, Belém
Andrew Paterson	Food and Agriculture Organisation
Nelson Vieira	Fundação João Pinheiro, Belo Horizonte

3. Forest Regeneration

Dr John Proctor	University of Stirling
Dr João B. S. Ferraz	INPA–Silvicultura
Dr Valerie Kapos	University of Mérida, Venezuela
Dr Robert Marrs	Institute of Terrestrial Ecology
Robert Miller	INPA–Silvicultura
Duncan Scott	University of Stirling
Dr Jill Thompson	University of Stirling
Virgílio Viana	EMBRAPA–Belterra/Harvard University

4. Soils and Hydrology

Prof. John Thornes	University of Bristol
Flávio J. Luizão	INPA–Ecologia
Dr Jo Anderson	University of Exeter
Dra Lucille Marilyn Kriege Antony	INPA–Ecologia
Fabiano Biancucci Apolinário	INPA
Maria Carmozina de Araújo	INPA–Roraima
Sulineide Ataide	Federal University of Amazonas
Arnaldo Carneiro Filho	INPA–Solos
Bridget Gregory	University of Bristol
Maria Regina Costa Luizão	INPA–Ecologia
Dr Stephen Nortcliff	University of Reading
Maria Lúcia Pinheiro da Paz	INPA–Solos
Elizabeth Franklin Ribeiro	INPA–Ecologia
Dr Daniel Robison	University of Reading
Dr Sheila Ross	University of Bristol

5. Medical Entomology

Dr Victor Py-Daniel	INPA–Entomologia
Dr Derek Charlwood	Liverpool School of Tropical Medicine
Nelson Antunes	INPA–Entomologia
Dr Toby Barrett	INPA–Entomologia
Dr Sixto Cascaron	University of São Paulo
Dr Eloy G. Castellón	INPA–Entomologia
Assad José Darwich	INPA–Limnologia
Júlio Dellome Filho	University of Amazonas, Manaus
Sandra Tonetti Magni	Fundação Zoológica do Rio Grande do Sul
Dr José Mauro Martini	Departamento Nacional de Produção Mineral, Manaus
Renato Pigoraro	University of Santa Catarina
Ílea Brandão Rodrigues	INPA–Ciências Médicas
Dr Wanderli Pedro Tadei	INPA–Entomologia

6. Administration

Dr John Hemming (leader)	Royal Geographical Society
Steven Bowles (fleld leader)	Royal Geographical Society
José Antônio Alves Gomes	INPA–Roraima
Daphne Hanbury (home agent)	Royal Geographical Society
Sarah Latham (nurse)	Royal Geographical Society
Debbie Macklin	ICI–Brasil
Guttemberg Moreno de Oliveira	SEMA–Roraima
Eronias dos Santos Oliveira	SEMA–Roraima
Carlos Paredes	INPA–Roraima
Luis Berto Pestana	
Lorival Araújo dos Santos	INPA–Ecologia
Antônio Alves da Silva	SEMA–Roraima
Patrícia Silva dos Santos	SEMA–Roraima
Amazonas Valquimar Felix de Souza	SEMA–Roraima
Francinete Valquimar Felix de Souza	SEMA–Roraima
Fiona Watson (administrator)	Royal Geographical Society

Index

Note: **Bold** entries refer to tables and figures. In some cases there are also textual references on these pages.